Shadow
of the Hunter

Richard K. Nelson

Shadow of the Hunter

Stories of Eskimo Life

Illustrations by Simon Koonook

The University of Chicago Press • Chicago & London

The University of Chicago Press, Chicago 60637
The University of Chicago Press, Ltd., London

© 1980 by The University of Chicago
All rights reserved. Published 1980
Phoenix edition 1983
Printed in the United States of America
90 89 88 87 86 85 84 83   1 2 3 4 5 6

Library of Congress Cataloging in Publication Data

Nelson, Richard K
  Shadow of the hunter.

  1. Eskimos—Alaska—Hunting.   2. Eskimos—
Alaska—Social life and customs.   3. Indians of
North America—Alaska—Hunting.   4. Nelson,
Richard K. I. Title.
E99.E7N44   970.004'97   80-11091
ISBN 0-226-57179-3
      0-226-57180-7 (paper)

This book is dedicated to the Ulgunigmiut, who taught me their life and so profoundly influenced mine;

and to their grandchildren, who may wish to look back along the trail;

and to my faithful friends, who have helped and encouraged me along the way.

Contents

Acknowledgments	ix
Introduction	xi
Moon of the Returning Sun (January)	1
The Moon for Bleaching Skins (March)	27
The Moon When Whaling Begins (April)	55
The Moon When Rivers Flow (May)	89
The Moon When Animals Give Birth (June)	111
The Moon When Birds Raise Their Young (July)	133
The Moon When Birds Molt (August)	159
The Moon When Birds Fly South (September)	179
Moon of the Setting Sun (November)	209
The Moon with No Sun (December)	241
Appendix: The Setting	273
Glossary	281

Acknowledgments

This book is the result of some fourteen months spent living among the Eskimo people of Wainwright, Alaska. My studies during that time were generously supported by the United States Air Force, Arctic Aeromedical Laboratory, at Fort Wainwright, Alaska. Additional support was given by the Office of Naval Research, Naval Arctic Research Laboratory, at Point Barrow, Alaska. A later return to the village was made possible through a Patent Fund grant from the University of California at Santa Barbara. For all this assistance I am sincerely grateful.

I am deeply indebted to many people for their kindness and help during and after my stay in the North. My warmest appreciation goes to the people of Wainwright, who took me into their village, gave freely of their hospitality and friendship, shared their knowledge and experiences, and taught me a different way of living. I earnestly hope that what I have written of them finds approval in their eyes and helps in teaching others to respect and understand their way of life.

Almost everyone in Wainwright helped me in some way, but I want to express my special thanks to the following people: Waldo and Mattie Bodfish, the families of Wayne, Dempsey, Barry, and David Bodfish, Homer Bodfish, Weir

ix

and Roseanna Negovanna, Burrell Negovanna, Wesley
Ekak, Jack Ekak, Alva Nashoalook, Glenn Shoulda, Peter
Tagarook, Walter Nayakik, Moses and Marietta Nayakik,
Benny and Florence Ahmaogak, Luke Kagak, Rossman
Peetook, Jimmy Nayakik, the late Raymond Aguvuluk, and
the late Reverend Roy Ahmaogak.

Dr. William S. Laughlin and Dr. Frederick A. Milan
brought me the opportunity to live among Eskimos, gave
thoughtful advice and guidance, and greatly influenced the
outcome of my work. For all these things I am very grateful
indeed. My sincere thanks also to personnel of the Naval
Arctic Research Laboratory, especially to Dr. Max C. Brewer,
its former director, for doing so much to make my stays in
Wainwright pleasant and fruitful.

A number of friends helped me along with much-needed
personal support during my time in the North, and I want to
say thanks to them all. I especially want to mention Dr. Ken-
neth I. Taylor, Mrs. Carol Pooley, and Ray and Barbara
Bane. And a very special belated thanks to Ms. Cathy
Romano, whom I was too foolish and inhibited to mention
the last time around.

Many persons read parts of this book during its preparation. Their thoughtful critiques were invaluable, and their
encouragement kept me going when my confidence and energy waned. My deepest appreciation is to Ms. Kathleen
Mautner, who provided inspiration and would not allow me
the luxury of giving up. Donald Harvey made an important
contribution by editing the entire manuscript. And my parents, Robert and Florence Nelson, have been unfailing in
their support and encouragement, even when my interests
must have seemed unfathomable to them.

Finally, my thanks to Simon Koonook for the skill and
sensitivity with which he has illustrated these stories about his
own people.

Introduction

The Eskimos who live in widely scattered settlements along the Arctic Coast and North Slope of Alaska call themselves *Inupiat,* which means "the real people." In this way they set themselves apart from, and above, the rest of humanity. Perhaps, considering the harshness of the environment in which they live, they are entitled to this distinction. I hope the chapters that follow will give you some basis to judge for yourself.

The *Inupiat* are one of many distinct Eskimo groups living in the North American Arctic. During their four-thousand-year prehistory, Eskimos have spread over the entire northern face of the continent. Today they are found in eastern Siberia, throughout the western and northern coastal fringe of Alaska, across all of Arctic Canada from the Mackenzie to Labrador, and around the coasts of Greenland. By the time of first contact with Europeans, Eskimos had become one of the most successful peoples in all of human history, spanning almost half the earth's poleward circumference. They had pushed the human animal to the northernmost limits of its endurance. They had learned to live on the sparest resources, in the virtual absence of external warmth, where the sun vanished for months on end and where no moment of life was bought without the fullest use of the human genius.

This book will explore and experience that genius through a series of narratives. These stories are drawn from the year I lived as anthropologist and apprentice hunter in a small North Slope village. Their focus is sharply on the hunting life, the complex array of skills and knowledge that Eskimos depend on for success and survival in the high latitudes of the Arctic. But they also portray the Eskimos as people— their personalities, their social relationships, and their view of the world.

The book is intended as an ethnography—a descriptive account of a living culture—but as one that emphasizes the raw material of the senses as a means of communicating something of a people and their lifeway. It is in some ways a counterpoint to analytical scientific description, which is of course valuable in its own right but often has the sense of *life* taken from it. I have tried to avoid this by recounting events as they actually occur rather than distilling and analyzing them.

These narratives are fictionalized to varying degrees. All are based on my actual experiences among Eskimos, sometimes combined with stories I was told about the experiences of others. Some episodes are written just as I saw them happen; others are made up of several events put together as one. There is nothing in this book, to my knowledge, that has not happened or could not happen precisely as it is described.

All the characters are also fictionalized, as are their names. I have in no case drawn upon a single person in making an individual character sketch. But the people, like the events, are collages based on what is real. Because the book is about the hunting life, most of the characters are men, and the episodes take place away from the village. This is true simply because I have chosen to write about what I know best.

In all of these stories I have tried to write accurately and without exaggeration. Yet the book does not claim to be *truth* in any absolute sense. It is only one person's view of Eskimo culture, and so its accuracy is always open to question. In ethnography there are perhaps as many truths as there are observers, and even Eskimos looking at themselves would each see a different image. From this perspective, ethnography might best be considered a form of descriptive art, each observer creating a picture of humankind as accurately as his or her senses will allow. In spite of these potential shortcomings, I have written this book in the hope of teaching people about the Eskimos and the land in which they live.

Although I have focused on the modern Eskimo culture of north Alaska, the stories in this book are already somewhat historical. In the years since 1964, when I first arrived on the North Slope, the Eskimos' lifeway has undergone considerable change. The discovery of oil on their traditional lands has created great change, and the years ahead will undoubtedly see enormous transformation of both the people and their environment. Thus, what is written here preserves something of what was and what might someday vanish entirely from the earth.

This book is not only about the North Slope people, it is also *for* them. It is my profound hope that as life in the north country changes, accounts such as this one will help the coming generations of Eskimos and other native Alaskans to maintain a strong sense of pride and commitment to their cultural heritage. It is always difficult to know where the trail is leading, but the difficulty is eased somewhat by knowing where it began.

Before moving to the narratives themselves, some readers may want to begin with a short introduction to the Eskimos, their environment, and the research that led to my writing this book. This is found in the Appendix, "The Setting." A glossary of Eskimo words and certain English terms appearing in the stories is also found at the end of the book. Finally, I should mention that I have greatly simplified the spelling of Eskimo words here to accommodate readers unfamiliar with the *Inupiat* language. I can only ask the indulgence of those whose language I have represented in this way and note that I intend no disrespect for its beauty and complexity.

Siqinyasaq Tatqiq

Moon of the Returning Sun

(JANUARY)

MAIN CHARACTERS

Sakiak (Sah-*kee*-uk) *an old hunter*

Kuvlu (*Koov*-loo) *Sakiak's adult son*

Nuna (*Noo*-nuh) *Kuvlu's wife*

I T WAS NEAR DAWN, a few days past the New Year. A half-moon, low above the northern horizon, threw gray light across a featureless expanse of snow and ice. Featureless except for the silent cluster of houses set atop a low cliff where the tundra ended and long drifts sloped away to the ice-covered Arctic Ocean. The houses made up a small Eskimo settlement called Ulurunik, "where-the-bank-crumbles," Thin streamers of smoke, glowing pale in the moonlight, trailed from each house and diffused into a haze above the ocean ice.

A large husky sat near the edge of the bank, its outline dimly silhouetted against the horizon. Then it stretched forward, lifted its head in a gentle arc, and began a deep, moaning howl. Its voice started low and hollow, rose slightly in pitch, then dropped and faded. The dog howled again, this time higher and louder, its head thrown back and wavering slowly from side to side. The third time it howled several dogs nearby rose to their feet and added their voices. This aroused still others, and the chorus spread, like a drift before a growing wind, until almost every dog in the village was howling. Their sound, eerie yet wild and beautiful, carried for miles through the clear, frigid air. After several minutes it faded away except for the shrill barks and howls of a few diehard pups. Silence closed back over the land.

A midwinter day was about to begin. Toward the south-east, pale blue was gradually spreading along the horizon, where flat tundra plain met arching sky. The sun would never appear above the horizon on this day, nor on many more that would follow. For more than two months each year it remained hidden from sight, unable to climb above the curved edge of the earth. Even during this season, however, the twilight was strong enough to create a "day" several hours long. What little light there was, the Eskimos appreciated to its fullest.

The dog that began the howling was one of eleven tethered alongside a small frame house that was almost buried under a broad snowdrift deposited by the prevailing northeasterly gales. On one side a trough dug through the snow led to a small door that opened into a very low hallway. A second door at the far end of the hallway gave entry to the single large room in which the family of Kuvlu lived.

The dawn light was still too faint to be seen through the small window in the east wall of the house, but the dogs' spirited howling had awakened an old man, Sakiak, father of Kuvlu. He knew despite the darkness that it was morning, so he lay on his side, head braced on one hand, waiting for the sleepiness to leave him. No one else had awakened. He could barely make out a large bed near the south window where Kuvlu, his wife Nuna, and two of their smaller children slept. Three more children occupied another bed, and an older son, Patik, used a small mattress on the floor. Sakiak, whose wife had died many years earlier, also slept on the floor.

He could hear a breeze blowing gently in the stovepipe, and he hoped it would grow no stronger. Some mornings the house rumbled and shook as if there were an earthquake, but it was only *nigiqpak*, the northeaster, which howled across the tundra so often at this season. If the wind remained light today, Sakiak would go far out onto the ocean ice to hunt.

He felt around near his bed until he found a match, which he struck against the wall and used to light a kerosene lamp. The flame caught quickly, and yellow light filled the room, which was dingy and unpainted, cluttered everywhere with the necessities of life. In addition to the beds there were several chairs and box stools, a table, containers filled with clothing, and a large iron-topped stove. Sakiak pulled several chunks of seal blubber from a box, put them into the stove, and let the glowing embers set them afire. The blubber sputtered and burned with a hot, smoky flame that quickly drove the chill from the house.

Nuna slipped out of bed, set a kettle of water on the stove, and picked up a caribou skin she had begun scraping the day before. "Perhaps you will hunt," she said in a low voice, as if she were talking to herself. "It is possible," he answered. Men were usually indefinite when they spoke of hunting, because the fickle moods of weather and ice too often mocked their plans. Sakiak ate cold slices of boiled caribou meat left from the night before, dipping each one into a saucer of fermented seal oil to give it flavor. When he finished, he drank the cup of strong coffee that Nuna had set before him.

She used the remaining hot water to make a pot of black tea, which she poured into a battered thermos. Sakiak slipped the thermos into a cylindrical pouch made from caribou hide with the thick fur inside. This pouch would help keep the tea hot, since a thermos alone was inadequate when the temperature was far below zero. He packed the thermos, a few biscuits, and a small frozen fish into an oblong sealskin bag that he always carried when he hunted. The bag also contained binoculars, an ammunition pouch, matches, a sewing kit, and a seal-pulling harness.

Sakiak opened the door and stepped into the dark hallway. Supercooled air rushed into the house, condensing instantly to a thick cloud of steam that spread along the floor. He returned in a moment, carrying a voluminous bundle of clothing, all made from caribou hide. Two of the children,

who had awakened, sat quietly watching as he pulled a pair
of bulky fur pants over his cloth trousers. He slipped his feet
into fur-lined inner boots and tugged his outer boots over
them. Then he put on two wool shirts, a nylon jacket, and a
knit watch cap. Over it all he pulled a bulky parka, its fur
turned inside and white cloth covering the scraped skin
outside.

The caribou hide clothing was light and comfortable, but
its loose fit and thick fur made Sakiak look almost twice his
normal size. A ruff of stiff-haired wolverine fur encircled his
wrinkled face. He smiled at the children and gave one of them
a pinch with his stumpy, leather-skinned fingers before
turning to leave. On the way to the door he picked up his
hunting bag, gloves, and fur mittens.

Moments later he emerged from the long hallway, now
carrying a rifle in a homemade sheath of white canvas. He
straightened up outside the door, peering into the early
twilight. Needles of cold stung his face, and each time he
drew breath a deep minty chill spread down his throat into
his chest. "*Alapuu!*" he spoke to himself. "Cold!" It was
thirty-five below zero, with a gentle breeze from the east
lending added chill to the air. He pulled his gloves on before
his fingers numbed but stuffed his mittens into the sealskin
hunting bag. His hands would perspire if he wore mittens
during the long walk out onto the ice.

Sakiak stood atop the hard drift beside Kuvlu's house. The
moon was low above the northern horizon, its white profile
drawn sharp against the deep black sky. Millions of stars
stippled the heavens, each one standing out clear and unwavering. These were good signs. If the horizon was hazy
and the stars twinkled erratically, it forewarned of a gale that
could crack and move the sea ice. Looking southeastward,
Sakiak saw the black sky lighten to pale blue. Gold streaks
flowed upward from the invisible sun, illuminating a few
wisps of high cloud. If the east wind held, he thought, to-

morrow would be bitter cold. But this was a good day to
hunt.

He turned and walked along a hard-packed sled trail that
led to the edge of the village and onto the frozen ocean.
There were lights in several houses now, but Sakiak was the
first man out to begin his day's activities. Only the dogs
watched him pass, aroused by the noisy squeaking of snow
beneath his steps. He was careful to stay clear of the chain-
tethered animals, knowing they might lunge at any stranger
who passed within reach. Some dogs stood up to bark or
growl as he walked by. Most, however, remained in a tight
curl on the snow, breathing into the thick bushes of their tails
and conserving the warmth of their bodies.

Beyond the last house, the trail followed a gently sloping
ravine that opened onto the snow-covered beach. The trail
split at the ocean's edge, one fork going north along the coast
and the other heading out onto the sea ice. Sakiak chose the
seaward trail. He walked with short, brisk steps, rather
stiff-legged and somewhat bent at the waist. His hunting bag
and rifle were slung horizontally on his back, each suspended
from a strap that passed across his chest and shoulders. He
carried a long iron-pointed staff, or *unaaq,* that he would use
primarily for jabbing the ice to test its safety.

For the first half-mile the ice was almost perfectly flat, except
for a few low hummocks, or ice piles, where the floes had
moved and been crushed the previous fall. The surface was
also punctuated by the minor undulations of snowdrifts,
packed hard as a wooden floor by the pounding winds.
Sakiak's practiced eye could tell which drifts had been shaped
by the cold northeasters and which by the warmer south
winds. If fog or a blinding snowstorm caught him, he would
navigate by watching, or even feeling, the configuration of
the drifts.

Shortly, he reached the first high ridges of piled ice. He

picked his way up the side of a huge mountain of tumbled slabs and boulders, from which he could look far out over the pack. When he stood at the top, he scanned the vast expanse of snow-covered ice that stretched beyond him. It was still gray twilight, but in the crystal air and brightness of snow the sea ice stood out sharply to the distant horizon. From his lofty perch, Sakiak looked over an environment that appeared totally chaotic and forbidding. Huge ice piles and ridges interlaced the surface everywhere, encircling countless small flat areas and occasionally fringing a broad plain of unbroken ice.

To the unpracticed eye this jumbled seascape would have seemed utterly impenetrable and unattractive. But to the Eskimo it held a different promise. He would find an easy trail by weaving among the hummocks, crossing them at low places. And he would find his prey, the seal, that now swam in dark waters beneath the pavement of ice. For although this world appeared silent and lifeless, the sea below was rich with living things. The currents carried millions of tiny planktonic organisms, the basis of a long chain of biological interrelationships. Larger invertebrates and fish fed upon the drifting clouds of krill, and they in turn fell prey to warm-blooded animals that rose to the surface for air. Seals lived all winter among the congealing floes, gnawing and scratching holes through the ice to reach the air above or rising in the steaming cracks. And, on the ice surface, polar bears and Eskimos stalked the seals.

Sakiak searched the pack with his binoculars, their cold eyepieces stinging his skin. He was attentive to minute details, hoping to pick out the yellowish color of a polar bear's fur against the whiteness of the snow. He looked also for the fresh black lines of cracks and for rising clouds of steam that would mark open holes and leads. Long minutes passed before he took the binoculars from his eyes, satisfied that there were no bears or open places in the area. The ice was packed firm against the coast and would not move today unless the wind or current changed. It was a perfect time for an old man to wait for a seal at its breathing hole.

In a moment Sakiak was down from the ice pile, walking seaward again along the sled trail. About a mile out from the coast he passed the frozen carcasses of two old dogs, half-covered by blown snow. They had been shot early in the winter by their owner, who was replacing them with strong pups. This fate awaited all dogs that outlived their useful-ness, for though Eskimos appreciated their animals they could ill afford the luxury of emotional attachment to them. Sakiak had used dogs all his life, but like all the older hunters he often preferred to walk. Animals frequently saw or heard a dog team long before they could detect a lone man afoot, so it was better to hunt this way. If the kill was heavy, a man could drag part of it home and return with a team for the rest.

The trail wound and twisted across the ice, which made it long but relatively smooth. Still, it crossed many ridges that the Eskimos had laboriously chopped and smoothed to make the passage as easy as possible. About two miles out the trail entered a field of very rough ice, with some ridges forty to sixty feet high. Broad slabs of ice four feet thick had been tossed on end and pushed into the air like huge monuments that towered high above a man's head. The far edge of this rough area was marked by a single ridge that stretched un-broken for miles, its direction generally paralleling the dis-tant coast. The outer face was a sheer wall of pulverized ice, ground flat and smooth by the motion of the pack.

Sakiak sat down to rest and cool off beside this ridge. His long walk had generated too much warmth, and if he did not stop he would begin to perspire. He knew that moisture robbed clothing of its warmth, so he always tempered his labors during these cold months to avoid overheating. The long ridge where Sakiak rested marked the outermost edge of the landfast floe, an immobile apron of ice that extended far out from the land. An early winter gale had driven the ice against the coast and caused it to pile so high and deep that the entire floe had become solidly anchored to the bottom of the ocean. The ice beyond it was the mobile Arctic pack, which moved according to the dictates of current and wind.

Hunters knew that landfast ice rarely moved during the winter unless a tremendous gale arose, with an accompanying high tide that lifted the ice free of the bottom. Landfast ice meant safety because it would not drift away, carrying men out to sea with it. But the pack was different. Hunters who ventured onto it were suspicious and watchful, constantly checking wind and current to be sure the ice would not break away from the landfast floe. If this happened, and it sometimes did, they would be stranded beyond a widening lead, an open crack that blocked their return to shore. Men who drifted away often died without seeing land again.

A week earlier, powerful onshore winds had driven the pack against the landfast ice, where it had remained without moving ever since. Sakiak would now decide if it was safe to go beyond the final grounded ridge. He walked along its edge until he found a narrow crack covered with dark, thin ice. With the point of his *unaaq*, he chiseled a fair-sized hole through it. Then he cut a bit of sealskin thong from his boot tie, chewed it until it was moist, and dropped it into the black water. The white thong sank slowly downward until it cleared the bottom edge of the ice, then drifted off eastward, toward the land. Finally it was enveloped in the blackness.

Sakiak stood up and looked out onto the pack. The current flowed from the west, from the sea toward the land, gently but with enough force to hold the ice ashore against opposing pressure from the easterly breeze. He had studied the movements of ice throughout his life, and he remembered well the lessons taught him by old hunters during his youth. With this knowledge and experience he could judge to near perfection the mood of the pack. Today it would be safe, so long as the wind and current pushed against each other. He would look for breathing holes somewhere not far from the landfast ice, where he could scurry to safety if conditions changed. Old men knew there was no point in taking chances. "The ice is like a mean dog," they warned. "He waits for you to stop watching, and then he tries to get you."

Sakiak climbed to the top of a nearby ridge and scanned the pack with his binoculars. Jagged lines of hummocks pierced sharply into the brightening sky. The day was now full and blue, brilliant refracted twilight glowing high above the seaward horizon. He smiled as he squinted into the brightness. Indeed, it was *Siqinyasaq tatqiq,* "moon of the returning sun." But the cold needling his cheekbones reminded him that it was still midwinter, and that he must work fast to hunt before darkness closed over the sky again.

He saw no hint of life on the pack, but the configurations of ice told him where best to look for it. Just beyond a low ridge several hundred yards away there was a long plain of flat ice, its color and lack of snow cover indicating that it was not more than three feet thick. This would be an ideal place to search for the breathing holes of seals, because they were easy to see on such ice. The sled trail had ended at the edge of landfast ice, so he picked out an easy route before heading toward the flat. Younger hunters often failed to reconnoiter in this way, considering it a waste of time. But instead of moving faster they were forced to clamber laboriously over the rough ice, and they often came home bruised and exhausted.

It was not long before Sakiak stood at the edge of the big flat. Its surface was completely free of snow but was covered everywhere with large, fluffy crystals of frost, some so thin and feathery that they shivered in the breeze. They were made flexible by salty moisture from the ice, which prevented them from freezing hard, and when Sakiak walked on the frost his tracks were slushy despite the intense cold. This was why ice hunters wore boots soled with waterproof seal hide, which kept their feet dry on the moist surface.

He moved quickly along one side of the flat, searching for

the telltale signs of a breathing hole. Presently he stopped, looking at the ice nearby. He saw a little group of thin ice chunks frozen into the surface, scattered in a circle about a handbreadth in diameter. When this ice was newly formed, a seal had broken up through it to breathe, leaving a small opening with bits of ice around it. The hole was never used again, but this frozen scar remained.

If the seal had continued to use such a hole as the ice thickened, it would have looked quite different. Each time the animal returned, water would slosh out over the ice and freeze, eventually building up a small, irregularly shaped dome with a little hole in its top. By scratching and gnawing, the seal kept this dome hollow inside, like a miniature igloo. Beneath this structure the hole widened into a tunnel through the ice, large enough to accommodate the seal's body when it came up to breathe. The Eskimos called such breathing holes *allus*.

Sakiak walked to the far end of the flat without seeing an *allu* or even another scar. So he turned back, following a low ridge that flanked the opposite side. He had not gone far when he spotted an *allu* just a few yards from the base of the ridge. It was very large and nearly cone-shaped, so he knew at a glance that it had been made by the huge *uguruk,* or bearded seal. He bent low, stiff-legged, moving his trunk from side to side and peering into its opening. The interior was very dim, but he could make out its round entryway, covered by a layer of dark gray ice. This was a disappointing find. The ice was almost a day old, indicating that the seal was not using this *allu* often.

If the days were longer he might wait there, for a bearded seal was a fine catch indeed. But with few hours of daylight he needed a hole that was visited more frequently. He would remember this *allu,* and if the ice did not move he might check it again to see if the seal returned. Sakiak memorized the shape of the ridge nearby so he could easily guide himself to this spot another day.

Breathing holes were often somewhat clustered, so he looked carefully around the area. Seeing none, he climbed the ridge to inspect a small flat on its opposite side. He was surprised to find that the flat was cut by a broad crack, perhaps ten yards across, covered with newly frozen ice. The crack, which must have opened during the past week's storm, made a jagged swath across the flat and sliced cleanly through a ridge on its far side. Sakiak marveled at the power of moving ice, which could split a heavy ridge into two sections as a man would cut through blubber with his knife. The crack probably ran for miles, and there would almost certainly be a few breathing holes in its covering of young ice. It also offered Sakiak an easy trail through the hummocky areas.

Sakiak made his way down the ridge and onto the frozen crack. He followed it across the flat, through the chasm of the split ridge, and onto another flat. There he saw what he was looking for. Almost in the middle of the crack was a nearly perfect little dome, the *allu* of a ringed seal, or *natchiq*. He peered closely into its opening and saw deep black inside. "It's good," he murmured softly to himself. The blackness was a circle of open water with a transparent skin of new ice forming at its edges, just a few inches below the quarter-sized opening of the *allu*. Not an hour before, while Sakiak walked out across the landfast ice, a seal had risen here to breathe.

There was no time to waste. For all he knew, the animal might be heading for this hole now, and he was not ready for it. He slipped off his hunting bag and rifle, laying them on the ice together with his *unaaq*. Then he went quickly to the nearest hummock and kicked free two blocks of ice for a stool and footrest. After carrying them back, he again inspected the interior of the *allu*. Its opening was slightly off center, and the tunnel appeared to angle somewhat away from the vertical. From this Sakiak knew which direction the seal would face when it came to breathe, and he would angle his rifle slightly for the deadliest possible shot.

Now he placed the two ice blocks about a foot from the hole, along its southeast side. He calculated automatically, almost without thought, the effects of wind and light. There was enough brightness to create a faint shadow, which must not fall across the hole. And he must not sit upwind lest the seal be frightened by his scent. He also preferred to face away from the biting chill of the breeze. He emptied his hunting bag onto the thick ice alongside the crack and pulled his rifle from its canvas sheath. The bag would insulate and cushion his stool while the sheath insulated the footrest. Eskimos always took pains to minimize loss of heat from their bodies in every way possible, and Sakiak knew the wait would be a cold one even in the best circumstances.

He placed his *unaaq* on the thick ice, where its shadow would not be visible from below, and he adjusted the ice blocks so they could not jiggle or squeak noisily. Then he sat down on one block and put his feet on the other, so that his legs were held straight out before him, Eskimo fashion. He could sit this way for many hours without tiring. When he was seated atop the ice blocks, his menacing presence could not be detected by a seal looking up through the glowing translucence of the gray ice.

The bolt of his rifle clicked loudly in the brittle cold as he thrust a shell into the chamber. Then he placed the weapon crosswise over the tops of his boots, where it was least likely to compress his clothing and cause chilling. Its muzzle faced the *allu* but did not hang over where the seal might see it. He had taken the precaution of standing a flat chip of ice alongside the little opening to screen his intrusive shape from the seal's eyes as it rose to breathe.

Now he would wait.

It was impossible to know when the seal would appear. In fifty winters of hunting at breathing holes, Sakiak had learned not to think too much of time. It might be fifteen minutes, perhaps an hour. Perhaps many hours. Sometimes the animal never returned.

Sakiak knew of old men who, in times of starvation, had waited beside an *allu* for twenty-four hours. Nowadays the young men refused to hunt at breathing holes, preferring to wait until a wide crack or lead formed so they could shoot seals in the open water. When Sakiak was a boy the men had relied upon harpoons, which could not be thrown far enough to strike a seal swimming freely out in a lead. But a harpoon was as good as a rifle for hunting at breathing holes, perhaps better. When a seal was harpooned, a line attached to the point ensured that the animal would not sink or be carried away by the current.

Young men said that breathing-hole hunting was too cold, that it involved too much waiting. The old men said only that people must eat. They had learned the art of enduring patience, as if they could merge their thoughts with the timeless physical world that surrounded them. Life, after all, was a game of waiting. One could not expect that the weather, ice, and animals would do a man's bidding. If a man would live, he must persist, wait, endure.

Sakiak was enveloped in still silence, interrupted only by the occasional buffeting of wind against his parka hood. His breath condensed on the ruff around his face and on his scraggly moustache, coating each hair with thick white frost. He could feel the immensity of the pack surrounding him, its quiet, latent power.

Radiant amber flowed up the wall of the sky before him, hinting of warmth in some distant world, while the pervasive cold drew closer around his body. Time faded away to a dim consciousness at the core of the hunter's mind.

Twilight grew and spread slowly southward, then edged toward the west. The fullest light of midday came, then imperceptibly began to fade. Sakiak drew his arms from the sleeves of his parka and held them against his body for

warmth. He was shivering. Frost had collected on his
eyelashes and brows. Occasionally he poked a bare hand up
through the neck of his parka and held it against his cheek to
warm the stiff, numb flesh. His toes felt large and icy cold.
Perhaps the temperature was falling, he thought. Indeed, it
was now minus forty, but the wind was fading as it grew
colder.

Sakiak wished he had brought the boy along. His grandson
Patik was old enough to hunt and could make the seal come
to the *allu* where he waited. If he walked in a broad circle
around Sakiak, he would frighten the seal away from its
other holes and force it toward the hunter's station. Had the
ice been perfectly smooth, Sakiak could have accomplished
this alone by finding every breathing hole in the area and
urinating on it. The powerful scent would frighten the seal
away, leaving it only the hunted *allu* to use. It was funny to
think how a seal must plunge away in frightened surprise
when it smelled urine in its *allu*. But in rough ice many
breathing holes were concealed in open spaces beneath
hummocks and snowdrifts, where a man could never find
them.

Almost two hours had passed. A growing ache spread up
Sakiak's legs and back, but he dared not move to relieve the
discomfort. The seal might be near enough to hear any noise
transmitted through the ice to the water below. So he moved
only his head and arms, even then very carefully.

It was also important to watch the surrounding ice in case a
polar bear happened to approach him. Bears would occasionally stalk a man, if they were so thin and hungry that
starvation drove fear out of them. But today it seemed there
was no life anywhere, except for the silent lives beneath the
pack. Sakiak wondered how deep the water under him might
be. And he thought the current could soon shift and flow
from the east, as it always did when intensely cold air moved
in off the great expanse of land that stretched eastward away
from the coast.

He was now shivering hard, and he wondered if his shak-

ing might jiggle the ice stool, making a noise that would scare
away the seals. He smiled, thinking what a great joke that
would be after such a long, cold wait!

But beneath him at that moment a seal torpedoed through
the black-gray water, darting and arcing in pursuit of the
fleeting silver of fishes. It dodged between the blue and
emerald-green walls of ice protruding downward beneath
the hummocks. Huge inverted ice mountains blocked its
path, but it sensed them and turned away before striking
invisible barriers deep in the blackness.

In the freedom of its dense medium, the seal could ignore
the encumbrances of gravity. It swam on its side, then upside
down, then coasted to a stop in midwater. There it hung
quietly in the dark silence, drifting slowly with the current,
like a footloose star in the vastness of space. But this space
was far from an empty void. Nervous shoals of fish left
glowing trails as they spun and needled through luminescent
plankton. Tiny jellyfish pulsed and parachuted, trailing deli-
cate streamers beneath them. And, far below, crabs littered
the bottom, waiting for those above to die and become their
food.

For more than a minute the seal remained motionless, ignoring the fish that swam too near. It was in need of air and
was listening. Then it suddenly whirled and shot upward
toward a circle of white that glimmered faintly in the high
distance.

When it reached the underside of the ice, the seal turned
slowly beneath the circle. It hesitated a moment, then swam
slowly upward into the narrow passage. Reaching the surface, it poked its nose out for an instant, sampling the air,
then dropped again. The air was fresh and stinging of cold.
It rose again, emerging into the bright igloo of ice, globed
eyes wide and black, nostrils flaring and closing.

In the silence of the pack, after a long wait, the seal's approach was startling and exciting. Sakiak first heard, almost
sensed without hearing, a pulsation of the water inside the

allu. Then he saw water flow through the opening and over the ice outside, where it instantly froze to a fresh glaze. This water was forced up ahead of the seal as it rose from below.

Sakiak heard scratching as the seal cleared away newly formed ice at the tunnel's upper opening. He quickly slipped his arms into the sleeves of his parka, then remained perfectly still. The cold had vanished. Shivering ceased as warmth spread from mind to muscle.

He fixed his eyes on the *allu*, consumed with intense concentration. His lips moved slightly, almost imperceptibly. "Come seal," he whispered, asking the animal to give itself to him. "Come. . . . " It was only a thought this time.

In a moment the seal obeyed Sakiak's will. It took a first short, hissing breath, smelling the air for signs of danger. He did not move. He expected the brief silence that followed, knowing the next breath would be a deep one.

Whoosh!

It was a long, drawn-out hiss that sent a misty spray from the opening. This noise was loud enough to drown out the sound of Sakiak's movement as he reached down and picked up his rifle from his legs. He was careful to spread his arms so his clothing would not scrape noisily, and he was still before the deep breath was finished.

Whoosh!

Again the animal breathed. Sakiak lifted his rifle and held it vertical, with the thumb of his upper hand against the trigger. Again he waited, as the second breath stopped.

Whoosh!

On the third breath he moved his rifle straight above the *allu*, its muzzle inches from the opening. His face was expressionless. His resolve was complete. Without a second's hesitation, he deliberately squeezed the trigger.

For the seal, breath cut short. A sudden *crack!* only half heard before the world was shut out in closing clouds of black.

For the hunter, a sudden deafening explosion. The *allu*

split and shattered. Fragments of ice dyed crimson. The seal bobbing on the pulse of water, grotesque and broken, instantly detached from the reality of life.

Sakiak ran to fetch his *unaaq*. Using its sharp point, he chipped the rest of the *allu* away, then snagged the animal with the metal hook on its other end. The seal was still quivering, so he held it until movement stopped. With the knife he carried on his belt he slit the skin of its upper lip, then he pushed the loop end of his seal-pulling harness through this cut and fastened it around the animal's nose.

This done, Sakiak held the line under one foot while he chiseled the hole until it was large enough so he could pull out the seal. If he had not secured the seal quickly with a line, it might have been carried off by the current. In thicker ice, where the seal would enter through a long, cigar-shaped tunnel, this would be unnecessary; winter-killed seals were buoyant from their thick layer of blubber, so they would float well up into the tunnel where the current could not take them away.

Finally, Sakiak pulled the seal out onto the ice. It was completely limp and flexible, like a sack full of liquid. Blood flowed and coagulated on its skin, freezing in thick layers around the wound. It was large for a ringed seal, about four feet long and weighing perhaps a hundred pounds. And its hide was deep black, patterned with small whitish circlets. The *Inupiat* called a dark seal like this *magamnasik*.

The warmth of excitement that had flared inside Sakiak died quickly, and he found himself shivering again. Before starting back he should eat something and drink the hot tea in his thermos. Eskimos knew that food kindled heat inside a man's body, so it was important to eat well and often during the cold hunts. Heavy steam billowed from the thermos when he opened it. He drank quickly, feeling the hot liquid flow down his throat to the cold pit of his stomach. Refreshed, he took the hard-frozen fish he had brought along and peeled off its

skin. Then he cut it into small sections and hungrily ate the
raw chunks. Its oily fat would bring him quick warmth and
energy.

More hot tea and a couple of frozen biscuits finished his
meal. When he had drunk his fill of tea he spilled the remainder out onto the snow, staining its white surface yellow
brown. It made sharp, crackling noises as it immediately
froze to a brittle crust. He felt deep appreciation for the food
and for the seal he had killed. He could remember his grandfather chanting thanks to an abiding spirit that helped him,
but Sakiak thanked the Christian God with a short prayer in
Eskimo.

He rested for a few minutes, looking at the distant sky.
The light was fading, and he had a long walk before him.
Perhaps in a few days he would return to this *allu*. Often
several animals used one hole, and they might eventually
come back in spite of the damage done to it. But now there
was little time to waste. Sakiak lighted a cigarette and put his
equipment back into the hunting bag. When this was finished
he took his knife and made a long slit down the seal's belly.
Then he cut a wide slab of blubber from the abdomen and
both flanks, laying it aside on the ice. Along each side of the
slit he made a series of holes in the hide, and through these
he laced a piece of heavy cord, sewing the animal back together. Removing the blubber made it almost ten pounds
lighter, and ten pounds would make a noticeable difference
to an old man pulling a large seal home over the ice.

Now he slung his hunting bag and rifle case across his
back, placed the strap of his seal-pulling harness around his
chest, and began walking toward the landfast ice. The limp
seal, still warm inside, slid along easily behind him. Sakiak
had pulled hundreds of seals this way, however, and he knew
that its weight would grow as he crossed the piled ice.

Once, when he was young and strong, Sakiak had shot two
bearded seals weighing several hundred pounds apiece and
decided to pull both of them home. He cut every bit of meat

from one animal, discarding the bones, skin, and entrails. Then he removed the entrails of the other, stuffed the meat of the first seal into the empty carcass, and sewed the skin back together. The load was still very heavy, and he had pulled late into the night before reaching the settlement, completely exhausted.

Thinking of that experience seemed to lighten his load, and soon he could see the edge of the landfast ice. This was good, because he wanted to be off the pack while there was still fair light. He was taking a long route, because by weaving back and forth he could stay almost entirely on flat ice. In spite of the deep cold he soon became overheated from pulling, and so he decided to rest at the base of a small ridge.

He was about to sit down on a large ice boulder when he noticed what appeared to be an *allu* in the flat ice some distance away. Curious, and hoping to find a place to hunt another day, he walked quickly to it, leaving the seal behind. Even before he reached it he could tell that something was wrong. The little dome was partially caved in, and along one side the ice had been dug away. He knew immediately what had happened. "Ah, *nanuq!*" he whispered. Wandering away from the hole was a set of broad footprints, the track of a polar bear. It was not fresh. A haze of frost crystals already filled the prints, showing that a day had passed since they were made.

Sakiak inspected the tracks again and again, looking off in the direction they faced. The bear had hunted at this *allu* and, like him, had found success. It first dug around the dome until the ice was very thin. Then it filled the excavated area with snow scraped from the ice, so the seal could detect no change as it came up inside. Finishing this, it stood beside the *allu* at a right angle to the wind, awaiting the seal's return. Eventually, perhaps many hours later, the bear heard its prey breathing within the dome. In an instant it smashed the surrounding ice with both paws, simultaneously crushing the animal's skull. Then it pulled the seal out onto the ice, squeezing it through a hole so small that many bones broke inside the lifeless body. So it was that Eskimo and polar bear hunted the same animal in almost the same way.

The hole was now frozen over. Flecks of blood spotted the bear's tracks, showing that it had carried the seal away to eat it elsewhere. Sometimes bears slept long and soundly in the rough ice near a kill site, digesting the meal before moving on. Sakiak saw darkness moving up the eastern sky and looked away along the tracks. The bear might be somewhere nearby, or it might be far away over the ice horizon. From the age of the tracks he suspected it had moved on, but he would follow them for a short distance to look for more signs.

Several hundred yards away, near a broad field of rough ice, he found the seal's carcass. The bear had eaten only its skin and blubber, leaving the rest behind to be gnawed by the little white foxes that so often followed bears. They had already eaten half the meat, showing that many hours had passed since the bear's meal. The bear must have been fat and in its prime; otherwise it could not afford to eat only the choicest parts. Sakiak was sure now that it was far away, but he climbed a ridge and scanned the surrounding floes for a long time to be sure. Seeing nothing, he returned to his seal and resumed his trek toward the landfast ice.

Now he was careful to look behind him every few minutes, to be sure no bear was following. Bears often followed a man's trail over the sea ice, especially if it was scented with the blood and oil of a seal. Sakiak knew men who had felt a tug on their seal-pulling harness as they dragged their catch home in the dim hours of evening. They turned to see a white bear, ready to stake claim to the animal. Old-timers often warned the young hunters to slip out of the harness quickly and grab for their rifles if ever they felt something strange while pulling a seal.

A man named Takirak, who lived in the neighboring vil-

lage of Utqeavik, had an unexpected encounter with a bear
when Sakiak was still a boy. He was setting fox traps on the
landfast ice and carried only a long knife. A skinny bear
appeared nearby, looking as if it might attack him. Takirak
was a brave man who knew much of animals, so he handled
the bear wisely. He drew his knife and walked threateningly
toward it, speaking in a firm, low voice. "Go away, bear, or I
will cut up your handsome face." The animal backed away,
but it persisted in following as Takirak walked homeward.
Each time it came too near, he threatened it again. Finally,
when they drew within earshot of the village's howling dogs,
the bear ran off and did not return.

It was not long before Sakiak reached the ridge that marked
the edge of landfast ice. He followed it southward until he
found the sled trail, and there he rested briefly before heading landward. Twilight was fading rapidly now, and distant
ridges loomed mysteriously in the growing gloom of evening.
The trail crossed many low ridges, and Sakiak found himself
becoming warm and a little tired. Fortunately the snow had
been pounded slick by the passage of many dog teams over
the previous months, so the carcass slid along easily. In any
case, old men, like old dogs, were tough and long-winded.
The young were faster and had more brute power, but they
often tired long before their elders.
Sakiak thought of these things as he trudged across the
silent floes. He was alone, one small old man on the vastness
of an ice-covered sea. The breeze had died away to an occasional puff, and his footsteps squeaked loudly in the steel-
hard cold. Beads of perspiration covered his forehead, just
inches from the rime of thick frost that whitened his parka
ruff. He melted ice droplets from the long whiskers of his
moustache by holding his tongue against them, refreshing
himself with the cold moisture. Ahead he could see the vil-

lage, sharp and black against the snow-covered tundra that
swept away to meet the sky. Smoke from the chimneys rose,
then flattened out in a thick haze that hung over the houses.

Soon he was crossing the last stretches of flat ice that
fringed the shore. It had been a long, slow walk from the
edge of the landfast floe, and Sakiak thought fondly of the
comfort that awaited him. Nuna would have hot tea ready,
and stew made from caribou meat. Behind him the last
streaks of flaming gold spread widely along the sea horizon
beneath the overarching blackness of night.

He could see a dog team returning home amid a chorus of
envious howls and challenging barks from tethered animals.
Someone was hauling in large blocks of freshwater ice cut
from a tundra lake near the village. He wondered if any
hunters had killed caribou today far inland where tall willows
broke the sweeping wind. Fresh tongue and heart, boiled
together in a large pot, would await the families of the lucky
ones.

Sakiak walked slowly up the ravine that ended atop the
bank and followed the trail toward Kuvlu's house. Children
of all sizes ran out to walk beside him, asking endless admiring questions. "Where did you catch the seal?" "Did you see a
bear?" "Will you eat the seal's boiled intestines tonight?"
Sakiak said little, letting the older children invent answers for
him. He loved to hear the laughter of children and was
always happy when they ran to meet him. Someday, perhaps,
they would hunt to feed him when he no longer walked out
over the ice.

Migalik, a young man, was feeding his dogs when Sakiak
passed. "Ah, Sakiak, you have killed a seal. *Azahaa,* you're a
man!"

"And you," he answered, "perhaps you have traveled
today." Migalik said he had gone far south along the coast,
nearly to Qayaqsirvik, searching for polar bears. But he saw
nothing except a few wolverine tracks and a fox caught in
one of Nauruk's traps. The two men talked briefly, their

conversation raptly followed by several young boys who wished they could hunt instead of spending their days inside the village school. Some of the boys had already killed their first animals and passed the meat out among the old people to ensure luck as they grew to manhood.

When the men had told each other the events of their day's hunting, Sakiak pulled his seal the rest of the way home. His grandchildren, bundled in parkas that were miniature replicas of his own, ran out from the house to meet him. He joked briefly with them, then told the oldest boy to pull the seal in for his mother to skin and butcher. When she finished, he was to carry a piece of its meat to Saatuk, the old woman who lived in a sod hut at the far end of the village.

Sakiak stood looking out over the sea ice. He wondered about the bear whose tracks he had followed. It was a big one, with meat that would drip with fat and a pelt that might bring a handsome price indeed. He did not think about killing it, lest he bring bad luck upon himself. Tomorrow would be very cold and still, perhaps so cold it would be wise to stay at home. But he would like to walk out and look for the bear.

The moon, enormous and brilliant white, was lifting itself into the southern sky. Long gray shadows stretched out over the snow. The sea ice emerged again from darkness, looking distant and utterly detached from the world of the land. Sakiak brushed a shower of sparkling frost crystals from the ruff of his parka, turned, and disappeared into the long hallway of the house.

Paniqsiqsiivik Tatqiq

The Moon for Bleaching Skins

(MARCH)

MAIN CHARACTERS

Pauluk (*Pow*-look) *an old hunter*

Kakivik (Kah-*ki*-vik) *Pauluk's adult son*

Tupik (*Too*-pik) *an adult hunter*

Kakivik's cheekbones felt chilled and numb, so he held the palm of his bare hand against his face until feeling returned. Then before his hand began stinging from the cold he slipped it back into the thick warmth of his caribou-hide mitten. In a short time the numbness would return, as it had so many times that day, and he would warm his face again to avoid the painful nip of frostbite. "*Alapparah!*" he whispered. "So cold!" The temperature was forty-five below zero when he awoke in Ulurunik that morning, and it seemed to have changed little during the day. At least, he thought gratefully, the wind had been very light. And the dogs had pulled well, perhaps because exercise warmed them.

Kakivik clapped his mittens together and called out to the huskies, encouraging them to keep up their quick pace. He often spoke cheerfully or sang Eskimo songs to entertain them, remembering the old hunters' advice that dogs worked best when they were happy. "Avvak!" he shouted to the lead dog, "Hurry now. The camp is not far ahead. Let's go!" Avvak looked off to one side, recognizing her name and listening for a command. She was a smart one indeed, the kind that knew her master so well she often sensed his next order before it was given. Ten winters now she had been a

leader, and although she no longer ran with a pup's graceful
speed she was nearly tireless and had far more strength than
any young dog.

Long shadows danced over the snow, casting surrealistic
images of dogs, lines, sled, and rider. Looking all around
him, Kakivik saw the endless expanse of tundra, almost perfectly flat and monotonously white to the horizon's sharp
edge. Here and there a small patch of brown showed where
gales had swept away the snow, exposing tussocks of grass
and creeping willows. The tundra was so featureless, so devoid of landmark or irregularity, that the land all around
appeared to lift upward toward the crest of a gentle encircling ridge—as if a few hundred yards ahead he would sur-
mount this ridge and stand above the surrounding country.
But it was an illusion; it never changed, hour after hour. The
land was so uniform and the air so clear that what appeared
to be a nearby crest was in fact the remote horizon, miles and
miles in the distance.

The only breaks in the landscape were occasional abrupt
river or creek valleys, carved down into the flat surface like
outsized gulleys. These usually could not be seen until they
were just ahead, and inattentive travelers sometimes found
themselves careening down a creek bank behind the running
dogs. Farther inland, a full day's travel from the coast, there
were gentle hills and willows nearly as tall as a man, which
made the terrain very different and exciting to look upon.

The cold numbed his cheeks again, so Kakivik turned to
stand backward on the sled, facing away from the chill
breeze. He squinted directly into the sun, which was now
very low and silver gold in the west. A halo of frost sparkled
on the wolverine-fur ruff encircling his face. He looked the
classic Eskimo in every detail—an extraordinarily handsome
man with narrow eyes, smallish nose, high cheeks, and broad
smiling mouth that gleamed with bright teeth worn flat by
years of chewing on tough meat and gristle. And Kakivik's
physical strength matched the power in his face; he stood

more than six feet tall and had the hard, sinewy musculature of a wolf. Yet for all this he was a humble man who laughed easily and never asserted himself over anyone. Now in his thirty-fifth year, he was at the prime of life for a hunter.

Kakivik thought it must be the beginning of the lunar month called *Paniqsiqsiivik tatqiq,* "the moon for bleaching skins." For the past few days his wife, Qavlunaq, had been very busy scraping skins from the previous summer's hunting. It was a tedious job, sitting for hours on the floor with outstretched legs, pushing a bone scraper over the dense hide, peeling away stubborn bits of membrane. But Qavlunaq was strong and good-natured, and she loved the work of preparing skins for sewing. Before Kakivik left that morning, she had hung two scraped sealskins on poles outside their house, where they would bleach white in the long hours of late winter sunshine.

From the sun's position, Kakivik knew that about four hours had passed since he left the settlement, and he was now more than thirty miles inland. Thus he was not far from his destination, the trapping camp he shared with Pauluk, his father, and Tupik, a hunter about his own age. They had left Ulurunik three days ago and would probably return home in just a day or two. Kakivik planned to check both his traplines and to hunt for caribou, which meant he would stay in camp a day or two after the others left.

He brushed the accumulation of frost from his eyelashes, eyebrows, and moustache, then stood listening to the familiar sounds—snow squeaking beneath sled runners, dogs' feet patting staccato rhythms, the sled creaking as it twisted one way or another over the drifts.

Pauluk and Tupik had returned early from checking their fox traps, and now after a brief rest they were preparing to feed their dogs. Tupik stood looking westward, toward where the sun was a molten red hump flattening out along the horizon. "Something is moving far over there," he said.

"Perhaps it is someone traveling this way." Pauluk looked for a long moment, then spoke in agreement. "*Eee.* . . . A dog team. Perhaps it will be Kakivik, coming at last to check his trapline." All they could see was an elongated dark fleck, a tiny moving flaw in the vastness of white. Impossible to tell how many dogs there were, the size of the sled, the color of the traveler's parka—all things that would help them identify who was coming. They went back to chopping pieces of meat from a frozen quarter of caribou, about two pounds for each dog, setting aside enough to feed the newcomer's team.

A short while later Kakivik's dogs ran headlong down a steep bank onto the frozen surface of the Kungok River, crossed at a fast gallop, and pulled up to the top of the opposite bank. Just ahead, on a little point overlooking the confluence of the Kungok, Mioagaiak, and Kolipsiun rivers, was the camp. Kakivik dragged his sled hook to slow the dogs and shouted "Haw! Avvak, haw!" trying to steer them away from the tethered animals. Avvak did her best, but several powerful males behind her managed to pull themselves within reach of Tupik's dogs, and a snarling battle erupted. Pauluk ran up and pulled them away, and the event was reduced to a great commotion of yaps, barks, and growls.

Tupik walked over to Kakivik, smiling broadly. "What lively dogs these are, who can work all day and still have energy to fight!" He spoke with real admiration as the two men pulled off their mittens and shook hands with a single abrupt motion. Kakivik could not conceal his pride, but he appropriately changed the subject. "Ah, this is *cold* weather indeed." Tupik agreed and commented on the cloud of steam that surrounded them all, created by condensed moisture from the breath of dogs and men. "Go ahead, stake out your dogs while I unload the sled," he added. "Hot tea and meat are waiting inside."

When they had finished, Kakivik paused for a look around in the fading daylight. There was the rectangular snowhouse, with low walls, a gabled roof, and its entrance at the end of a long snow-block hallway. Paraphernalia of various sorts was stored on the roof, including a box of traps, several skinned fox carcasses, an ax, caribou hides, and a frozen caribou stomach. Off to one side was a miniature snowhouse Pauluk had built for storing meat and trapped foxes. And on three sides were the dogs, each team in its own area and every dog tied so it could reach no other. This was the only sure way to prevent having to run outside in the dead of night to break up fights.

A moment later, just before he ducked into the low hallway, Kakivik noticed a full moon lifting above the eastern horizon. It looked a bit hazy, and he wondered if tomorrow might be stormy or less cold. The hallway led to a narrow canvas-covered entrance that opened into a large room with a tent inside. The tent, which neatly filled almost the entire snowhouse, transmitted a bright luminescence from Tupik's gasoline lantern. Kakivik wriggled out of his heavy caribou-hide parka, then crouched through the tent door, fastening it behind him.

"The old man loves to keep his shelter warm," he puffed, gesturing toward his father. Warm indeed—it was a sweltering ninety degrees in the tent, which was heated by the gasoline-burning camp stove and lantern. A snowhouse alone would have to be kept near freezing inside or it would melt. But with a double shelter like this there was no such problem, and the heat was limited only by the men's tolerance. Eskimos often compensated for the intense cold they had to endure by keeping their homes and shelters very hot inside, sometimes to the point where they were forced to lie on the floor to cool off.

If the tent was warm, it was also small and cramped. The roof was high enough so a man could kneel but not stand, and its floor space was only about seven feet square. Along one wall were three grub boxes, one for each man, and beside the entrance was another box with the camp stove on it.

Steam billowed from two pots on the stove, one filled with boiling meat and the other with jet-black tea. A strong smell of cooked wild meat hung heavy in the moist air, adding to the impact of excessive warmth. The remaining floor space was covered by caribou skins, fur side up, with sleeping bags spread over them. For pillows and backrests, the men's heavy clothing was piled along the tent's far wall.

Pauluk lifted a piece of caribou meat from the pot and concluded that it was cooked. "Let's eat," he muttered in his soft voice. Hé pulled an old tin can full of seal oil from behind the stove, opened it, then speared several large chunks of meat with his knife, placing them between the men on a flat piece of wood.

The men looked at their food with pleasure and gratitude. Eskimos never took food for granted, not in a spare land in which all things came only with effort and a measure of good fortune. And so, before they ate, Tupik looked at Pauluk and said, "We will pray." Being the eldest, Pauluk was expected to speak the words. When he had given thanks and asked for protection from bad fortune, the men said "amen" in unison. Now they could eat.

"This is very fine indeed," Tupik muttered to himself as he cut a thick slice of hot meat. It had been a hard day for each of the three men, with long hours of travel in temperatures that drained enormous amounts of energy from their bodies. Small wonder they ate voraciously, cutting healthy bites from the meat, dipping them into the viscous, pungent oil, and savoring the taste to its fullest.

Tupik sat in a far corner of the tent, legs straight out before him. He was a fairly tall man, lean and hard-muscled, known for his quickness and agility. Like his father, Uli-maun, he was a clever craftsman, especially skilled in making sleds and skin boats. And he was a diligent man who loved hunting caribou and seals, which meant that his family was never short of fresh meat. Among people, he could be sullen when things did not go his way; but most often he was talkative and jovial.

For several minutes no one spoke, then Tupik smiled and looked toward the old man. "Ah, Pauluk, three more foxes today. That makes ten this trip." Turning to Kakivik, he smiled even more. "Your father traps like a young boy, full of enthusiasm. He hopes to get rich and make a new house, then ask the old widow Saatuk to marry him." With this Tupik broke into gales of laughter. Kakivik smiled broadly as well but avoided laughing too heartily at his own father. Pauluk, meanwhile, grinned between bites of meat but said nothing. "You had better hurry for Saatuk, though," Tupik continued, "before your cousin Sakiak beats you to her." This time Kakivik could not help joining the laughter, and Pauluk said something about young men who seemed unable to catch foxes but laughed at the successes of their elders.

Pauluk was a fine man, fondly admired by everyone and the object of constant, affectionate teasing. He had a very full, round face with heavy cheekbones, a thick, somewhat pug nose, smallish eyes, and very short hair that was thinning at the crown. Although he was getting old, his squat body was still full of strength. Pauluk had never been a very successful hunter, but he was a diligent trapper with a genius for catching the white fox. Few men were more quiet than Pauluk, but he loved to be with people and he was never angry. Perhaps that was why everyone cared so much for him; he could be teased and teased, yet the soft grin never left his face.

After they had eaten, the three men leaned back against the tent wall and drank tea, talking of the day's events. The discussion turned to dogs, as it so often did among Eskimo men, particularly to the qualities of this or that team, one dog or another. Tupik, who was perhaps overly proud, boasted of his dogs' speed and energy, recalling that several weeks earlier he had passed Kuvlu's excellent young team and left it

well behind. Kakivik was less boastful, but like the other men
he was very attentive to the good qualities of his dogs, often
overlooking their shortcomings. He was especially fond of
Avvak, the leader, and said that a man could hardly expect to
have more than one dog that intelligent during his lifetime.

This eventually led to gossip, Tupik describing in animated detail the way young Puviak had beaten one of his
dogs far beyond what was reasonable, apparently angered by
its laziness. "That is very bad," Pauluk interjected. "I can tell
you that one should never lose himself in such a way. Many
years ago there was a man living at Ataniq who often treated
his dogs with great cruelty, beating them for even the
slightest misbehavior. One day he whipped a dog more mer-
cilessly than usual, and as he did the animal's face suddenly
changed to that of a man. It turned and spoke out loud,
warning him to stop his cruelty, and then its face reverted to
its original form. Never again did this man treat his dogs
badly, and he often warned others by telling the story of his
frightening experience."

While they were talking, Kakivik pulled a little sewing kit
from his grub box and began repairing a tear in his mitten.
Using a heavy steel needle and a length of braided sinew, he
made tight, even stitches, almost as good as the original sewing done by his wife. Eskimos knew that clothing was their
most essential defense against the lethal cold, and for this
reason they would never travel anywhere without sewing implements. When Kakivik was young, Pauluk had frequently
reminded him of this, telling how he had once torn the bottom right off his skin boot while hunting far from camp. He
might have frozen his foot badly had he not cut a piece of
skin from his parka and sewed it on in place of the damaged
material.

After Kakivik had finished sewing, Tupik challenged him
to a finger-pulling contest. "*Eee,*" he agreed, smiling; and so
they faced each other, hooked their right index fingers, then
pulled with all their strength. Tupik grunted and strained,

but in less than a minute his finger went straight. They went on to try the other fingers, and Kakivik won all except two.

Pauluk watched, then spoke thoughtfully. "People say Kakivik is strong, but perhaps they forget about old man Apuktok, who was never once beaten in a game of strength. It was he who carried the Big Stone across the frozen mouth of the Kuk River and put it where it remains today. When Kakivik tried, he could not even lift the stone. Before Apuktok died last winter I heard him say that it was too bad he would never live to see a man stronger than himself."

A short while later Tupik and Kakivik spoke of tomorrow, that perhaps they should travel farther inland looking for caribou. Tupik had seen fresh tracks east of their camp, and he felt sure there were many small herds scattered over the country in that direction. Pauluk said he would check his south trapline, and he advised the younger men that hunting would be difficult unless the weather changed. They should hope for warmer temperatures that would make the snow less noisy, or at least for a wind to cover their sound; otherwise they would never get within gunshot range of caribou. And they should sleep now, so they could start out before sunrise.

The old man turned off the lantern and crawled into his sleeping bag, and within minutes his deep breathing showed that he was asleep. Kakivik, still awake, felt the cold creeping in around him and thought of his wife and young son in their warm house back at the settlement. When he was half-asleep he heard and felt a heavy boom pierce the ground under them. It was the frozen tundra, or the permafrost that extended for a thousand feet or more beneath it, cracking in the penetrating cold. A moment later he slept, a deep and dreamless sleep.

The moon had crept to its zenith and dipped off into the northwestern sky. A faint breeze whispered over the snow. Whatever hint of warmth the earth might still retain was

released upward into the clear immensity of the Arctic night.
Miles from the camp, far up where the Mikigealik River cut a
shallow valley into the tundra, a ghostly creature skittered
across the drifts. Thick white fur made it nearly invisible
against the snow, but the moon shadow beneath it traced the
animal's outline perfectly—an Arctic fox. It was trotting into
the breeze, alternately lifting its nose and drooping to sniff
the ground, following a faint scent of carrion.

Several hundred yards upwind it weaved and turned
around a spot marked by dark flecks on the hard surface of
the snow. The fox was nervous, its long whiskers twitching
and its black eyes searching out details of the ground. Then it
circled below the wind again and walked forward, following
the smell.

Suddenly its step was caught short by a metallic *snap*. Snow
flew upward. The fox leaped into the air squealing and
knotted. It twisted and pulled in a frenzy of pain, breaking its
teeth on the thing that gripped its paw. Then finally it sat
whimpering and licked away blood that oozed onto the jaws
of a steel trap set there by Pauluk. In an hour pain would
vanish as the leg slowly numbed and froze. But the fox would
live until the deep cold, a hungry wolverine, or a man put an
end to its waning vigil.

Next morning Pauluk woke the others before dawn, and
after a quick meal of cold meat with steaming black coffee
they all pulled on their warmest clothing. Outside the snow
crunched loudly underfoot and sharp cold pinched their
faces. It was a morning that tempted even the best of men to
go back inside and wait for the cheer of the rising sun. But no
one gave this a serious thought. The eastern sky had begun
to lighten, and already the nearby landscape was clearly visible. Time to hitch the dogs and be off for a full day's traveling. They were somewhat lucky, Tupik thought, because it
was no colder than yesterday.

Pauluk took the dog harnesses from his sled and stretched them out on the snow. "I will check my short trapline," he said, "the one that follows the Mikigealik River to its junction with Irak Creek. The last time I was there, ten days ago, I saw many fox tracks, and a wolverine's track as well." The old man walked stiffly back and forth, bringing one dog at a time to its place in the line of harnesses. He looked like a squat little fur man, bundled in caribou-hide pants, boots, and mittens and two parkas, one underneath with fur turned inside and a second over it with fur on the outside.

Tupik and Kakivik were busy loading grub boxes, rifles, and equipment bags onto their sleds, but they paused to watch the old man finish hitching his team. He had six aged dogs, and their slow, calm demeanor matched his personality to perfection. All of them sat quietly, looking almost bored, as he prepared to leave. "*Azaah,* Pauluk," Tupik laughed, "you had better hurry up and leave before your dogs fall asleep on the snow!" Pauluk smiled and kept on with his work. A moment later the dogs trotted down onto the frozen Kungok River and turned toward the west, where the Mikigealik was visible as a distant low spot in the curving bank.

Tupik and Kakivik turned quickly to the job of harnessing their own teams. Now a great commotion disturbed the early dawn—twenty-one dogs barking and leaping at their tethers in a frenzy of excitement. Kakivik hitched nine dogs, a beautiful team of matched gray-brown animals, all from a single litter of pups born to Avvak two years before. And Tupik harnessed eleven, leaving behind a young pup that was too noisy and might frighten caribou with its yapping.

When they were ready, Kakivik sat on his sled, held on tightly, and lifted his sled hook. Tupik followed seconds later, and both teams swept away down the bank, angled off southwestward into the narrow Kolipsiun valley, and within moments became small in the distance.

Behind at the empty camp the lone pup let out a long melancholy moan, unable to comprehend why it was denied the joy of traveling with the others.

Pauluk's team settled into their usual leisurely pace, somewhere between a fast walk and a slow trot; but the old man did not hurry them, knowing there would be plenty of time to check the trapline and return to camp well before dark. He followed the heavily drifted surface of the Mikigealik River for several miles, stopping occasionally to climb the bank and check a trap. The first three were empty, still perfectly concealed beneath a thin covering of snow, and he scattered a few chunks of frozen caribou stomach contents upwind of them to replenish their bait. Near the third trap he also dug around until he found a large flat stone, which he stood upright in the snow. This made an attractive urinating post, visible for half a mile over the tundra, and when foxes came to it they would probably go after the trap bait as well. Pauluk stood there briefly, silhouetted against the bright orange of the morning sky. The air was clear and nearly calm, but a few streaks of high cloud made him wonder if a wind might arise soon.

Farther up the Mikigealik, one of Pauluk's traps was set beside an old drifted-in caribou carcass in a low spot several hundred yards from the riverbank. As he approached it, he could see that it had been disturbed. The carcass had been overturned and heavily gnawed, and its entire front shoulder had been dragged away over the snow. "Wolverine!" he whispered excitedly. Although it weighed only thirty pounds itself, this stocky animal had easily moved a three-hundred-pound carcass. And it had tracked the snow all around the trap but was too wise to let itself be caught. In fact, it had dug up the trap and batted it around until it snapped harmlessly shut. Pauluk smiled, contemplating this evidence of the elusive wolverine's strength and cleverness. Even if it had been caught the animal would surely have escaped, chewing off its frozen foot if necessary.

The old man had recently heard of people living at Utqeavik who not only trapped wolverines but also hunted them with the new snowmobiles. Because the machines were fast and completely tireless, they were far better than dog teams for chasing wolverines, or wolves, spotted on the open tundra. As yet no man in Ulurunik had ridden on a snowmobile, though many wished to try it. Pauluk shared their excitement about such new things, but he was very fond of dogs and would prefer to travel slowly and quietly as he always had. Dogs would never break down, he thought, and if he became stranded in a storm they could help keep him warm in his tent or snowhouse.

At his next trap Pauluk found that he had been lucky. Here was a fox, still very much alive. Tracks leading to the place were so fresh that the animal must have been caught just last night. The fox recoiled in fear, threatening its enemy with open mouth, jerking its frozen paw in a final desperate attempt for freedom. But Pauluk pinned it deftly with one foot and then pressed hard on its chest, killing it almost immediately without causing a wound that would stain its valuable fur. In a moment it lay soft and limp on the snow, its sightless eyes meeting the remorseless stare of the hunter.

Pauluk saw that its fur was thick and white, except for a yellowish patch under the chin where it had soiled itself feeding on the putrid fat of an old walrus or whale carcass out on the pack ice. The hide would someday hang from the shoulders of a woman as white as itself, he thought; but for him it meant twenty dollars in trade at the village store. And the meat would be used for dog food, unless it was very fat and he decided to eat it himself.

He quickly bent to his knees and smoothed the snow with his knife. Then he cut a shallow depression in the drift, put the opened trap into it, and laid a thin slab of snow over the top. Using his knife again he shaved this slab down until it was very thin and fragile, then smoothed the area with the furry back of his mitten. The trap was now completely hidden and remained anchored to a stick buried down under the snow. He had scattered several bits of meat on the northeast side of the set, so that a fox following the scent on the prevailing wind was likely to walk onto the trap before reaching the bait.

When he had finished, Pauluk carried the fox to his sled and carefully secured it with the lashings. The warm body and thick fur gave a welcome dose of heat to his chilled fingers as he tied his catch in place. Then he stood behind the sled, pulled up the hook and called to the dogs. They arose, stretched, and waited until he called out again before setting off at their usual leisurely trot.

Several hours after leaving the camp, Kakivik and Tupik stopped to make tea with the camp stove and kettle they had brought along. It was bitter cold, still near forty below zero, and the chill had penetrated their furs. They had traveled in the Kolipsiun River valley, climbing the banks here and there to scan the tundra, but as yet there was no sign of game. Sitting on their sleds drinking the strong, hot tea, they saw the sun's rays slanting over one bank of the river, pouring their brightness onto the other.

"Not far ahead there is a small creek that enters from the north," Kakivik said. "Perhaps we should leave the river there and travel across the land." Tupik agreed, saying that they were near the first low hills, which they could ascend to overlook miles of terrain. He knew that caribou had been moving through this area several weeks before, so he was a bit surprised that they had seen no tracks yet. "A little wind appears to be stirring from the northeast," he added. "If it grows stronger we may have good hunting in spite of the cold."

At that same moment, only a few miles from where the two men sat, a small herd of caribou stood placidly near the top of a gentle rise. Powerful winds had stripped away much of the snow cover here, exposing patches of matted vegetation—the mosses, grasses, and crisp lichens that were the caribou's food. They were beautiful deer, their heavy bodies tan with a frosting of white on the neck and shoulders. Several large bulls, weighing perhaps four hundred pounds, stood among the scattering of cows and younger bulls. A few animals lay quietly on the snow, looking attentively over the surrounding terrain. The others grazed slowly along, digging through the drifts with their sharp hooves to find fresh plants, occasionally lifting their heads for a look around.

The herd ambled slowly down off the rise and up onto another, searching for fresh feed and perhaps yielding to their perpetual urge to move. Few animals wandered more than the caribou. During the winter they remained in small groups, dispersed widely over the Arctic plains and far southward into the northern fringes of the boreal forest. With the coming of spring they gathered into herds and migrated north, congregating at the age-old calving grounds. Then in summer they often migrated again, wandering to and fro over the land, apparently following no predictable pattern. And when the chill of fall arrived, great massed herds swept southward toward the mountains and forest, leaving only a fraction of their numbers behind to winter as far north as Ulurunik.

Although this little group of animals had spent the past month within fifty miles of the settlement, they had seen nothing of man beyond a few empty sled tracks cutting across the path of their wanderings. They had been chased several times by packs of wolves, but none had been taken except an old cow that had grown weak with age. And one other became sick in the darkest part of winter, finally dying near the end of a powerful blizzard that lasted six days. The

remaining animals were all healthy, and fatter than was usual
for this time of year. Now they moved along slowly toward
the northeast, completely unaware of the danger that would
approach them later that day.

Kakivik and Tupik finished their tea and were on their way
again, letting their teams trot along side by side. But at one
point the animals drew very close together and opposing
males began to growl antagonistically. Before anything could
be done a fight had erupted. Both men quickly stopped and
waded into the snarling animals, whipping offenders until
they cringed away from battle. Sled dogs were so tough, so
thick-skinned, that without a whip or stick no one could stop
them once a fight erupted. When they got under way again,
this time with Kakivik's team out ahead to avoid trouble, the
dogs galloped for a while, working off the energy that fighting had given them.

About a half-mile farther on they saw fresh caribou tracks,
where a dozen animals had crossed the Kolipsiun going
eastward. But when they looked from atop the bank the
country was empty, though they could not see far now because of scattered low rises. A short time later they found
more tracks, these about two days old; but again they saw
nothing through their binoculars. Even so, both men were a
little excited, and Kakivik recalled the fun they had had
chasing caribou during the huge migration that had passed
near Kangich the previous fall.

The day had now become very bright, and the low sun
shone directly on the men as they traveled up the narrowing
valley. Kakivik's feet were chilled and stiff, so he ran behind
the sled for short stretches to stimulate circulation of warm
blood to his extremities. Even Tupik, who often seemed impervious to cold, clapped his mittens and jogged a few times.
But he suddenly forgot his discomfort when he noticed a
very subtle quickening in the dogs' pace. Almost at the same

moment Kakivik saw Avvak's nose lift, her head turning this way and that, as she searched the air for a faint scent.

Shortly, several dogs in each team raised their snouts and looked from side to side, unable to establish direction for a scent that swirled around in the valley's confusing air currents. Their speed nearly doubled now, as the familiar urge to hunt charged their muscles; and just as they broke into a run Kakivik gave a low-spoken command, "Avvak, gee! Gee!" Avvak swerved to the right, leading the excited team in a dash up the face of a huge, steep drift that ended at the bank's edge. Tupik's dogs followed right behind, and in a moment they emerged onto the rolling tundra.

From the dogs' behavior the men knew that game must be nearby, but they were not quite ready for what happened now. As they came up over the lip of the bank they saw the animals, not more than four hundred yards straight upwind of them. "Caribou," Kakivik whispered. "Caribou!" There were eleven, standing in a scattered line against the side of a hill, staring directly toward the hunters. They had probably heard the sleds before seeing them—the air was so clear and the breeze so light. One of them, a magnificent antlerless bull, stood with a single hind leg jutting back and to one side. This was a warning posture, a signal of danger that other caribou could read from a distance.

The dogs, already stirred by the powerful scent, became frantic when they saw one caribou move a few steps. Before any of them could start barking, Tupik and Kakivik took a firm grip on their sleds, pulled up the anchoring hooks, and were off on a mad dash over the snow. Sometimes caribou would not run until a team got very close, and even then they might go only a short distance and stop again, looking back at their pursuers. Perhaps they mistook dog teams for wolves, which could manage to catch only the old, infirm, or newborn. The slow-minded caribou seemed never to learn that men and dog teams were something entirely different.

This time, however, the caribou quickly took flight, probably startled by the loud banging of sleds bouncing over hard drifts toward them. Each of them took a single splendid leap and ran off, head high and white tail erect. The men gave chase over the first low hill, into a broad swale, and up another long rise. But the caribou's stiff gait was much faster than it looked. Although they stopped several times to look back, they still remained far out ahead. Tupik encouraged his dogs with hushed commands, and they kept running at top speed, tongues hanging and clouds of breath puffing into the cold. Kakivik, with fewer dogs, dropped slightly behind.

In a flat area beyond the second rise, two miles east of the river, the caribou stopped a few hundred yards from their pursuers. The dogs were tiring, so both men quickly unlashed their rifles and prepared to shoot. Two loud cracks rang over the land, and the snow puffed twice, well short of the herd. Shots again, now accompanied by the dogs' wild barking. This time one puff was high and another off to the left. The men fired again and again, always sitting on their sleds to guard against losing their teams should the anchoring hooks jerk from the snow. But the caribou were now running full speed at an angle away from them, and no shot hit its mark. In a few moments they became small in the distance, running up the ridge and vanishing on the other side.

"*Azaah,* some of them looked fat," Tupik said. Kakivik agreed, smiling. They could not feel disappointment at their failure, for this was surely what one would expect on a cold day when caribou could hear sleds a mile away.

They were now far off on the tundra, seemingly lost amid an endless confusion of monotonous rolling terrain. But after a brief discussion the two men had their exact position pinpointed on mental charts of the area through which they traveled. The largest hill just north of them was named Kimigaak; and the faintly visible creek at its base, now a mere furrow in the snow, was called Imaktok. To experienced hunters this unvaried land was anything but an endless repetition of itself. Every small irregularity, every rise and dip, every pond or stream—all these things, even down to certain rocks on the ground, were unique. The oldest men could name hundreds and hundreds of landmarks in the region surrounding Ulurunik, many of them identifying features so subtle that they could never be detected by a stranger.

"Perhaps we should travel farther inland, straight east toward the headwaters of the Kugroak River," Tupik suggested, warming his face as he talked. "It seems possible that more caribou will be there, and if the wind grows stronger we may find easy hunting." Kakivik agreed but thought they should make tea again and eat *quaq,* frozen raw meat, before traveling on.

Eskimos knew the importance of stopping frequently to rest and restore themselves with food, especially with wild meat that would generate physical and mental strength. So while snow was melted for tea they cut thick chunks from a piece of raw, frozen caribou meat. It was hard and chewy, dark red, with a rich taste that made people prefer *quaq* over meat that had the flavor cooked out of it. With each piece they ate a slice of mesentary fat from inside the caribou, fat that would quickly restore their warmth and energy.

"Why do you suppose the *Tanik,* the white man, cannot bring himself to swallow something as delicious as *quaq?*" Tupik asked. "It can only be that he is foolish about food, as he is about so many other things," Kakivik replied. "I have seen them singe their meat on the outside, leaving it red and bloody inside; yet they believe it is not raw. And think how they are repelled by raw fat and seal oil; yet the *Taniks* use oil that they pour from bottles, and they love to smear butter, their own kind of grease, over much of what they eat. I have watched enough *Taniks,*" Kakivik concluded, "to know that they are strange."

By the time they had finished hot cups of tea and set out again, the sun had passed its zenith, moving around behind

them toward the west. The northeasterly breeze had increased to a fair wind that blew sinuous wisps of snow along
the ground. Traveling into the wind was very cold indeed,
and they crossed two broad knolls without seeing more than
a few tracks and one large flock of ptarmigan. The ptarmigan, Arctic grouse that turned pure white in winter, flew up
suddenly near Kakivik's team, startling him and his dogs.
These were tasty birds, and he wished he had a light rifle or
shotgun so he could follow them and try to kill a few. In the
spring, he thought, the old men and women would catch
many in baited snares, and everyone would eat ptarmigan
until they grew tired of them.

About a mile beyond where they saw the birds, the dogs
began showing excitement again. Several raised their noses
simultaneously, and the sleds surged ahead. Moments later
Tupik saw bits of grass blowing along the surface, and from
this he knew that caribou were not far away, digging through
the snow and scattering bits of vegetation. Coming over the
gentle curve of a rise, they saw what they had anticipated.
There, perhaps half a mile ahead, was a herd of more than
twenty caribou.

No matter how far sled dogs had pulled, and no matter
how dead tired they seemed to be, they still had the energy to
run like fresh puppies when they were chasing caribou.
Down the hill's gradual slope they went, sprinting over the
snow as if they were free of harnesses and sleds. The caribou
were feeding, moving into the wind with their backs toward
the approaching hunters. Because of this, and because the
brisk wind carried the noise of the sleds away from them,
they were not alerted to danger.

At the bottom of the hill Tupik turned his dogs off toward
one side of the herd, and Kakivik went toward the other.
They were not seen until they were two hundred yards away,
and then every caribou snapped to attention. But instead
of running they stood and watched—perhaps unafraid,
perhaps confused. Then they milled for a moment, unable to

find a leader or agree on which direction to run. Fairly close now, Kakivik saw that about half were bulls, with beautiful white manes and powerful haunches. The others were fat cows with small and gracile antlers, brown and gray coats striking against the background of white.

When the teams were seventy yards away, the caribou suddenly bunched, turned, and ran across in front of Tupik. He reacted instantly, setting his sled hook and jerking the team to an abrupt halt. Two shots cracked in quick succession, catching the lead animal in mid-gait. It stumbled and pitched forward to the snow, stiff legs flailing. Tupik smiled, knowing that a leaderless herd would become confused.

The caribou wheeled away and then stopped, milling and disoriented. Tupik shot two, three, four more times. Finally a young cow veered off from the herd, dashing toward Kakivik, and the others followed crazily—except for two that had been hit. One collapsed immediately; the other slowly dropped out from the herd, wobbled, stood still, and finally toppled sideways.

Kakivik fired three times at the new leader, and with his last shot it staggered and fell. Again the herd reversed its direction, then circled to and fro in confusion. Both hunters now shot repeatedly until at last the panic-stricken beasts galloped away on the heels of a large bull that ran east into the wind. Two animals fell behind, and the men gave chase.

The one nearest Tupik soon stopped and turned sideways, as if offering itself, and Tupik dragged his sled hook until his near-delirious team was forced to halt. It was difficult to aim—he was breathing hard and his heart pounded—but his second shot hit the caribou and knocked it powerfully down onto the snow.

Kakivik chased another that was wounded in the heavy muscle of its hind leg. It ran with an uneven gait just a few yards ahead of the rushing dogs, head turned to look behind, wide-eyed and fearful. Kakivik tried but could not stop his team, so he held the rifle at his waist and fired from the moving sled. On his third shot the animal jerked to one side and suddenly went slack, fell forward, and used its last strength to raise its head and look toward the oncoming dogs. Seconds later they charged right into the animal, tearing and shaking it, consummating all that went before. Kakivik gave them their time, reinforcing the urges that made them chase, then pulled them away and looked to be certain it was dead.

Kakivik stood there briefly, staring at the animal he had just killed, then looked over the land to where the others lay. "*Quyanaq*," he spoke softly, a single word that expressed thanks for what they had been given.

They had killed six and would have taken more—all of them—had they been able. Hunting, after all, was life for these men. But there was something beyond this, for life was hunting as well. Perhaps this was why they sometimes killed beyond their need, so powerful inside them was the urge to hunt. And from the elders they had learned that what was killed would become living flesh again through reincarnation of its soul.

Both men set to work immediately, dragging heavy carcasses onto their sleds and hauling them to one place. Kakivik looked over their catch and exclaimed joyfully, "Good, excellent indeed!" Tupik's pleasure was no smaller, but he said that not much remained of the day and they should perhaps work fast. Eskimos tried to avoid traveling at night, but it looked as if darkness would catch them before they reached camp. "At least we have the full moon, and the sky is clear," Kakivik mused.

Tupik took a small whetstone from his sled bag and sharpened his curved steel knife to a fine edge. Then he went to the nearest animal and looked at it carefully, "Ah, this *kulavaraq* [young cow that has never conceived] will be fat, with tender meat." With deft knife strokes, he slit the skin and pulled it away from the flesh inside, removing it completely within a few minutes. Then he turned the carcass belly up and cut into the tight-stretched, silvery layers of muscle. The intestines and distended stomach felt warm and slippery as he pulled them, steaming, onto the snow. They permeated the air with heavy smells of flesh and digesting vegetation.

Cutting along the soft cartilage, he severed the ribs and opened the chest cavity. Dark, hot blood swilled inside, dyeing his hands crimson as he worked. Each set of bones could easily be cut apart along its joints, and Tupik used his detailed knowledge of anatomy as he dismembered the animal, piece by piece. Lower leg was cut from upper leg, upper leg from shoulder, shoulder from upper body—each part had its own name and its own uses. Tupik was pleased by the thick layer of fat along this animal's back, and he hoped the others might be in equally fine condition. "Kakivik," he smiled, "we will eat an excellent meal tonight! If the old man is wise, he will wait for us before eating the skinny meat back in camp."

An hour later they were nearly finished. Tupik held his hands among the warm folds of a gelatinous mound of caribou stomach until finally the aching chill left them. The sun was just setting, pale orange and silver glowing over the crown of the nearest hill, and they could feel a steady drop in temperature. Working together, they loaded heavy chunks of meat onto the sleds, careful not to forget small delicacies like kidneys, hearts, tongues, and favored parts of the stomach. Tupik's family loved to eat *amaniilik,* boiled lower intestine, so he took a long section and pulled it through his fingers, squeezing out its unappetizing contents. When they had finished loading, Kakivik set two fox traps alongside the discarded stomachs, hoping to add still more to their measure of success.

It was slow going now with heavy sleds and dogs already tired, so they set a course just north of west, heading straight toward their distant camp. Evening gradually shrouded the sky, lifting up and over them from the east, finally closing down upon the last vestiges of sunset. But at the same time the moon rose, full and clear, with mottled patterns standing out sharply on its face.

Traveling by moonlight over this enormous, silent wilderness was like no other experience on earth. A beautiful gray cast spread over the land, illuminating it to the far horizon, but in this pale light even the irregularities of drifted snow were lost. The world was now divided between two halves, a great flat disk of white below and a limpid expanse of star-flecked black above. But the hunters' practical minds dwelt on other matters—picking out faint valleys, watching the low knolls pass by them, maintaining a steady angle beneath the faint arch of aurora overhead. Aesthetics were a luxury reserved for men not burdened by the all-encompassing concern for survival in a hard land.

The day's sparse warmth was quickly sapped, and the temperature dropped to minus forty-five. Tupik and Kakivik found it best to walk behind their sleds now, both to lighten the dogs' load and to keep themselves from shivering. It had been a long day out in the cold, and a good distance remained to be traversed.

Kakivik let himself think of the *Inyuiligaurit,* the Little People, though it was somewhat frightening to do so. These were tiny dwarfs, the size of a newborn puppy, who lived in little houses under the tundra. *Inyuiligaurit* did not hurt people, but they did not like them either. Once, it was said, a dwarf had challenged a man to a footrace along the edge of a lagoon. The man had insisted that they run on opposite shores, knowing that one side was straight and the other very crooked. Since he chose the straight shore, he had won easily; but then the angry dwarf had tried to kill him with a little ivory spear. Instead, the man had shot the dwarf with an arrow, then had taken its head to prevent vengeance by its relatives. Kakivik remembered being told that the head was like an owl's. Imagining this made him feel uneasy, so he urged the dogs to hurry and forced his thoughts away from dwarfs.

After two hours' traveling, Tupik, who was in the lead, very slowly became aware that it was growing darker. Finally he looked back over his shoulder at the moon, thinking that a cloud must be covering it. But what he saw was a shock. A curved black shadow crossed the moon's face, seeming to cut it in half. *"Azaah,"* he exclaimed out loud, "an eclipse!" Perhaps everything that happened in life was an improbability, but this...the one night when they happened to be traveling after dark. Tupik could not help wondering why such a thing would occur.

Earth's shadow moved very slowly upward, until finally the moon disappeared behind it. Now they were immersed in blackness that was near absolute, with only a dim glow of aurora to make the ground at their feet half-visible. When Tupik stopped, Kakivik might have passed right by him had his dogs not slowed to sniff the other team.

The two men discussed their situation, Tupik saying they should perhaps await the moon's return before going farther. But Kakivik said this would delay them for at least an hour or two, and by then they would be thoroughly chilled. "Avvak is an old lead dog, and she cannot get lost," he added. "If we let her find the way there will be no trouble. She has traveled in this country before, and darkness will make no difference to her." Tupik had seen the way old dogs could navigate, and so he agreed that they should continue.

Once they were under way again, Kakivik gave no commands to Avvak, even when it seemed that she might be veering off course. Once he stopped and felt the drifts with his hands, and from their shape he knew they were still heading northwest. The blackness seemed to grow even more complete, and for once Kakivik became impatient with the slow passage of time as he traveled. But Avvak went on and on without hesitation, guided by an innate directional sense that was as natural to her as sight and smell.

An hour passed without change, beyond the imperceptible motion of stars and the startling flash of a meteor in the

northern sky. But finally they noticed a crescent glow above
and behind them, then a thin sliver of moon gradually reappearing. In half an hour more, Kakivik thought, there
would be light again.

But a few minutes later he felt the dogs abruptly surge
ahead, almost trotting despite their heavy load. Perhaps
there were caribou nearby, and if so Avvak might deviate
from her course to chase them. They had traveled a long
time, however, and should be well beyond the area where
caribou had been wintering. Kakivik's thoughts were cut
short as the sled suddenly tilted and slid precipitously downward, the dogs fleeing ahead to avoid being run over.

"The river," he said aloud. "This must be the Kungok
River, the high bank just across from camp." In a moment his
thoughts were confirmed by the sound of barking ahead—
Pauluk's dogs giving them an excited welcome. "Good dog,
Avvak. *Azahaa,* you're a good one!" he shouted, as they
strained up the bank and pulled to a stop beside the
snowhouse. It was still pitch dark, but when Pauluk emerged
with the lantern they could see Avvak curled up next to the
spot where she had slept the night before. The hunters were
home.

Agaviksiuvik Tatqiq

The Moon When Whaling Begins

(APRIL)

MAIN CHARACTERS

Ulimaun (*Oo*-lee-mawn) *an old man*

Talimat (*Tul*-ee-mut) *Ulimaun's first son*

Nauruk (*Now*-rook) *Ulimaun's second son*

Tupik (*Too*-pik) *Ulimaun's third son*

Migalik (Mee-*gul*-ik) *Ulimaun's fifth son*

Ivisaak (Iv-ee-*sock*) *Talimat's wife*

Sakiak (Sah-*kee*-uk) *an old hunter*

Pukak (*Poo*-kuk) *an adult hunter*

Patik (*Pah*-tik) *Sakiak's grandson*

S IX LITTLE WHITE BIRDS fluttered over the snow, then
abruptly wheeled and landed just beyond the southernmost house of Ulurunik. They found a patch of grass poking up through the drifts and hopped about pecking at tassles
with seeds left on them, occasionally singing out clear, high-
pitched notes that identified them as snow buntings. Perhaps
they sang to commemorate the end of their long journey
northward from the prairies of southern Canada.

Nukatpiak, a ten-year-old Eskimo boy, heard the birds'
song and went quickly to his house. A few minutes later he
crept across the snow on his belly, eyes narrowed and face
determined, with a small bow and arrow in his hand. Ten
yards from the unsuspecting flock he stopped, drew the bow,
and shot. Much to his surprise the arrow struck a bird, and
only five flew away. The bird felt hot and plump in his hand
as he ran for home, excited almost beyond knowing what
to do.

Nukatpiak's father was also surprised and excited when
the boy proudly held out the little ball of ruffled,
bloodstained feathers. "This boy has killed an animal," he
exulted, "and it is *amautligaaluk*, the snowbird!" Two
momentous things had occurred. Nukatpiak had taken his
first game, marking the beginning of his life as a hunter. And

the snowbirds had returned, which meant that the whales would soon arrive on their annual northward migration. "The birds tell us," Nukatpiak's father said, "that it is now *Agaviksiuvik tatqiq,* the moon when whaling begins."

Events like this quickly became known to everyone in the settlement. The old hunter Ulimaun told Nukatpiak, "I see you have become a man, grandson. Perhaps someday soon you will bring seal and caribou meat to my house." The boy stood looking at the ground, then turned and ran away in embarrassment.

And Ulimaun admonished the younger hunters to procrastinate no longer, but to ready their skin boats and equipment for the whaling season just ahead. "Do you want to sit here in the village while someone else chases whales out in the open leads?" he asked.

One of the men who heard him was his second son, Nauruk. Although Nauruk was only in his mid-thirties, he had already taken five whales and was regarded as an *umealik,* or boat captain. This was not an ordinary achievement, but neither was he an ordinary man. First of all, he was the biggest and strongest man in Ulurunik, as well as the most agile and athletic. His blustering, somewhat egotistical personality seemed a natural outgrowth of these physical attributes; but underneath it he was a thoughtful and intelligent man who commanded great respect from his peers.

During the past year Nauruk had been especially generous to the members of his whaling crew, and all had agreed to hunt with him again this season. Now he asked them to help with cleaning and repairing the equipment, so they might be among the first out when whales appeared. In the next two weeks they carved a new set of paddles, repaired a broken whaling harpoon, made two sealskin floats, and helped to put a new cover on their *umiaq,* or skin boat. The *umiaq,* a large one made by Ulimaun ten years earlier, required seven bearded-seal skins to cover it. The skins had been allowed to rot last summer so that the hair would slip off easily; and now they were scraped, cut to size, and sewn by Nauruk's mother, his wife, and the wives of four crew members. Using special stitches that went only halfway through the thick hide, the women sewed double, overlapping seams that were completely waterproof. Finally the men helped them to stretch the finished cover over the frame and lash it to the gunwales.

When they were done, Nauruk spoke with pride and satisfaction, "Now we are ready to hunt. Our boat looks new in its fresh skins, and the equipment has been cleaned so that everything will be pleasing to the whale's eye." The people were invited to his house, where they feasted on frozen chunks of *maktak,* black whale skin with oily pink blubber attached. It was the last that remained from a whale killed the previous year by Nauruk's crew, and he had saved it for this occasion. Eskimos loved *maktak* like no other food, savoring its almond flavor and rich, chewy fat. When the feast was over Nauruk divided all that remained among his crew members and their families, and when he finished everyone went home.

In the week that followed, the whalers could do nothing more than wait. A persistent onshore wind held the pack tightly in toward the land, so an unbroken expanse of ice stretched to the horizon. Then finally the wind shifted to the northeast and rose to a gale that blew steadily for three days, dropping afterward to a gentle breeze. Now the people saw what they had hoped for—a dark streak in the clouds far out over the ice. This was *kissuk,* water sky, the black color of open water reflected in a low overcast. Strong winds had pushed against the mobile pack, breaking it free of the land-fast ice and opening a lane, or lead, of water several miles wide. This lead stretched along the entire coast from Ulurunik two hundred miles south to Tikerak, and who could guess how far beyond.

Nauruk stood outside his house on the bank overlooking the frozen sea, talking with Pukak, a member of his crew. "Whales are surely coming north in that trail of open water," he said, "if indeed some have not already passed during the storm." That evening his thoughts were confirmed when two men returned from hunting seals at the lead edge and reported that they had seen twelve whales in the course of the day. They even said that a very large one had surfaced right in front of them, blowing so close by that its noise had startled them badly.

Hesitation was no virtue in the Far North, where weather or ocean currents might change at any time, closing the lead and spoiling the hunt. It was early spring and there was no real darkness, only a period of dim twilight for a few hours around midnight; so Nauruk and his crew set to work immediately and continued all night making preparations for departure. Early the next morning four dog teams were assembled in front of Nauruk's house, three of them pulling sleds loaded with supplies and the fourth hitched to a large flat sled with the *umiaq* tied onto it. Everything was ready.

A large crowd of people, including jubilant hordes of children, gathered around the *umiaq*. Old Sakiak, who belonged to Nauruk's crew, stood near the bow of the boat and delivered a long prayer asking for protection and success in their hunt. As a boy he had watched the shamans chant sacred and powerful songs before the whalers left for the ice. Perhaps little had changed except the words that were spoken. When the prayer was finished, Nauruk's wife, Itiruk, threw handfuls of candy to the gleeful children, showing again that the *umealik* was a generous man who shared his wealth with those who assisted or encouraged him.

Throughout these final preparations, Nauruk was kept very busy making certain that nothing was forgotten, seeing that sled loads were properly secured, and bracing the boat so it would not break crossing rough ice. All the whalers were objects of great admiration, but *umealiks* like Nauruk were heroes of another order. No one in Eskimo society was so respected as the provider, and to become an *umealik* a man had to provide in abundance far beyond what was usual.

Nauruk had earned his status by his prowess as a hunter, by his extraordinary physical strength, and by his powerful personality. He and the other members of his crew knew well that this was their moment of glory. It could be surpassed only by the acclaim they would receive if they returned driving sleds laden with whale meat.

The crew gathered inside Nauruk's house to eat before departing. There were six men in all—Nauruk, his three brothers, Talimat, Tupik, and Migalik, his great-uncle Sakiak, and his friend Pukak. In addition there was Talimat's wife Ivisaak, who was to be the cook, and Sakiak's grandson Patik, who would help with chores in the camp.

While they ate, old Sakiak told stories of whaling as he knew it when he was young, and especially tales of hunts that ended in success. "Whaling is not easy," he warned. "Many seasons have passed when not a single whale was taken by any of the Ulurunik crews. If we are to succeed we must work well together, avoid noises that will frighten the animals, say nothing boastful of ourselves or demeaning to the whales, and make prayers several times each day."

A short while later they were on their way past the last village houses and down the bank onto the frozen sea. Crowds of children followed along behind, running until they could pursue the hunters no farther. Nauruk, riding ahead with the *umiaq,* felt thoroughly proud and happy. What more was there for a man then to be off on the ice to hunt whales?

Far to the south of Ulurunik, and twenty miles off the coast, an enormous bowhead whale swam ponderously northward against the gentle current. It rolled to the surface and breathed several times in succession, then arched its back and sounded, showing its flukes at the last moment of the dive. At twenty fathoms it leveled off, gliding slowly through clouds of living particles, the tiny planktonic organisms that sifted through its jaws and became its food. Here, at the lowest

edge of light, the animal was visible only as a black, tor-
pedolike shadow sixty feet long from nose to tail.

When the whale rose toward the surface again it tilted on
one side and saw a solid expanse of deep translucent gray
above, part of a broad ice peninsula that extended across the
lead. After swimming another half-mile, feeling a need for
air, it angled upward toward a bright glowing patch indicating ice only a foot thick. The heavy bones of its skull felt no
strain as it burst vertically through the frozen pavement;
then it emerged into the brightness above and took a long,
resonating breath of air.

Beneath the ice again, the whale heard distant waterborne
sounds, a strange orchestration of tones, metallic squeals,
and dissonant grunts. These noises came from others in its
group, about a dozen, that were all heading north in the lead
within a few miles of each other. Perhaps the sounds allowed
distant whales to communicate, or possibly they created
echoes that were used to locate food and trace the configurations of pack ice up ahead. The bowhead flipped its
huge tail several times and swept away into the darkness, tons
of water swirling quietly in its wake.

Nauruk and his crew traveled north along the coast for ten
miles, then turned out to sea just below Nunagayak. The ice
was smooth for several miles offshore here, unlike the very
rough conditions around Ulurunik; and from the dark cloud
they could see that the lead came closest to land in this area.
Still, it appeared to be about fifteen miles out, and reaching it
would involve many hours of hard work. Before long they
approached the first ridges and fields of piled ice, and they
found Amiksuk's crew already there, chopping a smooth trail
for the boats and sleds.

Using axes and chisels, the men slowly chipped their way
through the lowest parts of ridges, one after the other in
what seemed like an endless succession. Their trail wound
back and forth across the jumbled floes, following the longest

flat stretches and cutting across the least difficult rough spots. Throughout the afternoon the men labored, throwing their parkas aside and sweating despite temperatures slightly below zero. In the evening Kuvlu's crew joined them, and the work crept along somewhat faster. The little procession, twenty-five men, thirteen dog teams, and three *umiaqs*, made its way toward its remote goal. Near midnight, when they stopped to rest, Amiksuk laughed and said that the water sky still looked very far off along the horizon.

Early the next morning, when the sun was well up and snow crystals glistened brightly, Sakiak climbed a tall ridge and called to the others. "Open water just ahead. . . . I see the lead, and only a few rough spots still to cross." An hour later Nauruk's *umiaq* bounced through the last stretch of hummocky ice, Tupik and Migalik running alongside to steady it. And a hundred yards farther on they stopped at the ice edge.

The men sat down for a brief rest, drinking hot tea and looking out over the lead. The water was glassy calm, mirroring the weird configurations of ice pans and floebergs that drifted southward on a slight current. Floebergs were ponderous islands of ice, broad ridges with peaks and crags and tilted slabs, that had broken from the pack to float free. Because it was cold, about ten below zero, a haze of steam rose from the water and hung very low along its surface.

When they had finished their tea, Nauruk said his crew would make camp several hundred yards to the south, where Sakiak had found a good place surrounded by heavy ice. Kuvlu decided to move a short distance north, and Amiksuk would go beyond him. The spot Sakiak had chosen was ideal, a small flat area with large ridges north and south of it and a somewhat lower ridge behind, which they crossed to enter the flat. The high ice piles were solidly grounded on the ocean floor, their seaward faces scraped smooth and sheer by the pack ice that had crushed against them throughout the winter.

Sakiak gestured with a sweep of his arm as he explained to

the others, "This is the outer fringe of the landfast ice, and
the big hummocks will anchor it well. But we must watch
carefully when the pack ice moves swiftly nearby, because if it
rams powerfully into the edge close to this place we may have
trouble."

Nauruk and the others set to work immediately, removing
the *umiaq* from its sled and positioning it so the bow stood
right at the water's edge. Paddles were placed in readiness
along the gunwales, sharp butchering lances rested in the
bottom, and the weapons were set carefully at the bow. These
consisted of the shoulder gun, which was an oversized rifle
that shot explosive bombs, and a darting gun or harpoon.
The harpoon was about eight feet long, with a heavy wooden
shaft. It was armed with a sharp iron tip that would lodge
deep beneath the whale's skin. And near the tip was a trigger
mechanism that automatically shot a bomb into an animal
when it was struck. A heavy rope ran from the harpoon head
to an inflated sealskin float that was kept behind the harpooner's seat. If a whale was struck, the float would be
thrown from the boat and would drag along behind the animal, marking its position.

Young Patik stood looking at the *umiaq,* anxious for the
moment when he would help to slide it into the water and set
off after a whale. It was a sleek craft, twenty-five feet long,
with a narrow bottom and gently curved gunwales. Six men
could paddle it swiftly and quietly through the water like a
light canoe, yet it was so tough that constant scraping and
banging from the ice did it no harm.

When the boat was ready and waiting, everyone worked
together to set up the camp. In a matter of minutes the tent
was erected, with a floor of caribou skins spread out inside,
and a camp stove was lighted to make tea and provide
warmth. Talimat's wife Ivisaak, who had worked alongside
the men all night, started boiling a pot of caribou meat. But
by the time it was ready Patik, Migalik, and Pukak were all
sound asleep on the skins behind her.

The other men were still busy outside, making a snow-block wall near the *umiaq* to serve as a windbreak. In its shelter they put a large sled covered with caribou skins, making a comfortable bench for those who would keep watch for approaching whales. Finally, Tupik chiseled steps to the top of a large hummock at the water's edge, making a high lookout for sighting game in the distance. From this moment onward, throughout all the days and weeks of the whaling season, a continuous watch would be maintained. Only weather or ice conditions that drove them back to the land would interrupt their vigil.

Everyone except Nauruk and Talimat retired into the tent for a meal and long-awaited sleep. Old Sakiak lay back in a corner of the tent, eyes half-closed, speaking in a low monotone. "Eskimos have hunted whales for many generations, perhaps thousands of years, since long before the white men came into our country. When I was a boy we still followed the old ways, using only *ayak,* the big whaling harpoon, and stone-bladed lances that could puncture a whale's heart or kidneys. Although there were many whales then, it was hard to kill them without the bombs and iron tools brought here by men from the ships.

"We followed many ancient rules in former times," he continued, "rules that made whales consider us worthy of hunting them. For one thing, we were not allowed to be comfortable. Although we made sealskin tents and caribou-hide sleeping bags, in whaling camps their use was forbidden. We were also allowed no fires, no cooked meat, no warm liquids or broth, and we could never return to the settlement except when bad conditions forced us off the ice. We used windbreaks and double layers of caribou skin clothing, but *oh,* we were cold.

"Noise was also strictly forbidden, especially chopping sounds. Even people left behind in the village were expected to keep quiet, to avoid chopping wood or pounding things." Then Sakiak looked at Ivisaak and added, "The *umealik's* wife was expected to behave in special ways. She could not work or keep busy, because to do so made whales hard to catch. She could not use a knife, lest the harpoon line break when a whale pulled it. And she was forbidden to eat the meat of land animals, though I cannot say why."

Migalik said he was happy that they no longer followed these rules, and Sakiak replied. "Indeed, our ways have changed. Now we have tents, sleeping bags, warm food—and the only difficult rule is the new one told us by missionaries, that we must never kill a whale or any other animal on Sunday. I remember two springs ago, when a huge whale surfaced at the ice edge right in front of our *umiaq*, late one Sunday afternoon. Luckily, we were not foolish enough to kill it, because if we had I know that some bad luck would have befallen us. The missionary said later that we would surely be rewarded for honoring the Sabbath in this way." The old man sat quietly thinking for a few minutes, then pulled his arms inside his parka and nodded off to sleep.

Nauruk and Talimat sat outside on the bench watching the lead, each of them occasionally napping, then awakening from the cold a short while later. The sun rode slowly up and along the southern sky, finally dropping lower toward the northwest. Tupik, Migalik and Pukak emerged from the tent and let the two watchers sleep.

Sunset came, and high cirrus clouds flamed orange in the sky; breezes blew ripples across the water, then faded to calm again; it was twenty below zero. The oval moon, in its third quarter, rose above the deep blue eastern horizon and settled low just a few hours later. Everything was dead still, and the hours passed in silence, broken only by occasional hushed conversation and once by the distant thud of a rifle shot from the direction of Amiksuk's camp. Perhaps someone had killed a seal that rose nearby to stare at the intruders.

Midnight passed without darkness, and soon afterward the gloomy dusk began to lighten. The men outside paced back and forth, clapped their hands, and did short Eskimo dances to their own accompaniment, keeping themselves warm as they awaited the slowly growing dawn. Several times during the night's long passage they went into the tent and made tea, leaving someone behind to keep watch. Finally, it was sunrise—long shadows stretched out across the ice, and a hint of warmth could be felt in the air. When one person awoke and came outside, another would go to the tent for his rest; and so the shifts changed continually according to each man's energy and persistence.

So it was that the whaling began with a night of quiet waiting; and so it would continue, day upon day, week upon week, for some two months. Before it was over, it would test the men's patience perhaps as much as their skill and endurance. The hunters' lives would focus toward that rare moment when their prey surfaced within reach of the boats. "*Agavik!*" someone would call to the others, pointing out into the lead. "Whale!" Then they would set off in pursuit, hearts pounding, full of the energy that had built up inside them. But for now that was only a distant dream. Like everything else in the Arctic, a whale did not come without its price; and the price was mainly time spent patiently waiting.

For two days no one saw or even heard a whale, but the next evening several passed by. Only one surfaced near enough for the men to attempt a chase with the *umiaq,* but it eluded them. The rest were swimming too far out in the lead. If a whale was more than a hundred yards from the edge there was little point in chasing it, because chances of getting close were practically nil. They also saw a herd of belugas break surface on the lead's horizon, far out of reach. These were small white whales, the size of porpoises, that sometimes migrated through by the thousands later in the season.

On the morning of the fourth day the current shifted to the northwest, bringing pack ice very slowly inward until there was only a narrow lane of open water two hundred yards across. "This small lead is perfect for catching whales," Nauruk said, "because they cannot surface far out from the edge." Sakiak agreed but said that there would probably be few whales, if any at all, because this current would close the lead south of them near the great headland at Qayaqsirvik. Indeed, the entire day passed without sight or sound of game. One by one the hunters retired to the tent, leaving Talimat and Pukak outside.

For some time the watchers heard sounds of lively conversation and laughter coming through the tent walls. But as evening came the voices grew quieter, and finally there was silence. Talimat sat on the skin-covered sled, huddled inside his parka and shivering just a bit. "Everyone is asleep in there," he muttered, staring out over the water. Hearing no answer, he looked and saw that Pukak was also sleeping beside him. Everything was silent, even the majestic floes that drifted slowly by in the lead.

About an hour passed, and then Talimat thought he heard a faint noise somewhere toward the south. It was a protracted deep hiss that sounded like a whale, and so he listened carefully. There it was again, a little clearer this time. He hurried to the high ice pile and climbed up for a look around.

A minute later he came rushing down again. "*Agavik! Agavik!* A whale is coming," he exclaimed as he hurried past Pukak and went to awaken the others. "Come quickly!" he fairly shouted into the tent. "A whale, not far down the lead. I saw it rise twice right beside the ice edge, coming this way."

Men started piling out of the tent as Talimat ran back to look again. In a moment Nauruk stood beside him, holding the shoulder gun in his hands. "It was close enough to shoot from the ice," Talimat said, "so we may not need the boat." Then, just a few seconds later, they saw it. Several hundred yards down the lead a young bowhead rose to breathe. It did not roll its back above the surface as was usual but projected itself straight up into the air for half its length, then sank back tail first. The water slowly calmed after it disappeared.

Then it rose again, now a hundred yards away. *Whooosh!* The loud hiss of its breathing broke the silence. Talimat and Nauruk stood beside the boat, one with the shoulder gun ready, the other holding the harpoon. A minute later, fifty yards south, it came straight up to breathe once more. Glassy water shimmered as they waited, tensed and still, imagining a dark shade coming their way beneath the surface.

Suddenly the calm was pierced right before them, fifty yards beyond the ice edge. The huge head rose vertically into the air, black skin glistening wet, flippers laid against its sides, the chin white and barnacle-encrusted underneath. *Whooosh!* A misty spray blew from the peaked top of its skull.

At the same moment Nauruk fired the shoulder gun, its deafening crack cutting short the whale's protracted breath. Blue-gray smoke puffed as Nauruk's body jerked sharply behind the powerful weapon. Instantly there was a bright splash just beyond the animal's broad flank and off to one side. The whale slid back into the water unharmed, sending a circle of waves around it, and there was silence again. No one moved or spoke; they only watched up the lead for a sign of the animal. Minutes passed. . . . The lead went calm.

It was a very long shot, and Nauruk had aimed hastily. Perhaps they should have launched the boat and waited out in the lead, he thought out loud. He was filled with mixed excitement and disappointment, still watching in case the whale appeared near one of the other camps. But there was nothing. Sakiak finally turned away, musing softly, "It is gone," resigning himself to the loss.

No time was wasted on pessimism. There were many whales, and more would soon pass the camp. Even if they had shot the animal and it was lost, they would simply accept the inevitable. Eskimo tradition taught that animals had perpetually reincarnated souls, so that no death was permanent. Fortunately, also, bowhead whales spent their entire lives in or near the pack ice, where the white men with their modern ships and cannon-fired harpoons could not slaughter them to extinction. Half a century before, hardier whites had sailed north in wooden ships to kill bowheads by the thousands, but they were gone now and the whales remained.

The next few days passed uneventfully, and everyone lost track of how long it was since they had left Ulurunik. A brisk northeasterly wind opened a wide lead, and for a while they saw whales in fair abundance. But again conditions worked against them, because the water was rough and cluttered with drifting ice, making it impossible to give chase with the boat. Four more crews came onto the ice, making a total of seven whaling camps scattered for a mile along the lead edge. But among them all the only game taken was a few ringed seals, one large bearded seal, killed by Amiksuk, and some murres, little black seabirds that looked like ducks.

Then one morning the sky became hazy, a gray halo encircled the sun, and the air felt warm and moist. Sakiak predicted a south wind, adding that it would push the ice in to cover the open lead. Several hours later a gentle southerly breeze rippled the water, then not long afterward they saw a dark expanse of young ice coming very slowly toward them. The newly formed salt ice was like a flexible, slushy mat floating on the water, lacking the brittle hardness that would develop as it thickened. When it finally came in and met landfast ice, it either bent down underneath or crept slowly up onto the surface like a living thing, creaking intermittently as it moved along.

The current gradually increased and became almost parallel to the old lead edge, carrying fields of ice past the whalers' camp. That afternoon Sakiak climbed the tall hummock for a look around. Shortly he pointed out toward the horizon and called to the others, "I see the Mother Ice far out there—the heavy pack!" Looming up in the distance were the great rounded hummocks and ridges of the permanent Arctic pack, the most ponderous ice of all. It moved with tremendous inertial power, and when it nudged the landfast ice it could easily open cracks miles back from the edge, setting men adrift even when no wind was blowing.

That night everyone stood watching as the pack came nearer, until it drifted silently along right before them. It was strange to see these expanses of apparently solid terrain moving by like another world in fluid motion, as if the earth's stability had suddenly vanished and the land masses were sliding freely past one another.

Finally the pack pressed in against the fast ice, and huge ridges began grinding together. The sight was awesome, even for men who had seen it many times before. Colossal boulders of ice turned and fell, sending shivers through the floes. Low rumblings gave voice to the incredible power before them, as the faces of ice mountains met in slow, pulverizing collisions. It seemed that the pressure would slow the pack's drift, but the force of the continent-sized mass of ice was so great that these convulsions were significant only when measured against the microscopic scale of humanity.

Sakiak felt the wind increasing and considered the growing motion of ice before them; then he spoke to Nauruk. "It is perhaps time for us to move away from this place. There is danger here already, and a storm is coming." Without hesitating, Nauruk told the others to dismantle the camp and load the *umiaq* onto its sled. They would take everything far back onto the landfast ice where even the fiercest storm could not carry it away. "Patik!" Nauruk called teasingly to the youngest crew member, "tonight you will be in Ulurunik, and you can tell the other young men what it is like to be a whale hunter." A few minutes later the teams filed out through a notch in the nearby ridge, leaving the sounds of crushing ice behind.

Life was far more comfortable back in the village than out at the chilly ice camp, but it was also dull by comparison. All the

whalers, especially Nauruk, wished for an end to the south
wind that had settled in and refused to stop blowing. The
weather turned mild, with temperatures near freezing, and
wet snow fell from a low scud of overcast.

Then one evening a week after they had left the ice, the
skies cleared, temperatures dropped, and the wind shifted to
northeast. Late that night, Nauruk saw thin curtains of steam
rising along the ice horizon, indicating that cracks were
opening along the old lead edge. "Sikrik," he called to his
oldest son, "go to the houses of Sakiak, Talimat, and the
others in my crew. Tell them we will leave early tomorrow
morning if the lead opens and the weather is good." Then
Nauruk prepared his gear and went to sleep early.

It seemed that he had just drifted off when he was awakened by Tupik's voice. "Brother, wake up. Kuvlu and Amiksuk have taken their crews onto the ice. The lead is wide, and
Kavaasuk has returned saying they have already seen
whales." Nauruk was up immediately, pulling on his
caribou-skin boots. "Ah, those two are smart ones. We should
have gone out last night too, instead of staying home like
young boys. Well, we will go now, quickly."

When they arrived at the lead it was very wide, and a strong
wind blew whitecaps over the open water. They found their
camping spot as they had left it, except that hummocks
along the ice edge showed much evidence of fresh grinding
and piling. During the afternoon and evening they saw several whales surfacing not far from the edge, but choppy
water prevented them attempting a hunt with the *umiaq*.

The following day remained windy, and thick streaks of
pulverized ice were scattered over the water. At midmorning
they saw a whale; then they saw another and another; and in
the hours that followed they lost count of how many passed
the camp. There was hardly a time that day when at least one
whale was not visible, and often five or six could be seen at

once. This was the main body of the earliest migration, Sakiak said, but they would not be able to hunt unless an animal surfaced close enough to be shot or harpooned from the ice itself.

An hour later, Pukak called out from the high lookout, "Look! Down the lead. Whales are jumping." In the distance they saw an enormous bowhead, perhaps fifty feet long, burst straight up from the water until it hung for an instant in midair. At the peak of its jump the animal turned slowly to the side, tilted, and threw its entire bulk flat onto the surface. Great waves radiated outward, shimmering in distorted light over the long stretch of water. Moments later it leaped again, and this time another was just behind it. They turned in unison and came down with a tremendous splash. Once more they leaped together; then it was over. Ten minutes later the two whales blew several times just out from the camp, and everyone watched them pass.

The migration continued throughout the day, and although the men could not hunt they could still watch and learn. Sakiak never left the ice edge; he was too fascinated by the sight of these great creatures. He commented on the behavior of almost every whale they saw, counting the number of times each rose to breathe and carefully timing how long it remained submerged before reappearing. Even though Sakiak was old and already wiser than anyone else, he never stopped watching, never stopped increasing his knowledge.

"No two whales are exactly the same," he told Patik and Migalik. "The one that just passed stayed down eighteen minutes, then blew five times before disappearing again. Some remain down for only five minutes, some for twenty-five. The larger they are, the longer they can stay submerged; but the slower they are moving, the less time they remain underwater."

If the lead had been calm and free of drifting ice, Sakiak

could have used his knowledge to direct the hunt. If a whale surfaced south of them, he would watch its breathing pattern, judge its size and speed, then show the hunters where to paddle the *umiaq* to await its reappearance. But today he only sat looking. Scores passed by, perhaps two hundred in the course of the afternoon, and still he watched. Surely he had seen thousands of whales during his lifetime, yet his passionate interest never diminished. Small wonder he knew the whales so well.

That night the wind faded and a shoreward current brought the ice in until only a narrow lead remained. Conditions were perfect for whaling, but now there was no open water to the south and the run of whales ended. The lead before them was empty, its calm waters framed by silently drifting floes.

Shortly after the sun had set behind low clouds, a small flock of seabirds landed on the water south of camp. Migalik whispered, "Murres. Perhaps I will try to shoot some for fresh meat." But Sakiak said it was better to leave them alone for now. "I have seen gulls flying over us for the past few minutes, and more are coming. *Nauyaq,* the seagull, often flies over the water ahead of whales. If you shoot now," he advised, "your rifle's noise and the sound of bullets striking the water might frighten away larger game."

Migalik said nothing, but he abandoned his idea of hunting murres. Shooting was nearly always restricted in the camps, especially those farthest toward the south, because Eskimos knew that whales were highly sensitive to waterborne sounds. In fact, during good hunting weather when whales were running, men carefully avoided all unnecessary noises such as loud talking, stamping their feet, chopping the ice, or driving dog teams.

"The whale has excellent hearing," Sakiak thought aloud, "probably because he talks over long distances through the water. If you dip a paddle into the lead and hold your ear to the handle, you will hear the strange noises of whales speaking. And sometimes they send messages with their tails. When you see one arch sharply to dive, waving his tail high and then slapping the water at the last moment, that is a signal to the others coming behind. The old hunters say this means the way is clear and safe ahead."

Before Sakiak could continue, Tupik stiffened and spoke, "Wait. I hear something." A minute passed in silence. "There it is again," he said, "perhaps the noise of belugas rising to breathe." Migalik and Nauruk heard it this time, and Nauruk ran quietly to the hummock lookout. Everything was still again. Then Nauruk turned toward them smiling, shaking his head up and down, making little diving motions with his hand to signal the others: "Belugas coming; many of them."

He scrambled down again quickly and said that the animals were following the ice edge about a mile south of their camp, and there appeared to be hundreds of them. The hunters all picked up their heavy rifles and concealed themselves behind low hummocks near the water, sitting perfectly still to avoid making noises. Bowheads were easily frightened by sounds, but they were far less cautious than belugas. Old men like Sakiak said that belugas "talked" constantly as they traveled. If one of them heard a strange sound or saw a man as it surfaced to breathe, it gave a warning call and instantly the entire herd would disappear.

Now the sounds came again, as the whales surfaced five to ten times in quick succession, then swam underwater for several minutes. Nauruk and the other experienced whalers listened carefully, not only to keep track of the belugas' approach but also to be alert for the accompanying sounds of a bowhead. Belugas often swam along near their overgrown counterparts, perhaps as a measure of safety for themselves. If the lead closed and they were trapped beneath a solid cover of ice, they might suffocate unless they followed a bowhead and breathed at the holes it opened by bursting up from underneath. This time no large whales were nearby, but if there had been the hunters would have forgotten the belugas and gone for higher stakes.

Talimat, who was extremely fast and accurate with a rifle, positioned himself farthest south where he would have first chance for a shot, because after the first bullet the entire herd would dive in alarm and swim far before surfacing again.

Several minutes elapsed, and he began to wonder if the belugas might be passing in the still waters beneath them. He was wrong. Just to his left the first slick white head broke water, then another, and finally twenty or thirty at once. Talimat set the rifle against his arm and allowed part of the herd to pass, so the men near camp might also have a chance to shoot.

He saw a light form slipping along just beneath the surface, angling upward, then fixed his aim on the bulge of its forehead. When it broke water he hesitated a split second until it had filled its lungs but had not yet turned downward—the precise instant when a shot animal would have enough buoyancy to float until it could be retrieved. At that moment he squeezed the trigger.

The shot cracked deafeningly, followed an instant later by two other shots off to his right. Talimat saw the whale splash violently as it was struck; then it quivered for a few seconds, gliding slowly beneath the surface. Finally it stopped and floated so its back scarcely protruded above the water, as a cloud of red flowed out around it. He stood and signaled the others, urging them to hurry with the boat before the dead beluga expelled its air and sank. In less than a minute they had paddled to it, and Nauruk used an iron grappling hook to secure their prey.

Tupik and Migalik had also shot, but both of them had missed. The occasion called for teasing, especially toward Migalik, who was still young enough to be considered an apprentice. "Ah, I saw one bullet hit far behind a beluga's head," Nauruk laughed. "What kind of shooting was this? Or did you think the belugas would stop and wait until you aimed?" Everyone laughed, but Sakiak noted that none of them had tried to shoot at young, gray animals, which were smaller but rarely sank after they were hit. "All these whalemen," he mused, "and not one was wise enough to shoot at the right kind of animal."

Talimat's beluga was full-grown, nearly fifteen feet long, its beautiful, sleek body weighing close to a thousand pounds. Its white *maktak* would be a real treat, and many people back in the village would think well of Nauruk's crew when they received a share. Tupik butchered the animal and found a little gray fetus inside, a perfect replica of its parent but scarcely longer than a man's arm.

That night the lead narrowed to a mere crack, and the next day it closed tightly. The men remained in their camps, however, and two days later a wind arose from the east. The ice gradually loosened and pulled away, until finally there was continuous open water as far as they could see north and south. But no whales came.

"Perhaps the lead has not opened all along the coast," Sakiak speculated, "but when there is a clear pathway I think many whales will appear at once. They have probably waited south of us, below Qayaqsirvik and near the great point at Wevok, staying in open areas until they could head north again. If good weather holds until they arrive," he told Patik, laughing, "you will learn to hunt day and night without sleep."

But another full day passed without a sign of whales. They saw only a few early flocks of migrating eider ducks, some gulls and murres, and a seal that Nauruk missed because he shot hastily. Then Tupik and Migalik, holding the late night watch, saw a whale spout on the lead's rippled surface. "Ah, *ingutuq*," Tupik said. "A young female bowhead." This was the most desirable whale that could be caught, because its *maktak* was very soft and tasty. But the lead was a mile wide now and the whale was near its far edge, so they watched it pass without awakening the others.

An hour later, in the brightening light of dawn, they heard another whale. Tupik looked southward from atop the high ice pile and saw it rise twice, then disappear. Moments later he spotted another close to the first, and two more farther behind them. *"Ki!* Wake the others," he called to Migalik. "The whales are coming now." One by one, sleepy hunters emerged from the tent, shivering as they pulled on heavy clothing and tied their boot thongs.

When the whales surfaced again, Sakiak gauged the direction and speed of their movement, then told Nauruk that they should go out into the lead and wait. After the word was given everyone moved with smooth precision, slipping the *umiaq* quietly into the water, stepping inside and finding places, then paddling swiftly but silently toward the spot Sakiak had chosen. Once there, they sat unmoving, tense and excited, watching for the whales' appearance.

But when the animals surfaced, ten minutes later, they had gone well beyond the hunters and moved out to follow the lead's seaward edge. "Perhaps they heard the sound of wavelets slapping the boat's side," Nauruk suggested. They remained there for nearly an hour on the chance that more whales would appear. But none came, and the hunters finally returned to camp. No one went back to the tent now, because Sakiak felt certain that more animals would be along soon. And he was right.

Throughout the remainder of that day and the following night no one slept in Nauruk's camp or in any of the others. Sometimes five or ten whales passed in an hour's time, followed by an interval when none were seen; then another group would appear. The water remained fairly smooth and free of ice, but it was much too wide for effective hunting. Every crew paddled out at least once to intercept or pursue whales, but each time they kept beyond reach. Everyone felt hopeful and encouraged, however, as the run continued late into the night.

But the next morning Talimat commented that the lulls between sightings were growing longer, and by midday no more whales at all were passing. The hours crept slowly by, and when afternoon gave way to evening everyone except Migalik went into the tent for a meal of raw caribou meat with seal oil.

When he had finished eating, Sakiak lay back and closed his eyes, listening to the young men's hunting stories. Sakiak was seventy years old, but he was still almost as lively as a boy. His face was narrow and bony, with crow's-feet at the corners of his eyes, and his broad smile was almost permanent. Everyone knew he was the greatest living hunter in Ulurunik, and despite his years he still never missed a chance to be out in pursuit of game. Sakiak's knowledge of animals was legendary. But there was something beyond this as well, because he seemed to possess the ancestral gift of sensing what went on in an animal's mind.

Several of the men lapsed into sleep, but some remained awake talking late into the night. Talimat was in the midst of a long story about seal hunting when Sakiak had a peculiar feeling, a ringing in his ears that sometimes happened when game was nearby. He sat up and spoke. "I think a whale is coming, and perhaps it will surface very close to our camp." Nauruk, who was accustomed to the old man's extraordinary senses, pulled on his parka and said he had better go out and have a look. Talimat awoke the others, and eventually they all followed.

On his way to the lookout, Nauruk saw Migalik, the only man on watch, slouched in the stern of the *umiaq* sound asleep. He climbed the hummock and stood watching for less than a minute, then pointed south excitedly and ran down to the others. "Whale coming!" he whispered breathlessly. "Whale coming! Just down the lead, not far from the edge. We will need the *umiaq*."

No one said another word. In a matter of seconds they surrounded the boat and slid it off the ice so gently it hardly made a ripple. "Paddle up the lead toward the north," Sakiak directed in a soft but confident voice. "Otherwise it may pass by us underwater." The men stroked at half-speed, dipping their paddles carefully so they made almost no sound.

A hundred yards from camp they let the boat glide to a stop. The water was dead calm, reflecting deep blue and purple from the sky. Tiny bits of ice moved slowly along on the northward current. Every man's heart was pounding as they waited, their tension multiplied by the encompassing silence. Five minutes passed, and they began to wonder if something had gone wrong.

Suddenly their questions were answered. *Whoooosh!* The whale heaved up, breaking the mirror surface forty yards ahead and off toward their left. Before its single prolonged breath ended, the men lowered their paddles and stroked hard in pursuit.

The *umiaq* surged forward as excitement filled the men with extraordinary strength. Talimat sat high in the stern, alternately paddling and sculling to guide them in accordance with Sakiak's instructions. Nauruk was in the bow, the harpooner's position, pulling with all his might.

Whoooosh! It blew again, now just ahead as they swept over the ripples where it had first surfaced. Its broad hulk pushed slowly up through the water, raising waves from its sides like the wake of a small ship. The hunters looked up at their prey, thrusting their paddles deep and hard as they tried to close the remaining distance. "Perhaps two or three more blows," Sakiak whispered, "before it will dive and be gone."

The whale slid beneath the surface again, still unaware that it was pursued. Nauruk stood in the bow, holding the brass shoulder gun in one hand and pointing into the water with the other. They rushed swiftly forward now, passing swirls of upthrust water that rose behind the broad flukes. Nauruk looked down toward the deep black shade that moved almost directly below them.

The shade rose until it made a wave on the surface, then burst into the air, broad ebony back shining in the dawn.

Whooooosh! The sound was frightening, almost a roar. Warm mist blew into the hunters' faces, smelling of the whale's insides. They paddled again and again in perfect unison. Then Talimat dug in his paddle and the boat swerved nearer. Seconds later the bow nudged the animal's back. They were in perfect position, on the left side, even with its eye, where a deadly hit was most easily made.

Nauruk leaned over the gunwale, near enough to touch his prey, aiming downward. His body lurched backward as the powerful gun fired. Dense smoke filled the air, stinking like sulfur. Water splashed high as the bomb hit its mark, entering the whale's skull just below the waterline, straight above its eye.

Talimat saw the whale shudder as the shot's explosion rang out. Its back arched as he swung the boat off course to the left, clear of the huge tail should the animal thrash. But it only lifted its flukes a foot above the water and slid out of sight.

Nauruk turned and almost shouted in his excitement. "Quickly now...paddle ahead! It is hit well." A moment later they heard a muffled sound, like two large rocks striking together deep beneath the surface. "The bomb has exploded," Nauruk whispered to himself. They paddled up the lead, moving as swiftly as they could to keep pace with the invisible whale somewhere deep below. Talimat saw several other boats rushing out ahead and hoped the whale would surface near one of them.

His thoughts were cut short when the animal's back rolled up again thirty yards beyond the bow. This time the sound was different—powerful but gurgling and strained—and the spout showed a cast of red. They caught up quickly, as the whale moved with less speed than before. "Left side again!" Nauruk exclaimed, motioning with his arm.

Migalik, sitting in the forward paddler's position, saw the whale's eye come above water as they swept in alongside. The animal seemed to watch uncomprehending as its strange tormentor approached; and immediately its colossal body arched for another dive.

But Nauruk was too swift with the harpoon. He lifted the heavy shaft high, then thrust almost vertically into the thick hide, aiming just behind the eye. The iron tip sunk deep, piercing the skin and lodging in the thick layer of blubber underneath. At the same instant the trigger was released, firing another bomb into the whale's body. The shot cracked loudly, and its recoil threw the harpoon shaft high into the air behind them.

The whale shook again and sounded, this time for a deep dive. Tupik immediately grabbed the inflated sealskin float and tossed it over the gunwale, as rope flew out from a coil before him. The float moved swiftly along for a moment, then was suddenly jerked downward with tremendous force. The water became calm again. From the float's movement they could see that the whale was still heading north, toward the other crews. Nauruk had no more weapons except sharp lances that could only create minor wounds or cut tendons, so he said they should paddle slowly and let the others take over the chase.

"The float is attached and in this wide lead the whale will be easy to follow," Talimat observed, adding, "it is an *ingutuvaq,* a large female." Just then they felt the bomb exploding, only faintly detectable now because the whale must be deep and far ahead of them. If Nauruk's aim was true the bomb might have lodged near where the backbone and skull joined, which could cause instant death. But Sakiak said that Nauruk had struck a little too high and the whale would still have life in it.

About five minutes later the float bobbed up some distance away, not far from Amiksuk's boat. The whale was surfacing, its position faithfully marked by the buoy. Nauruk and the others watched as Amiksuk's crew paddled up behind the float, passed it, then pulled alongside the whale just as it spouted. Another harpoon was thrown, this one into its back, and again the animal sounded. Sakiak prayed, as he had when Nauruk made the first strike, asking for a swift completion of their hunt.

Now two floats bobbed across the lead's surface, but this time they did not disappear. The whale was turning, heading straight out to sea. "*Alyakaah*," Nauruk murmured, "this is bad." If it continued this way, it would go beneath the ice and die where they could never retrieve it. Two boats followed at top speed, keeping very near the floats.

Then, almost at the lead's outer edge, the whale surfaced again, spouting a crimson fog into the air. Kuvlu's crew was closest this time. They paddled in quickly and used a shoulder gun to fire a bomb just behind the animal's flipper, aiming for the heart. Nauruk saw it thrash and twist wildly, throwing the surface into a great turmoil. As they came nearer it managed to dive again, but the floats moved only a short distance, then stopped dead in the water.

The lead became still. All seven *umiaqs* converged on the motionless floats, stopping to wait at a safe distance. After five long minutes the water seemed to rise in one spot, then spill away. Very slowly, the whale's lifeless body emerged. Its white belly glistened in the clear air as streaks of water ran down its sides. The last shot had punctured its heart, and a tide of blood flowed from the wound, staining the water for many yards around.

Four crews that had not made strikes now raced in to touch the carcass. The custom governing division of a whale was based on order of participation in the kill. Nauruk's men were first and would therefore receive the choicest shares, second was Amiksuk, and third was Kuvlu. The remaining shares would be allocated according to who was first to touch the animal, since no further strikes could be made.

Nauruk watched until the last boat had made its touch. Smiling exuberantly, he said, "It is over. We have a whale! He was filled with joy and pride, not only in himself and his crew, but also in the ancient tradition of whale hunting, the quintessential expression of his Eskimo heritage. Then, because whaling was done only at the behest and benevolence of the animals, he looked with profound respect upon the whale he had killed. Silently, in the language of his ancestors, he gave it thanks.

Now everyone set to work. They tied a heavy rope to the carcass and fastened all the boats to it, one ahead of the other. During the several hours it would take to reach the lead edge, a messenger would rush to Ulurunik with the news. Nauruk's *umiaq* took its position in the lead, and before they started paddling Sakiak tied a small cloth rectangle to the end of a long-handled flensing knife. Then he raised the pole, fastening it in the gunwale lashings, so that the *umealik's* multicolored flag could be seen at a distance. When he finished they leaned on their paddles and began their tedious passage back to the landfast ice. It was two hours past midnight, and the sun's rim was just emerging from beneath the northeastern horizon.

Seven *umiaqs* pulling in tandem moved very slowly toward their destination, a camp just over half a mile down the lead. The men paddled until their arms throbbed and swelled, but they did not stop because once the whale's momentum was lost it took great effort to get it moving again. The ascending sun and amber sky reflected brightly on the still water before them.

Finally, after almost five hours, they drew near the ice edge. Nauruk saw dog teams pulling into the camp up ahead and people lined up near the water, straining their eyes to assess the whale's size. Despite their exhaustion, the whalers were full of jubilant pride, which they expressed by making the Eskimo shout of joy, a low-pitched yodeling sound that imitated the bellowing of a walrus.

A short while later they reached the camp and pulled the floating whale up against solid ice. Kuniun, an old man who

no longer hunted, greeted them enthusiastically. "*Azahaa,*
Nauruk, you are a hunter indeed! Now we will eat fresh
maktak and whale meat at last!" A crowd of men, women, and
children gathered around them—nearly a hundred people
who had come out to see the whale and admire the men who
had taken it.

Nauruk's elder aunt reminded him of the first time he had
killed a whale, when she and several other old people had
exercised their right to ask him for presents such as mittens,
boots, even his new rifle. Of course he could not and did not
refuse, for to do so was a violation of custom. Furthermore,
since it was his first whale, he received no share of the animal.
So it was that, although he had made gifts to persuade men
to join his crew, fed them throughout the whaling season,
and furnished all the equipment for the hunt, his only return
was the intangible but highly desired prestige accorded a
successful *umealik.* This time, however, he would receive
almost a ton of meat and *maktak* along with further en-
hancement of his standing.

Now the oldest and most experienced men took charge, as
they prepared to haul the whale up on the ice. First a weathered old block and tackle, acquired from a turn-of-the-
century whaling ship, was tied to the narrow part of the
whale's tail. Back from the lead edge, the lines were passed
through holes chipped down into the ice itself, making
another pulley arrangement in the traditional Eskimo fashion. Then fifty men and women began hauling on the rope,
pulling the great carcass, bit by bit, up onto the ice. The
animal measured about forty-five feet long, and following
the old whalers' calculation of one ton per foot it amounted
to a considerable weight indeed.

When it was halfway up, Kuniun told them to stop and cut
off some of the *maktak* before trying to pull it farther. Then
he took a sharp, long-bladed flensing knife and cut a series of
lines into the skin, marking the correct butchering pattern.
When he had finished, several men stood atop the whale and

began slicing the huge slabs of skin and blubber, while others used long-handled meathooks to pull them off. Each slab was cut into strips several feet long and a foot or two wide, weighing a few hundred pounds.

Young men were kept busy hauling the *maktak* away and making separate piles according to the traditional shares for each participating crew. Thus a large portion from the whale's midsection went to Nauruk, a part of the back from above the eye to above the navel was his crew's, the right belly section belonged to Amiksuk's crew, the left belly section was for Kuvlu's crew, and so on until every crew had its share. These were divided further among all the individual crew members, spreading the wealth as widely as possible.

After most of the *maktak* had been cut away, everyone heaved again on the thick ropes, inching the entire whale onto the ice. Although its size was reduced by removal of the thick skin and blubber, the animal's belly was still higher than a man's head. The lower jawbones, which measured almost the length of an *umiaq*, were now cut away. This exposed the rows of flexible baleen that the living animal had used to filter its food from the seawater. Many years before, when Sakiak was a young man, an *umealik* could make hundreds or even thousands of dollars by selling baleen to white traders. In those days "whalebone," as it was called, ended up as stays in the corsets of *Tanik* women.

Butchering continued through the entire day and well into the night, until nothing remained except a huge red stain on the ice where the carcass had been. Dark streaks radiated from it, drag marks leading to mounds of blubber and meat that awaited hauling to the settlement. Dog teams would go back and forth during the next few days carrying heavy loads that would be divided again among all the families, then stored in underground meat cellars. Everyone would feast on delicious *maktak*, raw and boiled, as well as on tender cooked meat. Some of the meat would be put in barrels kept inside the houses, where it would ferment for several weeks and become *mikigaq,* a sour treat that everyone loved.

When they had finished, the whale's skull remained, a voluminous thing almost half as long as the whale itself. A group of men slowly pushed it off the ice edge into the water. It made a great splash and sank into the blackness. Old men knew that this was done to show respect for the whale and to assure proper reincarnation of its soul, in the hope that it would return to be killed again. The younger hunters did it for reasons they could not define, perhaps simply because they knew it was right to follow what had always been done.

Now the activity and excitement came to an end. Everyone took a well-earned rest, watching the flocks of hungry gulls that still hovered over the water searching for bits of meat and offal. One by one the crews returned to their camps to begin the long watch again. The season was only half over, and so the others could still hope for a chance to share the honor that now belonged solely to Nauruk and the men who hunted with him.

In the days and nights that followed there would also be time to recount each detail of the hunt, and perhaps to consider the mysterious senses of old Sakiak, who knew that the whale was coming without seeing or hearing it. Indeed, that not a single bowhead was spotted for two days after the kill made his foreknowledge of the animal's arrival even more remarkable. Not that anyone would have attributed it to a mere coincidence. Most of the Ulurunik people simply accepted the event as a matter of course—Sakiak was a special man, a hunter who knew the animals, and that was all.

Suvluravik Tatqiq

The Moon When Rivers Flow

(MAY)

MAIN CHARACTER

Kuvlu (*Koov*-loo) *an adult hunter*

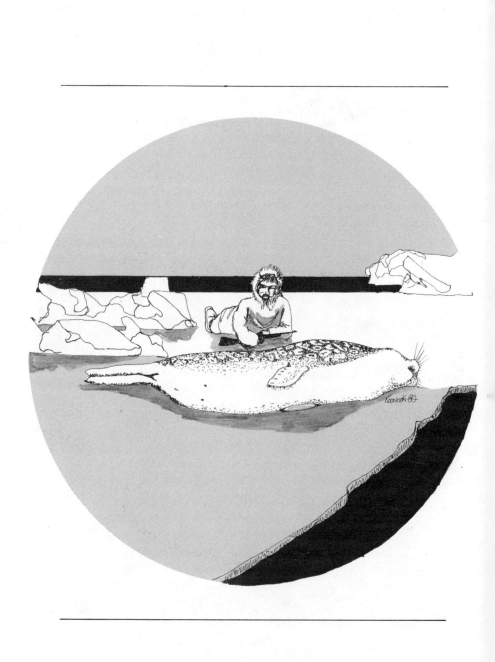

IN THE HIGH ARCTIC, winter always gave way begrudgingly to spring, but this year had been worse than most. Even the Eskimos had become impatient for warmth, and old men spoke of the hardest springs they had known. The days had grown steadily longer until there was no night at all, yet the cold remained, and gale winds blew clouds of snow down off the huge expanses of tundra to the east. But change was inevitable, and finally, in the space of a few days, masses of warm, moist air swept across the tundra plain on a powerful wind from the south. The snow quickly became heavy and wet, so that it could no longer drift. When the south wind dropped to a gentle breeze the warmth remained. A new season had settled on the land.

In the week that followed the weather was cloudy and dull. Saturating rain ate away at the snow until scattered patches of brown grass began to appear. Then came a day of near perfection. The sky was pure and pale blue, without a fleck of cloud. The sun crept slowly upward as it circled, while beneath it, from horizon to horizon, the ice-covered sea exploded in brilliant white. Darkness was sapped even from the shadows of hummocks, standing in bright silence like ancient tumbled ruins. This was the weather that beckoned men to journey southward to the great bight that cut the coast inward between Ulurunik and Qayaqsirvik. Within this protected embayment the sea ice flattened to a broad frozen plain, where large numbers of seals came up onto the surface to bask and sleep in the warm sunshine.

Half a day's travel south of Ulurunik, past the ancient campsite at Inyuktuyuk and beyond the silent old house pits at Qilyamittavik, the expanse of flat ice stretched for several miles outward from the land. Its outermost edge was marked by a single enormous ridge that stood above its surroundings, stark and bright in the sun. Water dripped steadily from the angular blocks of ice composing the ridge, some falling onto the surface of a large turquoise pond beneath its seaward flank. This water was all fresh, made so by percolation of salt from the ice boulders as they thawed. Now it would return to the sea. Near one end of the pond a whirlpool spun endlessly downward through a deep black hole into the ocean below.

An Arctic tern fluttered, hovered, and dipped to meet its reflection in the pond's glassy surface. Another tern flew nearby and they drifted off together, exchanging raspy calls. Beneath them, atop the tall ridge, stood an Eskimo hunter. He held a pair of binoculars to his eyes, scanning the surrounding floes for seals. He paid no attention to the birds as they turned and circled above his dog team, nor was he distracted when several minutes later a squadron of eider ducks flashed between the ice piles nearby. Their low croaking had faded in the distance long before he took the binoculars from his eyes.

The man was named Kuvlu. He was a hunter in his prime, neither so old that he was growing weak nor so young that he was not wise and experienced. His face was deeply tanned from strong sunshine and reflecting snow. It was also somewhat lined and wrinkled, especially around his eyes and at the corners of his mouth, showing him to be a man who laughed often. Indeed, Kuvlu was gifted with a great sense of humor. He was especially adept as a mimic, and when he visited other houses in the settlement people waited to see who would bear the brunt of his teasing. When he had said something funny, no one laughed harder than Kuvlu himself, showing his broad, white teeth and shaking his head from side to side, tear-filled eyes glistening. But when he hunted he was a serious man who put his cleverness to work in other ways. His father, Sakiak, was the best among the oldest hunters, and Kuvlu had inherited much of his skill.

From the peak of ice, Kuvlu could see the coastline stretching northward, the beach cliff furrowed and streaked with the blackness of exposed soil. And to the south the cliff, dwindling in the distance, traced a broad, perfect arc curving southwest, then west out into the Chukchi Sea. At the horizon, shimmering refracted light lifted the image of Qayaqsirvik from beneath the earth's edge so it loomed above the plain of ice, separated from the glare of white by a line of azure sky.

Kuvlu looked thoughtfully toward the remote headland that ended at Qayaqsirvik. Some people, like his father, had spent their childhood in a tiny village there, in the days when Eskimos still lived in half-underground sod houses with roof frames made from whale bones. This had been a fine place to hunt for whales when they passed near the point in spring. And in time the whales had been followed northward by sailing ships with crews of white men and *Kanakas* from the South Seas. When gales and currents brought the pack ashore, it piled into ridges as high as a ship's mast on shoals off the point. So the whalemen, who perhaps could not pronounce Qayaqsirvik, preferred to call it Icy Cape. All that remained of the village now was a few shallow depressions from the houses, bleached whale bones half-buried in the tundra, and thick tussocks of grass and willow blown flat by the winds.

Looking seaward over the frozen world of ice, Kuvlu could see many seals, lining the margins of cracks and surrounding open holes. But in such gatherings they were difficult to hunt. He was searching for a lone seal, lying on the ice somewhere away from the rest, and from this vantage none could be seen. He would need to find another ice pile, perhaps farther to the south, and look again from there. Kuvlu smiled. What did it matter, when the days were long and warm. It was *Suvluravik tatqiq,* "the moon when rivers flow," a season when everyone felt free and happy.

So he picked his way down from the hillock of ice, using his iron-tipped *unaaq* for support. A deep slushy drift sloped from the hummock's leeward flank, and he tested its depth with the *unaaq,* waded through it, then jumped stiffly over a narrow rivulet. The dogs whined and stretched in anticipation as he approached, but a low-spoken word silenced them. Then he quickly tied the *unaaq* onto the sled, slung his rifle across his back, and lifted the sled hook from a crack in the ice. The dogs surged ahead when they felt their towline loosen, and Kuvlu swung onto the sled as it hissed across the flat ice and bumped over a low pass between two hummocks.

Traveling over the spring ice was tedious work for man and dogs alike. Along the lee of each ice pile was an alluvium of snow, a long, tapering drift, sometimes many feet deep; and within the jumbled piles themselves, crevices and hollows brimmed with snow. It had been pavement-hard during winter's cold but was now soft and tacky, waiting like quicksand for a man or animal to step into it. The dogs tired quickly, wading chest-deep through the drifts, dragging their load over the ridges and across deep puddles.

Kuvlu had seven dogs. Of these, four had sore feet, one so bad that it left blood in its footprints. When the spring thaw began, the ice and snow surfaces became covered with sharp, icy needles. After several days of hard travel the dogs' feet were tender and raw from the steady abrasion, so they began to limp and pulled without enthusiasm. A week before, Kuvlu had been forced to shoot his oldest dog when it became too lame to keep up with the team. As was usual during the spring, he had run low on dog food and could not afford to feed an animal that gave nothing in return. By traveling during the warmest part of the day, when the ice needles became mushy and wet, he tried to spare his dogs' feet. But sharp spicules of ice always remained on the bottom of puddles and ponds. Even the polar bear, though he spent his entire life on the ocean ice, would make long detours to avoid wading across the pincushion-bottomed ponds.

The dogs, especially those whose feet were already sore, lived in constant dread of the next crossing. Some contrived exquisitely futile maneuvers to avoid or postpone the inevitable wetting. They hauled back at the water's edge until the necklines jerked them bodily toward it, then sprang madly into midair, heads high and eyes half-closed, as if hoping to reach the distant shore unsoaked. When they landed in the water they pulled frantically for the nearest edge, whether straight ahead or in a direction quite opposed to the line of travel. Kuvlu often stung these dogs with his whip, but it did little to change their acrobatics.

What a man needed most for travel on the wet spring ice was a good lead dog, and here Kuvlu was lucky. His leader, a large brown and white female named Maktak, willingly entered the water on command, and when she did the others usually followed without too much hesitation. Maktak was a young dog—it was only three years since she was put in harness—but she was quick to learn and always listened for Kuvlu's words. And she was fast for a dog of her size, built lean, with long legs and large paws that splayed broad prints on the snow. Maktak seldom tired of pulling. Even after a long day with a heavy load in tow she yipped and whined whenever the team stopped, anxious to be on the way again. Kuvlu was especially pleased when she came into heat, because at such times the males in the team pulled with twice their normal strength trying to catch her.

After about fifteen minutes of difficult travel, the team crossed a long, narrow flat that ended at the base of a

massive hummock. At its top a single colossal monument of
ice spiked skyward, leaning heavily off the vertical. Kuvlu
picked his way noiselessly up the jagged slope, binoculars in
hand. Before he reached the summit he stopped and
squinted intently into the sheet of sunlight that ricocheted
from the flat ice beyond. A straight crack an arm's length
wide split like a penciled line through the center of a featureless plain of ice before him, and lying alongside this
crack was a scattered row of seals, thirty-seven of them in all.
"*Azaah*," Kuvlu exclaimed softly. "So many seals!" He smiled
broadly at the sheer pleasure of seeing such abundance in
one place.

He would not hunt these seals. Only a long, tiresome crawl
over the wet ice could bring him within gunshot range of the
wary animals, and even then they would probably see him
and scramble into the water before he took a shot. Many
times before, he had found seals on big ice flats and tried to
stalk them; but he had nearly always failed. They slept only
in snatches, jerking to attentive wakefulness every minute or
so and scanning the ice to be sure no danger was approaching. In a large group like this there was never a moment
when several seals were not awake, stretching their necks and
blinking into the dazzling whiteness. A man could not penetrate such defenses undetected, and as soon as one seal took
fright the rest, accepting its judgment, were likely to scramble into the water. Even when only one or two seals were
lying in such a flat, too much time and energy was required
to approach them.

It was not like this for Kuvlu's grandfather, Ataaktuk, who
had hunted with only a harpoon. The old man had told how,
wearing clothing made from sealskin, he could fool the animals into thinking he was one of their own kind. He crawled
across the flat ice in plain sight, always presenting a side view
of himself toward his prey. When a seal watched him, sensing
danger, he imitated flippers with his hands and feet, lifted
his head high, and scratched the ice with his *azigaun,* a

curved wooden handle with four seal claws attached to it. Sleeping seals often scratched the frozen surface noisily, and when they heard this sound coming from someplace nearby it seemed to dispel their fear.

Eventually his guile was successful, and, secure in the belief that he was just another seal, the hunted animal refused to look his way. Ataaktuk crept carefully forward until he drew close enough to see whiskers on the seal's nose; then his harpoon flew. Twice in his life he had crept so near that he was able to run up, stand between the animal and the open crack, and kill it with only his knife as it tried to scuttle toward the water. This kind of hunting required great patience and perseverence, but there was no other way. Although the old man had been one of the best hunters, he was lucky to get one or two seals in a long day's hunting.

Kuvlu stood for some time watching the seals in the flat, picking out individual animals to see how long they slept and imagining how difficult or easy they would be to stalk. Like all Eskimo hunters, he was deeply fascinated by animals, and his tireless watching continually increased his knowledge. Whatever Kuvlu learned in this way he would tell the others in animated detail, and thus enhance the collective knowledge of his people.

A hunter had to know the secrets of whatever animal he would kill. From his understanding he would merge his thoughts with those of his prey, so that their minds were one. To hunt the seal he would become a seal himself; he would see through the seal's eyes and meditate with the seal's mind. Its tensing fright became his cringing terror. This was the hunter.

As he turned to climb down from the hummock, Kuvlu noticed a small dark spot, barely visible over a ridge several hundred yards beyond the dogs. When he looked with his binoculars the spot had disappeared, but he kept watching. In a moment it reappeared, and he recognized it as a seal's

head. The animal was on top of the ice, so close to a small
hummock that it was visible only when its head was lifted.

He watched it vanish and reappear several times, then
went quickly to his team. From a canvas pouch that hung on
the sled's upstanders, he pulled a wad of flimsy white cloth
that unfolded into a hooded tunic. He slipped it over his
dark cloth parka and pulled the hood forward so it covered
the wolverine-fur ruff that encircled his face. It was soiled
from the blood of numberless kills, but it was still white
enough to serve as camouflage on the spring ice.

Kuvlu left the dogs and walked toward the seal on foot. It
was not far away, and much of the ice between was too rough
for the sled to cross. He quickly reached the edge of the flat
and picked his way into a field of jumbled ice, the result of a
grinding collision between two immense floes. At the far side
of the rough ice, near the end of a high ridge, he expected to
find the seal. It was difficult walking, and despite a lifetime of
practice he slipped and fell in one place and in another sank
almost to his waist in mushy snow that concealed a narrow
crevice. He was perspiring heavily by the time he had made
his way to the ridge.

He moved along the base of the ridge to its end, then
peered cautiously into a narrow flat beyond. Near some low
piles of ice, not seventy yards from where he stood, lay not
one seal but two. Perhaps he had been unable to see the
second from his original vantage, he thought, or it might
have come out on the ice during the few minutes of his
approach. And these were not the small ringed seals, but huge
bearded seals, or *uguruk,* weighing perhaps four hundred
pounds each. This was an excellent find indeed. The *uguruk*
was an uncommon and highly prized animal. The tough
soles of Kuvlu's boots, and the coverings of his large whaling
boat and kayak were made from bearded seal skin. And all
that meat. . . . Kuvlu was very pleased with what he saw.

Bearded seals were much easier to hunt than ringed seals,
because they were relatively fearless and often slept very

soundly, occasionally refusing to awaken even when a man shouted at them. After a long and tedious stalk over the flat ice, it was sometimes disconcerting to find that a seal was unwilling to lift its head and present a good shot. But the *uguruk* had sharp eyes, and so a wise hunter always stalked it carefully. Kuvlu knew these things as he watched the two seals, and although they were almost within shooting range he felt sure that he could approach much closer undetected. He took the rifle from his back and prepared to begin his stalk.

As he stood quietly he heard a very slight creaking or budging noise, which he immediately recognized as the sound of moving ice. A storm several days earlier had caused much cracking and fresh piling in the floes everywhere, and now a persistent current from the south kept forcing the pack more tightly against the shore. So he was not surprised that some motion was still taking place.

The landward current, plus a slight onshore breeze, meant that there was no chance of being carried out to sea on a drifting floe. But any time the ice moved it could spell danger. Freshly piled ice did not freeze into a consolidated mass at this season, so it was best to stay away from it. Many times Kuvlu had seen entire hummocks suddenly disintegrate and crash down into the water, with no forewarning whatever. A man standing on such a hummock would be crushed in the cascade of ice boulders.

The sound of moving ice was also a warning to beware of open cracks and thin spots. Eskimo hunters were told early in their apprenticeship to look before they stepped whenever they were on the ocean ice. Those who did not eventually learned a hard lesson by plunging into the frigid water. Kuvlu saw many cracks in the ice between him and the seals, some narrow enough to jump across and others so wide he would have to go around them.

When the two seals dropped their heads almost simultaneously, he moved quickly around the end of the ridge and

into an area of low piled ice. By walking among the hummocks he could advance toward the seals, ducking out of
sight behind large upturned chunks whenever the animals
awakened. It was rough walking, and if a seal lifted its head at
the wrong moment he might be caught out where it would
see him. No hunt was without its difficulties, however, and
Kuvlu had learned never to expect otherwise.

He was lucky. Each time one of the seals snapped awake he
was hidden from its line of sight, or he stood still and
blended so well into the ice that the animal could not see him.
Finally he reached the end of the rough ice and had to cross a
small open area. A low ridge beyond it would afford concealment and a good brace for shooting. He waited until he
was sure the animals slept soundly, then crouched low and
scurried out into the flat.

Halfway across he ran into trouble—a jagged crack too
wide to jump over without detouring in plain sight straight
toward the seals. Without hesitating, he turned and ran for
the closest narrow spot. But before he reached it one of the
animals suddenly lifted its head. Kuvlu stopped dead in his
tracks, not moving a muscle, hoping that it would overlook
him. But the seal had awakened so quickly that he could not
react in time, and its keen eyes had caught his last step.

Kuvlu could do nothing. If he tried to raise his rifle, the
seal would flip into the open crack, and the other would
follow immediately. He began to speak, so low that only he
could hear the words, "Sleep, seal . . . sleep." Eskimos often
talked in this way to animals, which were said to understand
the words and thoughts of men. So long as they were not
ridiculed or slighted, they were often willing to allow themselves to be killed. People depended on the animals to live,
and the animals knew this.

When the seal finally lowered its head, Kuvlu dropped to
his knees and remained still. It awoke almost immediately,
staring straight at him; and it moved somewhat closer to the
open crack, preparing for a quick escape. This alerted the

other animal, which also turned to face the water. Probably neither had seen a man before, and they seemed torn between fear and curiosity. Clearly, Kuvlu was not their arch-enemy the polar bear, but he looked strange and perhaps menacing.

There was no chance to stalk closer, so Kuvlu attempted to move as slowly as possible to a sitting position from which he could shoot. Minutes passed. The seals watched as he gradually pulled his legs up before him and lifted the rifle to his shoulder. He set its bead on the closest animal's neck until it looked away briefly, then shot.

Both seals were gone in an instant. Kuvlu jumped a narrow place in the crack and ran quickly toward the spot where they had been. He knew his bullet had struck, but not well enough for an instant kill. Unless a bearded seal's neck bones were shattered, its body often convulsed so violently that it slipped into the water. From the way the animal had moved after he shot, Kuvlu was sure his bullet had struck its skull rather than its neck. He could only hope that the dead animal was floating in the crack where it could be retrieved.

In a moment he stood at the edge of the wide crack, peering into the deep black water. At one point a widening cloud of red slowly diffused and drifted away on the current. The thin cover of snow on the surface above this place was marked by two wet depressions, the spots where the seals had been. On the far side of the closest depression were spatterings of blood and fragments of bone. Had it been a ringed seal rather than a bearded seal, it would never have moved after such a hit.

Kuvlu looked once more into the water but saw nothing. Even the blood was gone now, as if the sea had cleansed itself. He had just lost a prized *uguruk* when it was nearly in his hands, yet he felt no sense of frustration or anger. In fact, what had happened seemed quite funny now, and the other hunters would enjoy the story when he told it that evening. Eskimos knew that things often went wrong in this way, and

they had learned to find genuine humor in their own mis-
fortunes. The old men sometimes laughed until tears ran
from their eyes when they told of how they had been fooled
by the animals, the ice, or the weather.

Missing the seal reminded Kuvlu of a time the previous
summer when his old uncle Ulimaun had been luckier. The
man had also sneaked close to an *uguruk,* but it took fright
and was about to plunge into a small open hole, so he aimed
and shot quickly. His bullet grazed the animal's skull,
knocking it unconscious. Ulimaun reached the big seal just as
it regained consciousness and began crawling into the water,
and he had only time enough to grab its hind flippers. The
uguruk paddled frantically with its short foreflippers, throwing up sheets of water and thoroughly drenching its captor.
It could not pull itself free, but the man was equally unable to
haul it back out onto the surface. Finally Ulimaun pulled out
his knife and cut holes through the webbing of the seal's hind
flippers. He slipped his fingers into the holes and could then
drag it out and across the ice to where he had dropped his
rifle. Using one hand to hold the seal and one to hold the
rifle, he managed a single deadly shot into its neck.

Kuvlu turned and followed his tracks back through the
rough ice toward the team. He walked quickly and was very
warm by the time he reached the sled. So he sat down for a
few minutes to cool off. Perspiration glistened on his temples
and forehead. Shortly, he picked up his binoculars and went
over to the tall hummock from which he had seen the bearded
seal. The sun was moving lower, and he wanted to make a
kill before evening's cool set in. He clambered up on the ice
pile and looked again over the wide flat, which still had many
seals basking on it.

From his high position Kuvlu could see across miles of
encircling floes; distant horizons and upthrown ridges
shimmered in distorted waves of warm light. Binoculars to
his eyes, he stood motionless, sheathed in white, invisible
amid the frozen silence. Inside the muffling hood of his

parka, he could hear his own heartbeat, feel the throbbing of pulse in his neck and behind his ears. Slowly he turned his eyes, probing the vastness of ice . . . south, southwest, west, northwest, finally north. There he stopped and stood and watched, ignoring the pain in his arms, which were tiring now.

There was something to the north. Beyond the margin of the big flat, quavering in the refracted light, he could see a small oval of flat ice. Near its middle, like a pebble in an open palm, lay a lone seal, a small ebony shape amid the white surroundings. He watched it for several moments to be sure it was not just a piece of dirty ice or the shadow of an over-hanging ledge. Twice he saw it move, lifting its head me-chanically and dropping it abruptly again. From this he knew which direction it faced, its back to the faint breeze and the sun catching it full along its side.

Kuvlu scanned the enclosing walls of ice and contrived a plan of approach. The hummocks would conceal the sight and sound of his coming. He must not move upwind of the seal lest his acrid human scent be lifted to it on the current of air. Beyond the seal, where it looked directly into the sun, were several hillocks of ice rubble, the last nearly within rifle shot of the animal. He would circle around below the wind and return through a long flat valley between two parallel ridges of piled ice, until he was between the sun and the seal. He smiled as he poked his way down from the mound and walked briskly to the waiting team.

He spoke softly to the dogs, *"Ki . . . Kya!"* and the sled cut furrows across a slushy puddle as they swerved off toward the west. The dogs, excited by a heavy smell of seals, pulled as if the hunt were theirs alone. High above, a glaucous gull sculled and circled in the clear air, arcing across the sun. To its eye the disk of horizon swayed and tilted, blue ponds flashed silver; and, far below, the tiny procession of man and dogs crawled slowly across the vastness. The gull set its wings and followed, slipping downward a thousand feet until it

hovered behind the intruders. Kuvlu glanced briefly toward
the bird as it lit on the shoulder of a nearby ridge, turning its
head to look first with one eye, then with the other. Moments
later it flew down to a large puddle and began pecking at
shrimp that had come up through a hole in the ice.

Kuvlu now approached the place where his stalk would
begin. With hushed commands, he turned his team north
into a narrow flat with ridges on each side and a peculiar
cone-shaped hummock at the end. When the dogs slowed in
confusion at the end of this cul de sac, awaiting a command,
he stepped off the sled and dragged his feet to stop them.
The seal lay somewhere across the ridge to his left, so he
would not use his voice or make any unnecessary sounds. He
set the sled hook firmly into a narrow crack, so the dogs
could not pull it out if they became restless or excited while
he was away.

   With rifle in one hand and *unaaq* in the other, Kuvlu walked
toward a low point in the ridge. It was late afternoon, but
still warm enough so the ice was very wet and slushy underfoot. After the sun dipped low near the horizon about
midnight, the surface would freeze and crunch loudly when
a man walked over it. Kuvlu bent low as he stepped up the
ridge and peered into the small flat beyond. Two hundred
yards away was a ringed seal, striking and dark, now perfectly still as it slept. How many seals had he stalked in thirty
springs since his first boyhood hunts? Hundreds, perhaps
nearly a thousand. Yet a surge of excited strength poured
through him as he looked.

   Kuvlu hid his profile in the space between two chunks of
ice, staring intently at the animal. In a moment its head
jerked up, then dropped to the ice again. He watched the
animal do this four more times to learn its pattern of
alternate sleeping and awakening. This seal slept for only
twenty to thirty seconds, then watched attentively for five to
ten seconds—a fairly cautious animal. Most seals would sleep

twice as long, and on warm days like this they often seemed barely able to lift their heads for a moment before dropping again into blissful unconsciousness.

The fifth time it slept Kuvlu crawled quickly over the crest of the ridge and jumped from an ice boulder to the surface below. He squatted there, hidden from the seal by several low mounds out in the flat. By lifting his head while remaining crouched, Kuvlu could watch the animal, now almost at eye level and well beyond good shooting range. It would not be an easy stalk. There were many puddles to cross without making noise, and he would have to keep very low as he moved. Fortunately the sun would shine from behind him, partially blinding the seal when it looked his way.

When the seal's head dropped to the ice, he began moving toward it, keeping his legs tensed hard in a crouch that would quickly tire a less powerful man. He bent just low enough so his eyes peered over the ice mounds and fixed on his prey. A few yards forward and the seal's head jerked up. Kuvlu froze, watching. The head went down. He moved quickly again, until he stopped at the edge of a shallow blue pond. After the animal's next awakening he stepped carefully into the water and moved very slowly across, balancing himself with his *unaaq* and making almost no sound. He wore sealskin boots that were impervious to water, sewn with caribou back sinew that swelled to fill each stitch hole when it became wet.

At the pond's far side he crossed the first ice mound, which was also the highest. Now he found that the animal would see too much of him unless he stayed on hands and knees whenever it awakened. His timing therefore became as crucial as his ability to move quickly and silently.

Kuvlu was now close enough to hear an occasional loud rasping sound as the half-conscious seal rolled on its side and scratched at the ice with its stubby foreflippers. This indicated ecstatic contentment, a sign that the animal was completely unaware of approaching danger. Thus Kuvlu knew the seal's state of mind. But as he drew nearer he would become easier to detect. He crossed two narrow rivulets while it scratched the ice, allowing its own sound to cover his noise in the water. Ice needles crunched loudly underfoot in one of the rivulets, and he nearly fell trying to move quickly across it.

The seal slept twice more while he moved to the edge of a large pond. Its dark blue water indicated depth, nearly to the top of his boots. If he crept around its edge he would lose what little camouflage remained from a single ice mound fifty yards ahead, so he decided to risk crossing. Kuvlu hunched low, allowing two sleeps to pass, gathering his strength. Next time the seal's head dropped he stepped slowly into the water and waded ahead, bent double at his waist, head still up to watch his prey. When the animal snapped awake he simply froze. Unable to drop to his hands and knees in the water, he could only hope that his white parka would blend with the ridges behind, and he would be ice to the seal's eyes. Its head dropped again.

Three more times the animal awoke and Kuvlu became ice still in the water. During the next sleep he took several long steps and reached solid ice again. He rested on all fours, his legs tired and his neck sore from holding his head up while doubled over. Kuvlu glanced around the flat and the encircling ice ridges. However deeply he might concentrate on his prey, he was continuously alert for the appearance of other game nearby and for signs that the ice might move or crack.

Several years ago his cousin Nauruk had noticed a slight movement out of the corner of his eye while he stalked a seal. The movement resolved itself into the hulk of a polar bear, flattened against the ice, creeping toward the same animal. Nauruk had slipped off his white parka cover and crawled into plain sight, where his dark form resembled a basking seal. The polar bear was tricked and had begun stalking him instead of the more distant animal. When it came within thirty yards, nearly to the point where it would dash in for the attack, Nauruk sat up and killed it with a single shot in the neck.

After he had rested, Kuvlu began crawling ahead, closing on the last concealing mound of ice. His thick cloth trousers were becoming soaked from slushy patches of snow, but he was aware only of uncomfortable warmth from the exertion of the stalk. The seal awoke, looking straight toward the sun that concealed the hunter in its blinding light. Kuvlu watched, careful now to avoid staring into its eyes. Old-timers had often warned him that animals would become frightened and uneasy if they looked directly into a man's eyes. The seal turned its head the opposite way before sleeping again.

Behind the last mound of ice, Kuvlu rose on his knees for a quick look while the animal slept. Along the seal's left side he could see a small open hole. This was an *allu,* or breathing hole, that had been enlarged to provide an exit to the surface. Kuvlu was pleased that the seal did not face toward its *allu,* because this lessened its chances for a quick escape.

During the next sleep he crept over the last mound and moved five yards beyond it. Now there was nothing between him and his prey but perfectly flat ice, so he inched ahead on his stomach. Suddenly the seal's head snapped high. Alerted by the sound of Kuvlu's approach, the animal stared along the surface directly toward its pursuer. Its eyes, black and wide, registered questioning terror. Kuvlu lay pinched and cramped, perfectly still.

The seal made a quick move and faced the *allu,* now just inches from its whiskers. It lay tensed, on the edge of flight. Then its head slowly settled to the ice again. Kuvlu watched unmoving, still able to make out the eyes wide open, as the seal feigned sleep. Minutes passed. The animal finally drifted asleep, awakened, slept again.

Kuvlu reached slowly under his parka and pulled out a long-bladed knife that he carried whenever he hunted. Then he began to scratch the ice, gently but with brisk, short strokes, careful to hold the knife so his body would shield it from the seal's vision. The animal awoke, half-startled, looking at him intently. He continued scratching, with brief pauses, as its head slowly lowered to the ice, lulled to sleepiness by what seemed to be the noise of another seal close by.

For several minutes Kuvlu kept this up, and when the seal awakened it did so only briefly before dropping to sleep again. Kuvlu felt pleased and certain now as he moved slowly forward, flat on his belly, eyes glued on the motionless black body of his prey. In five more sleeps he had crawled to within easy shooting range, scarcely a stone's throw from the seal.

He rested briefly, then pulled his rifle slowly forward and clicked the safety off. This took two sleeps, because he moved with deliberate slowness to avoid making a sound while this close to a kill. The weapon's rusty barrel glistened wet in the sunshine. Kuvlu lifted it above the surface, balancing it on the open palm of his left hand while he set the stock firmly against his shoulder and squinted along the sights. He saw the barrel lift and fall slightly with each pounding beat of his heart.

The seal's head jerked high, facing straight at him. He set the bead of the sight below the animal's chin, but did not shoot. The head dropped again, and Kuvlu waited. He wanted the best target, to ensure a perfect hit. Anything less than instant death and the animal might flip into the hole to die in the ocean below. Kuvlu did not wish to make the same mistake twice in one day.

The seal awoke again, turning its head to the side, nostrils flaring to smell the breeze. Kuvlu aimed where its neck met the base of its skull, and with both eyes open he slowly squeezed with his trigger finger.

The shot cracked. Kuvlu's shoulder was powerfully jarred, disorienting him for a split second. At the same instant the seal's head fell abruptly to the ice and no movement came from its body. He dropped the rifle, jumped to his feet, and ran toward the animal while the shot's thunder rolled and echoed across the surrounding floes.

He was breathing hard when he reached the seal and stood over it, staring down at the lifeless carcass, conscious of loud ringing in his ears from the shot's explosion. He grabbed a hind flipper and with one hand dragged the seal away from the *allu*. Its dry fur was silver gray, flinty and shining in the brilliant sun. Its eyes were still open but slightly askew in a broken skull. Blood trickled crimson from the left ear, spreading out and turning orange in the slush.

Relaxing now, Kuvlu heard excited barking and howling from behind the ridge. The dogs knew what the shooting meant, and they were leaping and straining at their lines in an effort to break loose and join the hunt. He hoped the sled hook would not jerk free, because if it did they might run away from him in their exuberance.

The seal seemed dead, but to make certain Kuvlu rolled it over, lifted its head, and bent its chin sharply toward its chest. He pressed hard until he felt the neck vertebrae snap. Wounded seals sometimes regained consciousness, so it was best to break their necks to be sure they were dead.

Kuvlu walked back to retrieve his rifle and *unaaq*. He disliked being away from his weapon on the sea ice, where a polar bear could suddenly appear or the ice might unexpectedly crack and separate him from it. Returning to the seal, he looked toward the horizon and noticed that the sun had dropped very low during his long stalk. A bit of a chill was in the air, and it would be good to travel quickly now before the ice needles started freezing. He pushed the hook of the *unaaq* through the flesh of the seal's chin then held the other end, using it to pull the limp carcass back toward his team.

A streak of blood trailed behind him across the whiteness of the flat. Some days or weeks later, Kuvlu thought, a polar bear would be attracted by the smell of blood and fat and would follow the streak where he walked now. He smiled and wished to be there when it happened.

Irniivik Tatqiq

The Moon When Animals Give Birth
(JUNE)

MAIN CHARACTERS

Kavaasuk (Kah-*vah*-sook) *an adult hunter*

Niutak (*Neew*-tuk) *Kavaasuk's wife*

Ikusik (*Ik*-oo-sik)

Illuktuk (Il-*ook*-took) } *Daughters of Kavaasuk and Niutak*

Suluk (*Soo*-look)

Migalik (Mee-*gul*-ik) *Kavaasuk's brother-in-law*

KAVAASUK ROLLED ONTO HIS BACK and slowly opened his eyes, listening to the laughter that had just awakened him. Ikusik and Illuktuk, his twin daughters, were playing beside the tent wall only a few feet from where he lay. "*Azaah,* so much noise," he complained. "The animals will avoid our camp." He tried to speak loudly, but his voice was low and full of sleep. Then he heard Migalik, his brother-in-law, laughingly reply. "Kavaasuk, you are finally awake. This is a fine day, and I have seen ducks flying out over the ice. If we hunt early we may get plenty."

It must be a beautiful day indeed, he thought, seeing bright sunshine and strong shadows on the tent's roof. He could make out the sun's image through the canvas wall, its position indicating that it was early morning. Not that time really mattered now, as they approached the longest day of the year. For several weeks the sun had followed a monotonous circle around the sky, a sloping trajectory that took it high in the south at midday and low toward the north at midnight. Everyone loved this season of endless day, especially the children. Ikusik and Illuktuk enjoyed sneaking outside to play in the middle of the "night." But Kavaasuk always made them come back to bed, lest they turn themselves "upside down," sleeping all day and staying active all night.

113

Kavaasuk's wife, Niutak, awoke and sat up beside him. She was a rather tall, handsome woman, with a lively and intelligent mind. Her manner was outgoing, assertive, even somewhat masculine, probably because she had grown up the only girl in a family of boys. But Kavaasuk, like any self-respecting man among his people, held all the overt signs of dominance over her. This restricted her to the covert measures that were the lot of all Eskimo women but that nevertheless brought her almost equal authority in their household.

"Look, little Suluk is still asleep," she said. Curled up on the thick mattress of caribou skins beside her was their youngest daughter, now in her fourth summer. "Suuuu-luuuk . . . ," Niutak cooed softly. "Wake up and see your father before he goes off to hunt." Suluk opened her eyes and smiled ecstatically as Kavaasuk nuzzled her soft little neck. Small children like Suluk were a complete joy to their parents, who showered them with endless hours of loving attention. But in a few months Niutak would give birth to a new baby, and Suluk, like her older sisters before her, would face the traumatic loss of her favored position.

Kavaasuk stood up and pulled his clothes from a line along the tent's ridgepole, where he had hung them to dry after returning from seal hunting the previous night. He searched for one of his sealskin boots, which Ikusik had hidden in a far corner under the hide mattress. The tent was a spacious one, taller than a man's head and measuring twelve feet along its walls. The back part was a sleeping area, with enough room for Kavaasuk, Niutak, the three children, and Migalik; and in front there was a small iron stove and some boxes that served as stools.

When he had finished putting on his boots, Kavaasuk picked up a battered tin bucket and slipped outside. Brilliant light made his eyes water as he paused to look around. Ikusik and Illuktuk stood near the tent juggling beach pebbles, trying to see who could go longer without dropping any, while

Migalik watched in amusement. The black, sandy beach on which they were camped stretched away for miles, curving westward in the distance. On one side of the beach was a narrow brackish lagoon, and behind it a low sea cliff rose to meet the tundra plain. On the other side a great flat desert of sea ice spread out to the sky's edge. Far off toward the southwest, a glimmering haze of white stood out above the icy horizon like a sheet of fog. This was *inyipqaq,* the ice mirage, caused by upward refraction of light waves in the clear, warm air.

"Such warm weather," Migalik remarked with a delighted smile. It was nearly fifty degrees outside, with only a gentle breeze coming from the southwest. He turned and walked toward the sea ice, just thirty yards down the sloping beach from their camp. The ice was almost perfectly flat here, with blue ponds scattered everywhere across its surface. Kavaasuk went by the nearest puddle, which was several feet deep. Lying in it were two seals that he and Migalik had killed yesterday and put here for cold storage until they were needed.

He walked to another puddle that was much smaller and rather shallow, then bent down to sample the water. It was fresh, deriving from ice that had lost its salt in the thaw, so he filled his bucket and headed back to the tent. Migalik was tickling one of the girls when he returned. "*Ninguaga* [brother-in-law], you wake up early like those children," he teased. "Be careful or you will get upside down as they do, and then I will be the only one who hunts." Niutak laughed approvingly as Kavaasuk slipped back into the tent.

Burning seal blubber sputtered inside the stove, and on top boiled a pot of meat left over from the day before. A short while later everyone gathered in the tent for a breakfast of boiled duck and black coffee. Migalik pulled the head of a king eider from the pot and bit the large knob of fat from its beak. This was a favored little delicacy, and so he gave half to Suluk, who smeared its grease all over her cheeks, smiling

with utter delight at having the morsel. Her sisters, who were
two years older, were each given a meaty leg with the webbed
feet still attached. They finished quickly and went back outside to look for a ptarmigan that was calling somewhere
nearby.

"I saw a male ptarmigan sitting on the cliff yesterday,"
Niutak commented, "perhaps the same one that is calling
now. Surely a female is nesting somewhere on the tundra
close by." Kavaasuk listened carefully, then added, "This is
Irniivik tatqiq, the moon when animals give birth. Last week I
discovered a tiny nest of *qupatluraq,* the longspur, when the
female bird fluttered up right at my feet. There were five
spotted eggs in a little feather-lined hollow beneath a creeping willow." Kavaasuk had a special fondness for birds, and
he derived as much pleasure from watching them as from
hunting them. He knew the Eskimo name for every kind of
bird, and no one was more adept at identifying and imitating
their calls.

Several minutes later Illuktuk burst into the tent, rosy-
cheeked and full of excitement. "Father, ducks! Many ducks!"
she blurted. Kavaasuk was up in an instant. He grabbed
the shotgun that stood beside the door and stepped out,
squinting southward along the beach. Niutak and Migalik
came close behind and watched him run down to the edge of
the ice. "You have good eyes, little niece," Migalik said. "The
ducks are still far away."

Kavaasuk found the only available hiding place, behind a
half-rotted walrus carcass that had washed up the previous
fall. He hunched down, watching the elongated string of
ducks wing low over the ice toward him. It was a large flock,
probably more than a hundred birds, flying side-by-side in a
sinuous line that flexed and rippled as it moved. Flies from
the carcass buzzed around his head. The ducks came nearer,
and finally he could hear their hoarse calls, *"kow, kow,
kow...."*

Now he saw that they were angling out over the ice,

perhaps frightened by the tent and the dogs tied alongside it. "*Kau . . . kau,*" he imitated their croaks to bring them closer. They turned toward him momentarily, then veered away and passed by out of range. "*Azaah,* too bad. So many ducks," he muttered softly.

Before walking back to the tent he looked at the walrus carcass to see if any meat or fat remained. It was a grotesque thing—shreds of dried flesh hanging from exposed ribs, wet innards crawling with maggots, deep gnaw marks where a polar bear had eaten from it last winter. He had chosen this camping spot partly because of the carcass, which still had some meat when they arrived here a week ago. Since then the remnants had been sliced off and fed to the dogs until everything usable was gone. So this walrus, which had sunk after it was shot far out at sea the previous year, eventually became food for a polar bear, several foxes, and two dog teams.

Migalik came down to meet Kavaasuk, talking excitedly. "It is good. Ducks are coming now. This southwest breeze may be the tailwind they have waited for to carry them swiftly northward." Kavaasuk agreed and added that they were fortunate to be camping here at Kilyamittavik, fifteen miles south of Ulurunik. "Ducks love to fly over the ice near land here," he said, "and there are no other hunters around to frighten them, as so often happens near the village."

Kavaasuk remembered the old stories told by Apuktok, who had camped here in a sealskin tent almost a century before. This spot was named "place-of-the-duck-bolas," he had said, because people stayed here all summer to hunt waterfowl with this weapon. The bolas consisted of six or seven ivory weights tied to sinew strings joined at one end. When birds flew low over a hunter, he whirled his bolas and flipped them into the air ahead of them. The weights spread out as they flew, and if a bird struck one it would become entangled, plummeting helplessly to the ground. "If you look around the shores of the ponds near Kilyamittavik," the

old man used to say, "you will find ivory bolas weights still
lying here and there. Ducks often flew so fast that the strings
snapped on impact, and when this happened the weights
were lost."

Kavaasuk and Migalik decided it was a good day to walk
out a mile or so on the sea ice, where they might find the best
duck hunting. Niutak packed some dried caribou meat and
biscuits into their hunting bags and rubbed seal oil on
Migalik's boots to make them waterproof. Kavaasuk said they
would stay out all night if the hunting looked good, because
ducks preferred to fly during the time of low sun.

An hour later Niutak sat in front of the tent watching the
men, who were now just specks moving across the distant
shimmering white. A breath of wind stirred, gently flapping
the canvas walls behind her. The three girls were drawing
pictures in the sand with sticks from a dead tree lying nearby
on the beach. The old bleached trunk was all that remained
of a tree that had once grown along a river in the distant
forests of Siberia. Although the girls had never seen a living
tree, they did not pause to wonder about the long drifting
journey that brought their toys to this Arctic beach.

Niutak found a small polished rock and began sharpening
her *ulu,* or woman's knife, drawing it quickly back and forth
over the pebble's face. The *ulu's* metal blade was shaped like
a half-moon, with its convex edge sharpened and a small
ivory handle fastened along its back. When she finished, she
walked down to the pond where Kavaasuk had stored the
two killed seals. The girls came running along behind. Like
most Eskimo children they were always eager to sit quietly
and watch adults at work and were delighted if someone
would allow them to help. Thus they could give assistance
and begin learning necessary skills when they were still very
young.

Niutak pulled one seal from the puddle and dragged it to a
dry spot on the ice. Then she bent over, in stiff-legged

Eskimo fashion, and made a long cut with her *ulu* down the middle of its belly. Using quick, deft strokes she cut between the inch-thick blubber and the meat underneath, until finally the carcass was laid bare of its skin. Then she slit open the belly, exposing the stiff, cold innards, After the stomach was out, she cut it open to look inside at the mass of small shrimplike organisms that had been the animal's last meal. Suluk picked some out and wanted to eat them, but her mother said, "*aqqah!* It smells bad. Put it down."

In a short while she had systematically cut through tough ligaments and separated the joints until the entire carcass lay dismembered on the ice alongside the pond. She stood straight for a minute to relieve the pain that came from bending over her work, then she spoke to the children. "*Ki,* go ahead, each of you take some meat to the tent." Even little Suluk did her share, picking up two bloody rib sections and toddling proudly across the beach with them. It hardly mattered that she dropped one halfway to the tent, coating it with sand.

Aroused by the smell of fresh meat, the dogs stood and began whining as Niutak carried the last of the butchered seal into camp. All twenty of them watched intently, shivering in anticipation, as she cut the least favored parts into small portions. Then a chaos of barks and howls erupted as she began tossing the pieces, aiming carefully so each dog could catch his meal in midair and gulp it down with a few lunging bites. It was important to keep the food off the ground, because when dogs ate sand they often became painfully constipated.

In a few minutes it was over. Half a seal was consumed, and the huskies sniffed around for any flecks of meat or blood they might have missed. They would not eat again for two days, needing very little food during the warm summer months. Their bodies used energy so slowly at this time that more frequent feedings would make them lethargic and overweight.

Everything was calm and quiet again. Niutak sat with her

back toward the sun to work on a pair of boots she was
sewing for Ikusik. She heard a strange sound off toward the
east. It was a series of high-pitched hooting noises, the improbable call of a whistling swan. Looking up, she saw only
empty sky, and beneath it the thin brown line of snowless
tundra that was barely visible atop the cliff. There was a large
lake not far from here, she thought, and perhaps the swan
had established a nesting site along its shore. Later on, she
might walk back over the soggy meadows to look for it.

Kavaasuk and Migalik had a long and difficult trek out over
the sea ice. Deep ponds and streams continually blocked the
way, forcing many long detours on their way toward a distant
field of ridges and hummocks. On the flat ice, which extended about two miles out from the land, there was no way
to conceal themselves for hunting. This was unfortunate,
because twice during the walk out flocks of eiders came
straight toward them, but they swerved away in alarm when
they saw the two strange figures ahead.

    Not far from the first ridges, they decided to wade across a
broad, shallow pond. Migalik went ahead, jabbing the ice
with the iron tip of his *unaaq* before every step. In this way he
not only braced himself to avoid falling on the pond's slippery, uneven bottom, but also tested its safety and hardness.
At this time of year, warm ocean currents steadily eroded the
sea ice from underneath while it was also melting in the mild
air above. A pond like this could sometimes look deceptively
safe to walk through, when in fact it was just a lens of water
resting on several inches of mushy ice. But this time Migalik's
unaaq struck with crisp, hard thuds, and it was solid all the
way across.

    Just as they reached the far side, Kavaasuk saw something
out of the corner of his eye. "Wait!" he whispered, pointing
off to the right. A few seconds later they spotted a small black
globe moving along the flat surface. "Ringed seal, swimming
in a narrow crack that we cannot see from here. It must have

heard us testing the ice and come to have a look." In a moment the seal's head vanished, as if it was pulled magically down into solid ice. Both men ran toward the spot until they could see a black line slicing the frozen surface ahead, then they stood watching. They were just thirty yards from the crack, close enough to shoot the seal with their shotguns. But minutes passed and nothing appeared. "The noise of our footsteps must have frightened it away," Migalik concluded.

Seals very seldom returned to a small crack once they sensed danger nearby, so the men waited no longer. They set off again at a brisk pace, and it did not take them long to reach hummocky ice. Kavaasuk said he remembered seeing an excellent place for duck hunting when he had passed by this area several days earlier. "There is a *qaiaqsuaqpak,* a very large flat area, not far from here," he said, pointing westward. "And a single broad hummock stands at its north end—a perfect spot to conceal ourselves." Migalik smiled and nodded approval, knowing that ducks would fly very low over the flat ice and would just clear the hummock as they passed. Here conditions would be ideal for the closest possible shots.

When they reached the spot a short while later, they removed their light cloth parkas and sat down to cool off in the hummock's shade. The sun blazed high, its full brightness glancing off the long white plain to the south of them. It was a day when no one could hope to venture onto the ice without sunglasses to protect his eyes. In the old days Eskimos had made goggles from wood or from caribou hooves, with narrow slits carved in them to look through. These cut down the glare, preventing snowblindness, but they also restricted the hunters' field of vision. So the people were happy to switch to the white man's sunglasses when the chance came.

Kavaasuk slipped on his white parka cover so he would blend with his surroundings and the sharp-eyed ducks would not see him. When he removed his sunglasses for a moment, Migalik had a good laugh. "*Azaah,* brother-in-law, your face is

tanned deep brown except for two circles where your sunglasses have been. You do indeed look like your namesake,
kavaasuk, the spectacled eider, with its dark head and white
patches around its eyes." Kavaasuk smiled a bit and looked
away southward, pretending to watch for ducks. Eskimos
loved to tease others about their names, though they were
somewhat sensitive when they had to bear the brunt of such
jokes themselves.

In the hours that followed a wind gradually arose, and
hazy clouds moved up along the southern half of the sky.
Migalik and Kavaasuk saw many flocks of eiders flying over
the ice both seaward and landward of their hunting spot. But
they all passed far out of range and the men could only
watch, hoping the next ones would come closer. They even
saw a few small bunches of *niglik,* brant geese, and Kavaasuk
wondered about them. "It is strange to see brants coming
north with the wind behind them," he said. "It is their habit
to fly against a brisk headwind from the north or northeast."
Migalik agreed but said it would surely be a fine thing if some
brants would fly near enough to be shot. "Boiled *niglik,*" he
said. "What tastes better than that?"

Time passed slowly, and Kavaasuk provided entertainment by telling stories, one after the other. "Did you ever
hear the old men talk of hunting ducks with only their
voices?" he asked. Before Migalik could answer, he launched
into the tale. "At this time of year the eiders are fat, and flying
is difficult for them even under the best conditions. But if
there is a heavy fog, so they become covered with moisture,
they must work doubly hard to stay aloft. According to my
father, men used to go out on the ice and conceal themselves
across the ducks' line of flight, waiting until they heard calls
approaching in the mist. When the birds were almost upon
them, they all jumped up and made a great noise. This badly
frightened the heavy, moisture-soaked eiders, and they
would bank so hard that they stalled in midflight and fell to
the ice. Then the hunters chased them down on foot."

Migalik smiled at the thought of ducks being startled this way, then quickly added, "You are so busy telling stories that you don't even see what is coming. Look! Down there." A long, dark string of birds was winging straight toward them, not ten yards above the ice. Kavaasuk and Migalik stood motionless, peering over the edge of their concealing ice pile. The flock changed shape continually, expanding and contracting, lifting and dropping. Low staccato croaks, with no pattern beyond endless repetition, became audible as the distance narrowed. This would be a perfect ambush, prey totally unaware of the predator now just seconds away.

The flock turned off slightly westward, so Migalik called, "*Kau, kau, kau.*" Obediently, almost as if they had no will to do otherwise, the birds changed course and headed straight toward the familiar sounds. Wings hissed in the air as they lifted slightly to clear the ridges before them. The hunters watched and hesitated, awaiting a split instant in the flow of time. When the birds passed even with them, reaching the precise angle where wings became most vulnerable to the fracturing shot, both men fired. *Whoom!* the explosions were simultaneous. . . .*Whoom!* again, and again.

Migalik had chosen one duck in the flock, a brightly colored male, and fired as its wings swept downward against the rush of air. Suddenly the order and shape of its flight disintegrated, its grasp on the sky was released, and it became a disheveled clump of feathers tumbling downward. It struck the ice hard, bounced, and skidded into a block of ice at the base of a ridge. At the same moment, Migalik aimed at another and fired again.

Three birds fell immediately, then another, and two more stayed with the flock for a moment before breaking off to a steepening plunge that ended in some low hummocks a hundred yards away. The rest of the flock gathered into a tight formation and continued northward, vanishing beyond a distant line of ridges.

Now the hunters ran to find their catch. Migalik picked up

two dead birds that had fallen very close by and a third that
was badly wounded but still alive. He grabbed it behind the
head and spun it around just off the ice, instantly snapping its
neck. Kavaasuk went to get the ones that had dropped
farther away. After some looking he found one, a dark
brown female, wedged in a crevice. The second was very
much alive, and he had to chase it down. It was a male king
eider in full breeding plumage. Its body feathers were con-
trasting black and ivory, and its head was aqua along the
crown and green on the cheeks, with an orange-yellow knob
atop the base of its bill.

The bird craned its neck and blinked, but did not struggle,
when Kavaasuk picked it up. Then he pulled a quill from its
wing and poked the sharp end deep into the side of its breast,
piercing its heart. There was no sign of pain, but in a few
moments the beautiful eider went limp in his hand.

The wind freshened, a thin overcast drew itself across the
sky, and the ducks seemed to come more frequently. An
hour after their first success, another flock went over. This
time they killed seven, including two spectacled eiders, which
caused Migalik to revive his earlier joke about the re-
semblance between the bird and the man who shared its
name. They were happy to have killed so many eiders, and
much friendly teasing went back and forth between them.
Both men were gifted with a sharp wit, and so their laughter
sounded like that of many men instead of only two.

Niutak sat behind the tent now, away from the wind, legs
straight out before her. She made careful stitches with her
needle and sinew, joining sealskin to caribou skin along the
sole of Ikusik's new boot. She called softly to the twins. "Look,
it is good." They watched patiently as she worked, ab-
sorbing knowledge that they would carry with them into
womanhood.

Suluk, on the other hand, was concerned only with gaining
some of the attention, so she began to sing. The words were

nonsense, but the tune was vaguely reminiscent of Eskimo songs she heard so often. "Cute little one," her mother cooed. "You want to dance?" Suluk smiled broadly, her narrow little eyes twinkling, cheeks puffed and brown. "*Aa kingak unaaah....*" Niutak began one of her favorite songs. "*Ki,* dance," she said, then sang again. Suluk dropped her eyes as a woman should, bounced lightly on her toes, and waved her tiny arms in a faltering imitation of what she had seen at the village dances. Then she stopped, midverse, and smiled ecstatically. Her delighted audience furnished ample applause, and the twins ran off to practice dancing by themselves.

When she finished sewing, Niutak called the girls and said it was time for them to catch an animal. She took a small stick, several inches long, and sharpened both ends; then she tied the stick onto a long piece of sealskin line. "Those two big white seagulls have been flying around our camp for two days waiting to steal meat," she said, "so we will give them what they want." Illuktuk brought her an old, smelly piece of seal meat, which she impaled firmly on the sharp stick. Then they walked a short distance from camp, tied the line to a heavy rock, and placed the meat conspicuously on top.

"You see, a gull watches us even at this moment," Niutak said as they walked back to the tent. High above, wheeling and hovering against the haze of cloud, was a large glaucous gull. Its arc widened, and very slowly it descended, beak pointing down toward the glint of wet meat far below. Moments later it flew toward the cliff nearby, planing for a moment on the breeze, feet hanging loosely as it lit on the precipice. Then it lurched out again and made a slow, curving glide down to the sand near the rock. Its head turned from side to side as it looked around suspiciously. Finally the gull decided. It walked briskly forward, snapped up the meat, and gulped it down.

It hopped twice, flew about ten feet, and was ignominiously jerked to a halt at the end of its tether. A great flapping of wings followed as the bird plunged to the sand, flew, fell, then rolled hysterically trying to disgorge its meal. The twins ran out but then stopped short, a bit afraid when they realized that this was a very big bird indeed. Moments later, Niutak grabbed the gull's head and wrung its neck. Because the seagull was not a tasty bird, its meat would be used for dog food. She would also dry its wings and use them for whisk brooms to clean the tent floor; and the wing tendons would be pulled out for later use as fishhook leaders.

As she carried the limp gull back toward camp, Niutak had a strange foreboding about the weather. A gust of wind scurried along the beach, lifting sprays of sand as it went. The clouds moved rapidly now from the south, and they had become heavier, with dark swirls and torn edges. When she looked out toward the horizon, she saw that its sharp edge had become indistinct and hazy.

Kavaasuk and Migalik had also noticed the threatening weather, but as the wind increased so did the flights of waterfowl. No hour passed without several long, twisting flocks passing somewhere nearby. Twenty-four ducks were scattered on the ice behind them, an exceptionally large catch; but they still hoped for more. It was late evening—the sun's hazy glow was visible through clouds toward the northwest.

Migalik began to think about the weather, wondering if a storm might be approaching. It was difficult to make accurate predictions in the summer, but there were clear signs now, as darker clouds hovered low toward the south. He walked to a high ridge nearby and looked over the scattered flats and hummocks surrounding them. Then he hurried back to talk with Kavaasuk.

"An hour ago when I stood on that ridge I saw many seals sleeping on the ice in two broad flats west of us," he said. "But now not a single animal is there." Migalik recalled the old hunters' advice that seals often went down into the water if a powerful storm was coming. Perhaps they did this because heavy winds could move the ice, closing the cracks or holes they had emerged from and trapping them on the surface.

"If a gale comes," Kavaasuk said, "it will blow from the south or southwest. This is good, because it creates no danger that the *tuvaq,* the landfast ice, might be carried away before we can reach shore. But warm water and sunshine have weakened the ice and eaten away at grounded ridges, so the entire *tuvaq* might move tighter against the land. If this happens there will be fresh cracks opening everywhere and perhaps ice piling as well."

Without further hesitation they prepared to leave. The ducks were gathered into two bunches, tied together by their necks, and slung on long straps. In this way the hunters could either carry their weighty catch on their backs or drag it along behind them. When they finished, they picked up their hunting bags, shotguns, and *unaaqs* and set off on a straight line toward the distant camp.

For some time there was little change in the weather except for continued lowering of clouds that swept overhead on the silent rush of air. The ice was dull and gray, ponds became a deep blue black, with ripples scurrying endlessly over their surface. But the wind held steady, and Migalik said perhaps it would grow no worse. Despite this possibility, they kept walking at their fastest pace, and both got wet feet when they hastily crossed a puddle that was too deep for their boots.

They were just past halfway to shore when Migalik was proved wrong. Quite abruptly, in a span of perhaps ten minutes, the wind increased to twice its original speed. Luckily it remained from the southwest, hitting the men from the side and slightly behind. If they had been forced to walk against such a gale their progress would have been slow indeed. They watched the ice carefully, but so far there were no signs of strain or movement. Nevertheless, fears that it would begin cracking or piling grew stronger in their minds as the storm continued to rise.

For a while they could still see the line of cliffs and the

greenish-brown tundra that climbed away behind it. But
finally the haze closed in before them, the coastline faded
and disappeared, and a few spits of rain pelted down.
Although the distance was fairly short now and they were
assured of reaching camp, the men felt tense as they quick-
ened their pace even more. Both of them were breathing
hard, soaked with perspiration, and nearly exhausted. At
one point a small flock of eiders passed right overhead,
hurtling effortlessly along on the wind—but the men were
too preoccupied for shooting, though they could certainly
have killed one or two.

Niutak sat inside the tent listening to the monotonous flapping of its walls and feeling the force of wind against the
small shelter. She could not help worrying, though she knew
the ice would not drift away. Every few minutes she poked
her head out the door to see if the men might be returning.
Suluk was sound asleep, wrapped in a thick cocoon of
blankets, but the twins sat quietly in a corner, excited but a bit
lonesome for their father and their playful uncle Migalik.

When it was near midnight Niutak thought she saw two
figures far out in the haze and drizzle. She watched for several minutes, until their shape and movement were clearly
visible, then felt suddenly relieved as it became certain that
the men were coming. Her face glistened with raindrops as
she turned to the girls and told them, "Someone is coming at
last. They must be very wet and hungry, but perhaps they
bring fresh ducks for us." She put several pieces of blubber
in the stove to heat up the tent and started making fresh tea
for the returning hunters.

When Kavaasuk and Migalik arrived they set to work
bracing the tent before coming inside. The wind was still
increasing, and they wanted to be sure that none of the ropes
would break or pull loose. By the time they finished the rain
had really started coming down, so they were drenched when

they entered. The air felt steamy and warm against their skin
as they undressed near the stove, hanging their wet things
along the ridgepole to dry. "Such bad weather this is!"
Kavaasuk puffed. But he added that twenty-four ducks were
outside, showing quite emphatically that the discomfort had
been worthwhile.

An hour later, Kavaasuk, Migalik, and Niutak sat eating a
tasty stew made with fresh-killed eiders. The pleasure of fat,
boiled meat after a long day's hunting made the men feel
happy, and they talked enthusiastically of the things they had
seen and done. When the meal was finished they rested on
the soft skins listening to the storm. Ikusik and Illuktuk had
drifted off to sleep shortly after the men returned, and their
mother pulled blankets up to cover them.

When she did this she noticed something—a small leak in
the tent roof. Water dripped steadily from it, and already
some of their bedding was soaked. "*Alyakaah,*" Kavaasuk
muttered. "This is bad. Our tent is facing crosswise to the
wind, so the rain is driven straight into the roof's slope." He
looked carefully and found drips starting in several more
places, then decided they would have to go outside and put a
heavy tarpaulin over the roof. Both men dressed immediately, pulling on wet clothes that felt icy cold and
clammy against their warm skin.

Grains of blown sand stung their faces and the wind
pushed heavily against them as they stepped outside. Migalik
remembered the morning and wondered how it was that
weather could change from one extreme to the other in the
space of a single day. He saw the dogs, curled up with their
backs to the gale, sand drifting against them the way snow
did in winter.

The big tarpaulin flapped wildly when they unfolded it,
and they wrestled the thing as if it were alive. After much
struggling they managed to pull it up over the tent, then each
set to work tying it firmly in place. Kavaasuk finished one

tie, then looked out toward the ice for a moment before moving on to the next. What he saw made him forget the tarp very quickly.

"Look there!" he shouted over the tempest. "The ice is warping near the beach!" Migalik snapped around and held a hand alongside his face to keep sand away from his eyes. Not fifty yards from the tent, where Niutak had butchered the seal that morning, he saw a broad arch of ice bending upward as the pack pressed in.

They went closer and stood watching for several minutes, unaware of the storm's raging. The ice here was thicker than a man's height, yet it continued to warp very gradually, without cracking, until it formed a dome ten feet high. Then it split down the middle and kept rising, while the ice around it began to crush into smaller hummocks. Finally an enormous slab rose thirty feet high, slowly tilted back off the vertical, and fractured under its own weight.

Niutak heard a muffled sound, like thunder, and guessed that the ice was crushing even before Kavaasuk shouted to her through the tent wall. "We are too close to the ice here," he said. "If it begins sliding up the beach our camp could be buried underneath it. Wake the girls and dress them, then cover everything you can. We will move back away from danger." Moments later she could hear them leading the dogs away as she hurriedly wrapped whatever she could in skins and pieces of canvas. The girls sat up in one corner, their eyes open but their minds still lost in sleepy confusion.

Kavaasuk and Migalik worked fast, glancing repeatedly toward the ice to check its movement. They both knew that it could slide onto the beach quite suddenly if enough pressure built up. And they had heard the old story of what happened at Utkeavik in the last century, when a terrible storm piled ice right up over the beach cliff. That time it was winter, and in the dark of night several sod houses were completely buried, killing all their occupants.

Rain fell harder now, but even though the beach was soaked the sand continued to blow along in thick clouds. Before long they were ready to take the tent down, and while Migalik and Kavaasuk unfastened the ropes, Niutak and the children scurried back up the strand carrying armloads of gear. Everything was assembled in one spot, and then they all worked together at putting the tent up, this time with its back wall facing the gale. It was no easy task erecting the shelter in such a storm. But by staking the walls out first and lifting the ridgepole afterward, they had it back up in a few minutes without the wind's tearing it apart or carrying it away.

When this was done Migalik remembered the seal in a pond on the ice. He ran down and saw it lying in the open, where the ice had bent and cracked upward. There seemed to be little motion just now, so he rushed out with an *unaaq*, hooked it, and retreated quickly to the safety of land. Shortly afterward, crushing increased again and broad slabs of ice inched up onto the beach, digging deep gouges in the sand. He turned and trudged off toward the tent, listening for the rumbling of ice but unable to hear it over the wind's roar.

Everyone was soaking wet, even the girls, so Niutak fed the stove until the tent was very hot inside. Dripping clothes were hung everywhere, but they would take many hours to dry. Luckily the blankets and skins were just slightly moistened, so they would have no trouble getting a good night's sleep. "Our tent will leak no more," Kavaasuk said cheerfully, "and the ice will not come sneaking after you, little Suluk." He kissed her face again and again until she laughed despite her tiredness. She was too young to comprehend what had happened, but when she grew older Niutak would tell her the story. Then perhaps she would recall what she had seen on this stormy night at the edge of the frozen sea.

Kavaasuk pulled the covers over himself and remembered a similar night he had spent not far away some years earlier. "This is a bad place for storms," he said. "Our tent was at

Milliktavik, five miles south of here, when a tremendous
south wind blew up suddenly. There were four of us—Amiksuk, Kuvlu, Tupik, and me. When the wind came there was
no rain, just sand everywhere, blowing so hard that you
could not face it. Three of us were inside the tent, but it blew
down within a few minutes. Since we could not hope to put it
up again, we stayed underneath it until the gale eased a
day later.

"Kuvlu was not so lucky. He was a mile north of camp
hunting ptarmigan when the storm came, and so much sand
was blowing along the beach that he could not walk against it.
A deep pond separates the beach from the land for a stretch
of several miles there, so he could not reach the tundra to
escape the blinding sand. Finally, after waiting several hours,
he became very cold and worried that it might start to rain.
So he walked north along the strand, the wind at his back, all
the way to Ulurunik. He had to go twenty miles on foot
because he could not walk a mile against that storm."

Everyone was quiet now, lulled by the steady pounding of
the wind and the exhaustion that made sleep come quickly.
Kavaasuk lay awake in the dim light, staring at the roof above
his head. The storm would last a day or two, he thought, and
then they could hunt again. It was good to be here at Kilyamittavik, far from the village, where they had solitude and
plenty of game.

The wind lifted powerfully, fell, lifted again. Raindrops
clicked on wet canvas. Kavaasuk felt the strong sense of security that comes when a storm whips outside the frail walls of a
tent, so close yet still powerless to reach one. He rolled onto
his side and saw Suluk there, fast asleep in the warm space
between her mother and father.

Inyukuksaivik Tatqiq

The Moon When Birds Raise Their Young
(JULY)

MAIN CHARACTERS

Ulimaun (*Oo*-lee-maun) *an old man*

Amiksuk (*Ah*-mik-sook) *an adult hunter*

Talimat (*Tul*-ee-mut) *Amiksuk's adult cousin*

Pukak (*Poo*-kuk) *Amiksuk's formal hunting partner*

Pamiuk (Pum-*ee*-ook) *an inland Eskimo hunter*

Nauruk (*Now*-rook) *Talimat's brother*

Itiruk (It-*tir*-ook) *Nauruk's wife*

Pauluk (*Pow*-look) *an old hunter*

Kakivik (Kah-*ki*-vik) *Pauluk's adult son*

IT WAS A MIDSUMMER MORNING, gloomy and chill-bitten. Thick overcast covered the sky with reticulated patterns of slate gray and silver. A cold breeze blew off the Chukchi Sea and through the houses of Ulurunik. Caribou skins, hung outside to dry, flapped monotonously on sagging lines.

The village looked timeless, ancient, like a cluster of scaling rocks thrust up through the tundra soil. Its dwellings were arranged helter-skelter, and they varied greatly in size, shape, and state of repair. Nearly all were colored like the sky, their unpainted lapstrake sides gray and weatherbeaten. Scattered everywhere around the houses were tall driftwood poles that supported clotheslines and meat caches. A variegated green of sedge and willow fingered into the settlement from the surrounding land; but in many places it was worn thin by footsteps, forming a network of trails between the houses.

Here and there, large bare patches marked the spots where sled dogs were tethered to wait out the summer's passage. Many of the dogs rested in deep, cool hollows they had dug for themselves after the snow disappeared. The ground nearby was littered with gnawed bones, tufts of shed fur, and moist piles of excrement. Not surprisingly, the air was heavy and fetid with smells of dung, rotting meat, blubber, and the boggy odor of saturated tundra.

135

Near the south end of the village, perched atop the beach cliff, was a very small, boxy house with blocks of sod piled halfway up its sides. Ulimaun, the old man who owned the house, sat on its roof looking out over the ocean with his antiquated binoculars. Each day throughout the warm months he spent several hours there, scanning the nearby ice and open water for game.

A few weeks ago he had seen an endless sprawl of solid ice, sometimes with an open lead in the distance. Then came a period of warm, sunny weather, when heat radiating from the land melted a strip of ice several hundred yards wide along the shore. After this, a powerful southeasterly gale with accompanying high tide carried most of the landfast ice away to drift with the pack. All that remained was a scattered band of grounded floes and ice piles less than half a mile offshore.

Ulimaun had been very pleased by these changes, especially by the storm, which blew fiercely for several days. It carried the ice far out beyond the horizon, opening a wide stretch of water so that seals and walrus could easily move northward from wintering areas farther south. The ice had been gone for two weeks, and people began to worry that the entire pack would drift north beyond Ulurunik, taking the game along with it. But then, just two days ago, a strong southwest current had brought the scattered floes shoreward again until they came within a few miles of land. Everyone knew the animals that had come north would be found in abundance out along the edge of the pack, where men could hunt them from skin boats.

The old man heard voices on the beach below his house and saw hunters carrying loads of gear toward an *umiaq* that rested upside down above the high-tide mark. There was Amiksuk, owner of the boat, with his cousin Talimat and his hunting partner Pukak. And coming behind was Pamiuk, the inland Eskimo, trudging through the sand cradling an outboard engine in his arms. Ulimaun wished he were young

again so he could go out with them among the broken summer floes to hunt the ringed seal and the large bearded seal.
Indeed, he thought, they might take many seals today,
perhaps even walrus if luck was with them.

Amiksuk stood looking over the gear scattered alongside
his boat and suddenly realized he had forgotten to bring the
harpoon. He laughed at his forgetfulness and called out to
his young son, who had tagged along to watch. "*Ki,* go
quickly! Fetch the harpoon, and bring the long line made
from walrus hide." Amiksuk always became a little excited
before he went hunting, partly because he was an emotional
man and partly because he threw himself wholeheartedly
into everything he did. People were often amused by his
energy and haste, which reminded them of white men, the
Taniks, who never did anything at a normal pace. But none
could help admiring Amiksuk for the success his ambition
brought him.

All four men lined up along one side of the *umiaq,* lifted,
and turned it right side up, then they laboriously dragged it
down the sand to the water's edge. Talimat fastened the engine to a small transom built onto the boat's stern. In every
other respect the *umiaq's* design was unchanged from the
time when paddles and gut-skin sails were the only sources of
power. After the motor was in place, everyone quickly loaded
food, rifles, clothing, hunting bags, and other gear inside.

Old Ulimaun walked down to speak with the hunters while
they waited for Amiksuk's son to bring the harpoon. He
made a teasing gesture toward Pamiuk, who had lived inland
since birth and had only recently brought his family to settle
along the coast. "Ah, I see you will travel far from the land
today," Ulimaun laughed. "Now you will become a real
Tareogmiut, a real sea Eskimo, and you will no longer dream
of chasing caribou and hooking fish up there." He swept his
hand away toward the bank and the tundra beyond.

Moments later the boy ran up with the forgotten harpoon.
He was smiling broadly, very proud that he had been asked

to help the hunters. Amiksuk inspected the weapon and gave it to Talimat, who placed it in the bow of the *umiaq* near his rifle. Then he turned to Ulimaun and spoke. "We will hunt toward the south, so if we should happen to return with a load, the strength of the north-flowing current will make our homeward travel easier." Ulimaun raised his eyebrows affirmatively and turned to walk up the beach. Moments later he stood atop the bank watching the boat make its way seaward, until finally it grew small in the distance.

Amiksuk was the steersman, sitting high in the stern. The engine droned monotonously in his ears as he scanned the water ahead, always watchful for signs of game. When they left the shore the pack ice had appeared only as a thin white line along the horizon, but now it began to resolve itself into the jagged outlines of separate floes with tall ice piles scattered among them. It had been nearly an hour since they set out.

A short while later they reached the outermost edges of the pack, marked by widely dispersed ice pans and occasional broad floes several acres in size. The surface of the ocean had been flecked with whitecaps outside the pack but grew nearly calm as they moved farther in amid the protecting ice. Floes became larger and larger, with less space between them, and soon they were following narrow lanes of open water. Amiksuk turned the boat southward, heading parallel to the edge of the pack to avoid going in where the floes would be dangerously close.

Pamiuk had never before traveled on the ocean during the summer, and what he saw was both fascinating and awesome. The winter sea ice had been much like the land, a solid frozen expanse. But now it had broken into millions of fragments in every conceivable dimension and shape. Yet the entire mass drifted as one—north, south, east, or west— according to the pressures of wind and current. In fact, at this very moment it was moving slowly toward the land, and so they would travel a shorter distance going home than they had coming out.

Pukak was sitting beside Pamiuk and saw the excitement in his eyes. "Look there," Pukak said, pointing off the bow, "the huge one is called *aulaylik*." It was an enormous floeberg, a tall ridge of piled ice formed the previous winter and now floating free. "Most of it is underwater," Pukak continued, "but if it melts down below and becomes top-heavy, it will overturn. That is why we never go close with the boat. If we want a place to look around from a high spot, we will find piled ice on a broad floe that will not tip over."

They had just passed the huge floeberg when Talimat, who sat in the bow, stiffened and looked sharply toward his right. Then he pointed with his whole arm and turned to look at Amiksuk. "Over there," he said. "A ringed seal!" His words were drowned out by the engine, but everyone quickly saw the animal. A small dark globe bobbed on the water's rippled surface perhaps a hundred yards away, near a large, flat ice floe.

To an unpracticed eye it might easily have been a swimming duck or gull—in fact, Pamiuk thought for a moment it was. But Talimat was a hunter, not a foolish boy who would speak out before he was certain. By the shape of its silhouette and the pattern of its movement, he could quickly tell not only that it was a seal but also the kind of seal it was. Its smallish head and pointed snout, and the way it bobbed up and down in one spot, showed clearly that it was a ringed seal.

Amiksuk immediately swung the boat and headed toward the animal at full speed. Now it rose high in the water, staring at the strange apparition that had suddenly entered its world. Talimat grabbed his rifle and pushed a bullet into the chamber, then quickly checked to see that the harpoon was ready beside him. A moment later he stood, bracing himself against the heavy, curved stem, rifle to his shoulder, the still-distant seal in his sights.

The animal sank straight down to listen under water but came back up a few seconds later, seemingly transfixed by

curiosity. Talimat gauged the seal's intentions, saw its head
turn to one side, then the other, and gambled that it would
stay a moment longer. Forty yards separated them now, and
he began squeezing the trigger.

That instant the seal took fright. All Talimat saw was a
quick splash, a sheet of water thrown up, as the seal dove
sidelong and disappeared. Amiksuk cut the engine and
turned in a circle, knowing that ringed seals usually surfaced
nearby after diving that way.

A minute passed before the animal's head bobbed up
again, not far from where it had gone down. But now it was
behind the boat, and before Amiksuk could turn it rolled
forward into a deep dive. Talimat could read the seal's direction from the way it went down, and he pointed toward the
nearby ice. "It is no use," he said. "The seal will rise somewhere among those ice pans, where we cannot chase it."

Amiksuk suggested that they go closer to the outside edge
of the pack, where seals could not escape so easily. Talimat
nodded agreement, and they headed off eastward. At the
same moment the seal sped away, deep beneath the water. It
still heard the strange metallic whining that had first attracted it to the surface; but now curiosity was smothered by
fear. Shortly the sound grew faint, and the animal angled
upward toward shimmering light.

The day grew brighter despite continued overcast, and hours
passed slowly as the boat made its way southward. The men
saw two more seals, but both disappeared quickly and did not
come up again. There were also seabirds in abundance, including a variety of ducks, gulls, loons, and terns. Talimat
kept his shotgun ready in case a flock of eiders happened to
fly over within range.

They were cruising across a wide area of open water when
Pukak pointed almost directly overhead. "Look there," he
said to Pamiuk. "*Isungaq,* the jaeger, chasing a seagull twice
his own size. Watch, he is a thief that flies." The gull darted
back and forth, climbed, circled, and nosedived; but the

jaeger followed just inches behind in perfect, mirrored flight. It had the shape of a dark, shadowy falcon, with narrow, pointed wings that angled sharply back, and adding to its rakish appearance were two long, pointed feathers that streamed out beyond its tail. Few birds could fly like a gull, but even the gull was no match for a jaeger.

The pursuing jaeger let out a harsh, squealing cry and hovered briefly above its victim. Finally the gull lurched in flight, opened its beak, and disgorged a large fish. In an instant the jaeger had folded its wings, swept downward, and plucked the fish out of the air before it struck the water. The contest was over.

"*Yahaii,* the jaeger is a bad one," Pukak muttered. "He lives by stealing and rarely catches a meal for himself." Jaegers were among the few animals that Eskimos genuinely disliked, and it was this habit of theft that earned them scorn. Few things were more unthinkable in Eskimo society than stealing, because if a person felt need he had only to ask and things would be given him. This was especially true of food, which was shared with no thought of debt or return.

Pamiuk watched the jaeger wheel and glide swiftly off on the wind. He thought of the many new and strange things he had seen since coming to live by the sea, and he felt a powerful longing for the tundra he knew so well. Pamiuk's family was among the last of the inland Eskimos to abandon their traditional way of life and move into a seacoast settlement. And, like the other inland people, he still held strongly to the old Eskimo ways.

The Ulurunik people admired Pamiuk for the traditions he represented, and they respected him as a man. They were also very fond of his wife, Nagliktuk, a warm, friendly woman who was kept continuously busy by her three children. Pamiuk guessed his age at about forty years, but he looked only half that. He was a short man, very strong and knotty, with a hard-set jaw and flashing, alert eyes. The winter before, when the young men raced fifteen miles on foot in forty below zero cold, Pamiuk beat them all. Few men were as quiet as Pamiuk, few were as honest, and none had more pride in being Eskimo.

But Pamiuk had much to learn about traveling and hunting on the sea. He could stalk caribou with the cunning of a wolf, but seals left him baffled. Their heads popped up suddenly out of nowhere, seldom stopped moving, and usually vanished again before he could put his rifle sights on them. He often laughed at his own ineptitude when it came to seal hunting, but at the same time he was determined to master it.

Pamiuk's thoughts were cut short as a pair of loons flapped along the water and took flight in front of the *umiaq*. Talimat, who was a fine mimic, imitated the loons' hoarse call, "*Qah-raoq . . . qah-raoq. . . .*" The birds turned and circled past the boat for a closer look. Pamiuk knew that they must have a nest beside a lake somewhere up on the tundra, with spotted eggs about ready to hatch. Summer was passing quickly, he thought, because already it was *Inyukuksaivik tatqiq,* "the moon when birds raise their young."

For some time they had been traveling into a stiff breeze that picked up from the southwest. Even though they were dressed in heavy parkas, with layers of clothing underneath, the men began to feel chilled. So Amiksuk decided to find a place to stop, make tea, and hunt seals from the ice.

He steered the *umiaq* toward a long, nearly level floe, but when they came alongside it the ice looked dark and wet. It was too rotten, and there was no reason to risk someone's falling through. Farther south they checked a smaller ice pan with a ridge down its center; but Amiksuk felt that it was top-heavy and might overturn. Nearby they found an ideal spot, a broad floe more than a mile long, with piled ice they could climb to look around and a low spot for pulling up the *umiaq*. A few minutes later they had the boat on the ice, emptied of its contents and tipped on edge to drain the water that had come in through a small hole in its skin covering.

Pamiuk and Talimat quickly set up a windbreak, using three *unaaqs* to support a large sheet of canvas. This offered protection for the gasoline camp stove, which they now lighted to boil water for tea. Talimat called to Pukak, who was jogging around to warm himself. "Ah, cousin, you are always cold. You must use all your energy at home with your wife! Perhaps if you fetch water for tea it will make you feel warmer." Everyone laughed, including Pukak, as he walked off to find a puddle of fresh water.

Talimat loved strong tea, and so he let the pot boil several minutes until the tea was deep black. When Pukak filled his cup and took a sip he sputtered, "*Azaah*, just like coffee! This man Talimat is a real Eskimo. His stomach is strong enough to take anything." Talimat smiled, opening a flour sack full of biscuits made by his wife. Each man took several, and then they spread out along the edge of the floe to watch for seals while they ate.

Pamiuk sat on a small ice pile looking out over the water, his rifle beside him. He noticed that all the ice pans seemed to be standing still, but he knew they were drifting along at the same speed as the floe he was on. If he concentrated hard it seemed he could detect a feeling of motion, together with a sense of the floe's immensity and inertia. But it was so vague that he wondered if the feeling might be imaginary. When hunters were this far from the coast the only way they could be sure of the speed and direction of their drift was to drop a weighted line and feel it dragging along the bottom.

Talimat stationed himself not far from Pamiuk and started scratching the ice with his knife. Eskimos often did this because for some unknown reason seals were strongly attracted by the noise. He scratched for a long while, but nothing appeared. Then, suddenly, Pamiuk caught a movement out of the corner of his eye. At the same moment Talimat sat down quickly, taking his shooting position. He whispered loudly, "*Uguruk!* Pamiuk, *Uguruk* close to you."

By this time Pamiuk had picked up his rifle and started

taking aim; but before he could shoot the seal rolled forward in a shallow dive. "Keep watching, to your left this time." Talimat scratched the ice again as he spoke.

A minute passed, then two minutes. Pamiuk thought the *uguruk* was gone, but finally it appeared again, farther away this time and off to the left as Talimat had predicted. No one shot, and the head vanished. "He will come close again," Talimat asserted. "*Uguruks* are always curious about people." He scratched several times, waited, scratched again, then sat with his gun ready.

Moments later the seal's dark silhouette broke water before him, just thirty yards from the ice edge. It rose high as the animal stretched to peer inquisitively toward the hunter. Talimat aimed quickly. His rifle cracked. The noise was deafening, and a split second later a dull thud could be heard as the bullet struck flesh and bone.

Everyone stood watching intently to see if the seal would float or sink. Oil from its lacerated blubber spread outward in a glassy slick. And in its midst the animal's head slowly appeared, floating just above the surface.

Amiksuk and Pukak ran to the boat, slipped it into the water, and sped toward the carcass. Pukak stood in the bow, ready to plunge the harpoon and secure their prey. But just before they reached it Talimat saw what he had feared. A stream of bubbles came from the lifeless seal as air was expelled from its lungs, and it vanished instantly. Pukak saw only a haze of red as they turned and circled the spot.

But Eskimos would not give up easily. Pukak quickly grabbed a small float with a long line and stone weight attached. He dropped the weight where the *uguruk* had gone down, and when it struck bottom the tethered float marked the spot. Talimat smiled and said, "Perhaps we will have this *uguruk* after all, if we use a snag hook before we drift too far away."

Talimat hurried over to where the boat had been and picked up a long coil of line with a four-pronged hook and a lead weight attached to one end. Then he ran back to his shooting spot, uncoiling the line onto the ice to be certain there would be no kinks or tangles in it. Standing at the ice edge, directly across from the marker float, he was now ready to throw the snag hook.

He grasped a small bone toggle tied into the line about three feet above the hook and weight, then began swinging it back and forth in a broad underhand arc. When his aim was correct he let it fly outward, guiding the cord loosely with his left hand. The hook splashed about ten yards beyond the marker. Talimat paused for a moment to let it reach bottom, then began pulling the line inward, coiling it at his feet.

He got nothing on the first try, nor on the second or third. Each time he threw the line he aimed a few feet to the right of his last toss, systematically covering the marked area. He also had to keep moving farther down the edge of the drifting floe to stay near the spot where the animal had sunk. The other men went back to hunting, but they also kept an eye on Talimat in case he struck the seal. He tossed again and again, but without any luck.

Soon he was quite far down the ice edge, and he decided to give up after a few more tosses. Another floe was drifting toward the marker, so they would have to retrieve it soon with the *umiaq*. Talimat decided to abandon his pattern and toss the hook well north of the float, in case the current was rolling the seal away along the bottom. He gave it an extra long toss.

Pulling the line slowly inward, he felt the hook abruptly snag. He gave a gentle tug, and his half-numbed fingers felt the line pull itself back, as if the hooks touched something soft and movable like a seal's body. So he grabbed the line tightly and jerked it hard. And when he pulled again it was very heavy indeed. "Ah, this is good!" he muttered to himself. He had snagged the *uguruk*.

Talimat did not call out to the others, but let them notice in their own time that he would need help. In a few minutes he saw them abandon their hunting places, quickly load the boat, and set out toward where he stood.

"*Azahaa,* Talimat is lucky today," Amiksuk blustered loudly as they approached. "It must be a big one, or have you snagged a rock?" Everyone laughed at this idea, because there were no rocks on the ocean floor anywhere along this coast, only fine black sand and pebbles. Pamiuk grabbed the float and hauled in its line, then they paddled up to the ice beside Talimat.

Looking down into the clear water, they could see the *uguruk's* outline slowly emerging from the blackness. In a few moments they had pulled it to the surface at the ice edge. Pukak grunted as he looped a rope around its flippers, "Ah, when have I seen an *uguruk* this big?" It was a huge male, light gray in color, nearly ten feet long and weighing perhaps a thousand pounds.

Amiksuk was clearly pleased. As owner of the boat he was given not only a double share of the meat but also the animal's valuable skin. And he would need at least six *uguruk* skins to re-cover the *umiaq* next spring.

It took all the strength the men could muster to haul their quarry up onto the ice alongside the boat. Then they tipped it so the gunwale was flush with the ice and lugged the seal inside. It was placed crosswise amidships, hind flippers hanging over one gunwale and head over the other. A deep-red stream of blood oozed from behind the seal's ear, ran down its side, and dripped into the bottom of the boat.

After loading the seal the men decided it was time to move. They headed southward, but before they had gone a mile they heard a strange thundering. The noise rolled and echoed among the floes, fading, surging, then disappearing in the distance. Several times it was repeated, loudly enough to be heard over the engine's sound. Amiksuk stood and pointed. "Someone is shooting," he said, "south of here and farther out among the floes." Everyone looked in the direction of the noise, but they saw only water and ice. Immediately, and without discussion, they set out to find the other hunters. Eskimos were intensely social people who would never pass up a chance to visit, especially when they were hunting far from the village.

Pamiuk spotted them. He was looking over a wide, flat ice floe and saw what appeared to be four black dots gliding along its surface. Then he realized that the dots were four people riding in a boat along the floe's far side. Only their heads and shoulders were visible over the ice; the boat was hidden from sight beneath it.

Amiksuk steered into a narrow passage that would intersect their line of travel. Everyone stared intently, trying to see who these hunters might be. "Perhaps it is Nauruk," Pukak said. "He left the village yesterday to hunt this way, and no one else would be so far south." The people of Ulurunik, particularly the hunters, generally knew where everyone was and what they were doing. It was a small settlement, and so news of people's activities spread very quickly. A few minutes later Talimat, who was watching the travelers through his binoculars, confirmed Pukak's guess. "It is Nauruk, with his wife and two men who look like Pauluk and Kakivik."

Nauruk had seen the others coming, and so he found a spot to pull up his boat and start making tea. When Amiksuk's crew landed, Nauruk looked inside their *umiaq* and exclaimed, "Ah, these men are hunters! Is this an *uguruk* I see, or is it a bull walrus?" This was fine flattery indeed. Amiksuk returned the compliment as he stepped out onto the ice and saw an *uguruk,* two smaller ringed seals, and a dozen eider ducks in Nauruk's boat.

Nauruk pointed to his wife Itiruk and spoke with pride. "This woman shot a ringed seal yesterday. And today she killed four ducks with a shotgun." Amiksuk was full of admiration. "Now you are a hunter, Itiruk! If you keep it up you will be like Ataakturak and hunt as well as any man."

Ataakturak was an Ulurunik woman of legendary skill as a

hunter. In her younger years she had gone out regularly
during the summer, and she had killed seals, caribou, ducks,
geese, even a few walrus. She was expert at fishing as well,
and sometimes she trapped foxes during the winter. But in
her middle years her eyesight had failed, and now she was
completely blind. Still, she cared for her children and grandchildren, and she was expert at sewing despite her handicap.
Every time the men spoke of Ataakturak there was respect in
their voices. It was a great pleasure to see a woman who could
hunt and provide like a man.

Itiruk was not so skilled as Ataakturak, but she was young
and anxious to learn. She had become discontented staying
behind while her husband hunted, and so she decided to
become a useful member of his crew. This was only her third
seal, but one could see that she would take more before the
summer ended. "As long as Nauruk will allow me in his crew
I will go with him," Itiruk said, "but if he refuses I will hunt
with another crew." Everyone laughed, but they knew she
meant what she said.

The two crews spent nearly an hour in animated conversation, talking of seals, ducks, the ice, and the weather. Nauruk
said they had hunted yesterday until the low sun near midnight, then had gone ashore to camp at Poktogavik. It had
been very cold, Kakivik added, because a chill wind blew in
under the tent and they had not bothered to bring sleeping
bags. Luckily they had caribou skins to put beneath them, or
it would have been very cold sleeping indeed.

The conversation lapsed, and everyone in the little group
sat quietly. When Eskimos had nothing to say they did not
speak, unlike the curious *Taniks* who seemed almost afraid to
sit together in silence. Finally Talimat spoke. "It is time for
aiviq, the walrus, to be drifting north on the floe ice. Perhaps
we should . . ."

Nauruk interrupted excitedly, "*Azaah,* I nearly forgot to
tell you. This morning, very early, we stopped to look around
from a tall hummock. It was nearly calm, and Pauluk heard

walrus bellowing from out that way." He pointed seaward. "We looked for a long time and finally saw them. It was a small herd, perhaps ten animals, on an ice pan far out in the pack. We might have reached them by following narrow lanes of water, but if the ice had closed and the water disappeared we would have been trapped."

This was the first report of walrus, and it was important news. Next to the whale, *aiviq* was the greatest of all sea animals. Walrus were tremendously exciting to hunt, and they provided tons of rich meat and fat. Amiksuk and the others could not help thinking they might spot a herd today, perhaps in scattered ice where they could safely undertake a hunt. So they became anxious to get under way again and began preparing for departure. A short while later the two boats droned off in opposite directions.

In the hour that followed, Talimat shot two eider ducks from a large flock that flew directly over the boat. And he missed a ringed seal that popped up unexpectedly in front of them. The water was choppy, however, making it nearly impossible to steady his aim. Shortly afterward it began to drizzle lightly, with lowering clouds all around.

Amiksuk was beginning to think about the changing weather when he saw something dark and round on the water far off to his right. It was not moving, and he thought it might be just a duck. Then it looked to the side, and its outline became clear—a seal. He turned the boat and pointed so the others would see.

Talimat, the sharp-eyed one, quickly noticed that it was an *uguruk*. Its head was large, with a shortened "bulldog" snout, and he saw its long back break the surface. The seal remained still, not even watching the *umiaq* that came toward it at full speed. Talimat picked up his rifle and shifted to his shooting position in the bow.

A hundred yards between them now, narrowing fast. The *uguruk* stared toward the boat, then began swimming

away on the surface, looking back over its shoulder. Talimat
raised his rifle and held a bead on his prey. At fifty yards the
seal began swimming along porpoise-fashion, undulating
above and beneath the surface, angling sharply toward
the left.

Amiksuk turned to follow, but at the same instant the
uguruk arched sharply and disappeared. Talimat lowered his
rifle and pointed eastward, indicating the direction they
should turn. His experienced eye had caught the direction of
the seal's dive, and he knew the hunt was far from over.
Amiksuk slowed the engine and cruised to a point about two
hundred yards east, then circled at idling speed. Luckily
there were no floes close by, and they were confident of
seeing the animal again. Time passed slowly, but Eskimo
hunters had never learned the notion of impatience.

Almost five minutes later the *uguruk* bobbed up nearly a
hundred yards east of the boat. Talimat instantly lifted his
rifle and shot toward it before Amiksuk had any chance to
turn the boat. The bullet struck water six inches from the
seal's head, making a bright splash as it ricocheted from the
surface. The startled animal took a sidelong dive, throwing
its hind flippers into the air and slapping the water violently
as it disappeared.

Pamiuk was baffled by this apparent wild shooting, but
Pukak explained. "Talimat is a clever thinker," he muttered.
"We were too far from the seal, and it would fill its lungs with
air before we got close again. But now it has made a deep
dive without getting air. From the way it plunged you could
see that it would head north; but it cannot go far."

They sped to a point fifty yards north of the seal's ripples
and began circling again. This time it came up in less than two
minutes, not far from the boat but almost straight behind it.
The *uguruk* looked for a moment as they turned, still drawn
by its insatiable curiosity. Then it made a shallow dive, and
the hunters followed the direction its snout had pointed
when it disappeared.

In a moment it was up again, straight ahead of them,

swimming at full speed but unable to dive deeply for lack of
air. Talimat positioned himself, leaning forward on the stem,
rifle steady against his shoulder.

Looking down the sights, he saw the *uguruk* torpedo beneath the surface then break water, a V-shaped wake plowing
from its neck. As the distance between them narrowed, the
seal turned to look back, its obsidian eyes wide and fearful,
head glistening wet, whiskers trailing on the water. Talimat
aimed behind the tiny pock that marked its ear, awaiting the
last instant before it would dive.

The rifle cracked, but he scarcely heard it. It kicked hard
into his shoulder, but he felt nothing. He saw only a splash
under the *uguruk's* jaw, saw it jerk powerfully, then drop its
snout onto the surface, blood streaming out behind.

Amiksuk cut the engine and swerved so the *uguruk* would
pass beneath the right side of the bow. Talimat dropped his
rifle and automatically snatched up the harpoon that was
braced in the skin lashings beside him. But he had shot the
seal too close, and they coasted beyond it before he could aim
and thrust. Then, as Amiksuk quickly swerved back for
another pass, the animal contorted and made a frenzied dive.
"*Alyakaah,* it is only wounded," Pukak said.

Talimat explained that he had shot low and too far forward, hitting the seal's jaw. "I do not think it will die and sink
down below. It will surface very quickly." He had scarcely
finished speaking when the *uguruk* appeared, swimming
slowly, nose held strangely high.

Talimat stood with the harpoon balanced in his right hand,
index finger curled around the small bone throwing knob,
coiled line ready in his left hand. The seal hardly moved as
they came swiftly from behind. Talimat raised his arm and
plunged the shaft downward, striking perfectly into its neck.
The harpoon's sharp head penetrated deeply and separated
from the shaft as the attached line jerked tight. At the same
instant the harpoon head flipped sideways and caught fast
beneath a thick layer of blubber.

Startled back to consciousness, the seal dived with a great

spasm of strength, throwing water on Pukak and Pamiuk. Talimat gave it twenty yards of the walrus-hide line, then braced himself with all his might. When the tug came it was terrifically powerful, jerking the bow down and tilting the boat until water nearly poured over the gunwale. Pukak jumped forward and grabbed the line to help Talimat. For several minutes the *umiaq* was pulled along sideways, but finally the *uguruk's* strength waned.

The men quickly pulled in line, drawing the seal toward them as it swam upward, desperate for air. "Hurry, Pamiuk, get ready with the .22 rifle!" Talimat shouted. The seal made a frantic lunge beneath the *umiaq*, but finally they dragged it in close. It was a medium-sized female, its lower jaw shattered and bleeding. Pamiuk put the rifle next to its skull and shot twice. "*Tavra?*" he asked. "It is enough?" Talimat nodded. The seal writhed slowly and went limp.

Pukak snubbed the harpoon line tightly onto one of the *umiaq's* heavy thwarts, then took out his knife and made an incision under the skin of the seal's cheek from its eye to inside its upper lip. He pushed a rope through the slit, tied it, and then lashed the other end inside the boat. Now, with the heavy carcass doubly secured, they headed for the nearest ice pan. Once there, they pulled it up and loaded it into the boat beside their first kill. Pukak slit its hide to free the harpoon head, which he replaced on the shaft so it would be ready again.

Everyone was pleased by their success. "Two *uguruks!*" Pukak exulted. "And if the weather does not worsen we may have more good hunting before we turn back." He looked up at the clouds and felt the prickly cold of droplets hitting his face. Meanwhile Talimat climbed a small hummock and scanned the area with his binoculars. He was hoping to spot walrus, but he saw only an endless patchwork of ice pans interlaced with dark lanes of water. Not far to the south he noticed a huge floe where they might stop to hunt from the ice edge. And he thought he could see a few seals sleeping on a flat along its west side. Amiksuk agreed that they should go there and have a look.

The big floe turned out to be a good hunting spot, as Talimat had suggested. They set up a windbreak so they could make tea and boil some meat, and before the tea was ready Amiksuk shot a ringed seal that surfaced nearby. After they ate, Pukak walked back onto the flat ice to hunt for sleeping seals. An hour later he returned dragging a large one he had killed, his clothes well soaked from crawling over the wet surface on his belly. Talimat could not help teasing. "Pukak, it looks as if you shot that seal in the open water and swam out to retrieve it."

Everyone was pleased, even surprised, that Pukak had gotten a seal. He was a hardworking and perseverant man, but he had little skill as a hunter, and only rarely did he catch an animal. He was somewhat clumsy and slow, but others less agile than he were far more successful hunters. No, what Pukak lacked was cunning—he could not look at an animal and know its thoughts; he could not deceive it; he could not turn its weaknesses and predictable flight to his own advantage. He was not a predator. Some men were gifted with the craft and guile of a wolf, but not Pukak. When Pukak killed an animal, it was largely a matter of luck.

Of course, one could hardly expect that all hunters would be alike in wiliness or passion or skill. There were masters and maladroits, and all shades between. Eskimo society had long ago adapted itself to such differences; so a man like Pukak was not shunned or disparaged for what was born into him. Nor did he and his family starve, though they were packed into one of the smallest and most ramshackle houses in Ulurunik. Pukak succeeded because he never missed a chance to hunt with others, with crews and partners; and the elaborate system of sharing sustained him. Although he seldom got his own game, he contributed his labor to support the hunt and took home a share of what others killed.

But, happily, today would be different. The catch of *uguruks* would be apportioned among everyone in the crew, but ringed seals were too small to be divided into shares—each man kept all that he shot. So when they returned to the village Pukak could drag his own kill home, and people would surely notice. It was something that made any hunter feel alive and proud, no matter what his usual measure of success might be. Talimat, who always watched closely, noticed a faint smile on Pukak's face as he pulled his seal to the boat.

Now only Pamiuk had made no kill, and without saying it the others knew he would be given first shot at any seal that came up nearby. It was always done this way when crews hunted together.

The skies became heavy and depressing, with cold drizzle now pelting continuously. It was late, close to midnight, but the sun remained high, so there was no darkness. The wind dropped to a breeze and then went calm. Tiny raindrops made a hissing sound as they struck the slick surface of the water. Otherwise there was no noise except the occasional clucking of a gull or shrill cry of an Arctic tern.

Despite the encompassing silence the hunters knew they were still drifting. Amiksuk stood for a long time looking toward the land with binoculars. They were many miles from the coast, scarcely visible as a thin black line toward the east. "We must be very far south," Amiksuk suggested. "Perhaps as far as Pingoqragaruk, where the old shelter cabin sits on the beach." The cabin was a tiny, dilapidated shack built many years ago as a stopover for Eskimo dog mushers hired by the government to haul mail along the coast. Hunters still made frequent use of it, both as a winter camp and as an important landmark along this monotonously flat stretch of shore.

Talimat said they might be wise to head for land. "Thick clouds and calm weather can be dangerous so far out at sea," he thought aloud. "Look, heavy fog toward the south, and if it spreads north we will have no way to navigate. The sun is hidden, so we cannot set a course by it; and there is no wind to follow at a constant angle toward the coast." Amiksuk agreed. Few things were more unsettling than to be caught out in thick fog with no wind. Perhaps they should leave.

"We can follow the beach home," Amiksuk said, looking toward Pamiuk. "If the mosquitoes are bad inland they may have driven caribou to the coast. Then you can show *us* how to hunt."

When the boat was partly loaded, Amiksuk tore his parka on a nail that had worked loose in the stern. He picked up the marking buoy's stone anchor and used it to pound the nail back in. Pamiuk stood beside the boat, rifle in hand, thinking of nothing in particular. Then, much to his surprise, he saw a seal's head appear in the water not far away. It swam along slowly, gazing toward the hammering noise. Pamiuk crouched and ran a few steps to one side, sat directly on the wet ice, aimed, and shot.

The boom of his rifle badly startled the others, none of whom had been looking. "What is it?" Amiksuk blurted. Pamiuk stood quickly, pointing toward the low, rounded profile of a seal's back. "Look!" he exclaimed, almost shouting, "I have killed a seal."

The boat was off in seconds, the harpoon was thrust, and the seal was secured. Pukak hauled the hundred-pound animal up over the gunwale while Pamiuk stood watching from the ice, thoroughly pleased. Talimat called out, "I heard the inland people were slow to aim and shoot, but Pamiuk seems to have learned to move like a *Tareogmiut* now." Then he laughed heartily at his own joking, and everyone felt happy.

They had gone deep into the pack, and getting out again was not simple. Amiksuk steered the *umiaq* through a maze of waterways, first one direction and then another, trying to find the quickest way to the open sea. At one point they sped down a narrow channel between two converging floes that collided just after they went through. But soon thereafter the ice began to look more scattered, and finally they reached the pack's outermost fringes. Nearly an hour had passed since they left their hunting place.

Amiksuk set a direct course for the distant shore. He could have shortened their trip by angling northeastward straight toward Ulurunik, but this would be risky. Haze and fog were settling in rapidly, and they could no longer see the land. Eskimos knew that it was wiser in such circumstances to aim far to one side of their target. Then when they reached the coast they would know for certain which way to turn.

The drizzle continued and worsened. Fog wrapped in tightly, surrounding them with impenetrable curtains of gray. The water was black, glassy, undulating slightly from the day's earlier winds. Amiksuk watched the boat's wake spreading behind them, trying to keep a straight course and resisting the hypnotic effect of staring into the void ahead.

The other men sat quietly, their clothing drenched and cold, water dripping from their parka hoods and running down their faces. They had all known discomfort since childhood—piercing winter cold, damp summer cold, hungry cold, tired cold, cold from the tips of their fingers to the pits of their bellies—it was a natural daily consequence of being alive. And for this reason they did not think much of it; they simply closed their minds to feeling, and endured.

Pamiuk saw a huge stray floeberg loom out of the fog like a ghost ship. Great ice slabs probed upward along its back, several of them looking weathered and about to topple. He watched it as they passed, wondering if it might be grounded, if the water was becoming shallower, if the land might not be far now. He felt the strangeness of the sea and feared it, then thought of the familiar tundra he had left behind.

Time passed immeasurably, without landmark or event to gauge it by. The men were all worried that they might be angling off course, turning in a great circle or perhaps heading back toward the ice. But they knew that Amiksuk was a navigator of high repute, with an uncanny sense for dead reckoning. It was said that he had never become lost in all his years of traveling, that although some men carried compasses he needed none because he was born with one inside him.

A pair of loons came out of the mist behind them and winged past, following an unwavering course. Amiksuk wondered if they had been feeding on the ocean and were now headed for a nesting site on land. He could not be certain, but it was a good possibility. He looked at his watch—it was nearly 3:00 A.M. If they did not soon reach land it would mean they had strayed off course.

At 3:15 they passed between two floebergs that appeared to be grounded. Then, shortly afterward, Amiksuk shouted, "Look ahead. The beach cliff!" Its dark face came up slowly out of the fog, looking heavy and forboding. But for the hunters it was a friendly sight indeed. Amiksuk idled the engine and examined the land's features.

"Do you know this place?" he asked the others, smiling. Clearly he already knew where they were. "*Aqlagavik,*" Pukak returned, "place-of-the-grizzly-bear. The narrow ravine just south of the ancient settlement at Milliktagavik." Amiksuk nodded agreement. Both men had recognized one of a hundred such gullies along the coast south of Ulurunik.

"Ah, Pamiuk," Talimat laughed, "you were looking worried. Perhaps you thought you would never see the land again." Eskimos often teased others this way to make light of their own fears or shortcomings. Knowing this, Pamiuk only laughed with the rest.

Amiksuk turned the *umiaq* northward toward Ulurunik. In two hours, perhaps even less, they would reach the village. Warmth, dry clothes, food, and much-needed rest would await them all. And by tomorrow night they would be ready to hunt again, for only foolish men stayed at home when the pack ice was nearby. A lazy man in summer would be a hungry man in winter. So it was that the Eskimos hunted until sleep overtook them, and then they hunted again. Eventually the pack would be carried north beyond the horizon and the game would go along with it. Then they would rest.

There was a break in the fog, and Pamiuk gazed toward the cliff and the expanse of tundra lying beyond. The great prairie was deep green, with purple and yellow patches where flowers bloomed. He could feel its richness, hear in his mind the call of nesting ptarmigan drifting on the warm wind. It was a fine thing to know the tundra was close again.

A gull flew from the black strand, crossed before the *umiaq's* bow, and headed out to sea. Pamiuk followed its flight, abandoning thoughts of the land. He remembered the great fields of broken ice, the strangely shaped floebergs, the silent motion of floes drifting inexorably on the current. And he thought of ducks winging along the water, of seals appearing from nowhere and vanishing again, of pursuing the *uguruk* and feeling its power on the harpoon line, and of shooting his own seal at last.

Indeed, the sea was a rich and exciting thing. It was a place of unexpected events, ceaseless changeability, abundant and unusual animals. At that moment Pamiuk began to feel differently toward the sea. He began to understand why the *Tareogmiut* devoted themselves so passionately to living by it and learning its secrets.

Aqavirvik Tatqiq

The Moon When Birds Molt

(AUGUST)

MAIN CHARACTERS

Sakiak (Sah-*kee*-uk) *an old hunter*

Kuvlu (*Koov*-loo) *Sakiak's adult son*

Kavaasuk (Kah-*vah*-sook) *an adult hunter*

Migalik (Mee-*gul*-ik) *Kavaasuk's brother-in-law*

Amiksuk (*Ah*-mik-sook) *an adult hunter*

Talimat (*Tul*-ee-mut) *Amiksuk's adult cousin*

Pukak (*Poo*-kuk) *Amiksuk's formal hunting partner*

Pamiuk (Pum-*ee*-ook) *an inland Eskimo hunter*

KUVLU SHADED HIS EYES, looking up into a bright, clear sky. After several hours' traveling, he had become unaware of the outboard's monotonous whining. And now that they had reached the sheltering pack ice, the skin boat rode smoothly over near-calm water. It was a fine day, he thought, a fine day indeed. At long last the ice was within reach and the weather was good. Perhaps now they would find *aiviq*, the walrus, which had eluded them for so many weeks.

He turned to look at the other members of his crew, seated behind him. Old Sakiak, his father, gazed placidly over the surrounding ice and water. Beside him was Kuvlu's second cousin Migalik, leaning against the gunwale half asleep. And in the stern was Kavaasuk, brother-in-law to Migalik, who for many years had been Kuvlu's formal hunting partner. These four men had hunted together all summer, sometimes on the ocean for sea mammals and sometimes far up the Kuk River for caribou. They were called *Kuvlurat koyaat,* "Kuvlu's crew," and were one of a dozen organized hunting groups in Ulurunik that summer.

Looking over the stern, Kuvlu saw Amiksuk's *umiaq.* The two crews had left the village together that morning, but Amiksuk had a slower engine, so his boat fell behind. "Perhaps we should find a lookout place," Kuvlu shouted to

Kavaasuk, "and that will give Amiksuk a chance to catch up with us." Kavaasuk looked back and then nodded agreement.

A short while later they coasted slowly in along the edge of a large floe. A broad ice ridge towered above the floe's surface, dwarfing the boat and the men as they pulled into its shadow. Rounded features, lacking sharpness and angularity, showed that the ridge was a solid old remnant from the previous winter. There was no danger that it would suddenly disintegrate; and the surrounding floe was wide enough to prevent its overturning.

"Watch this *kangataaq,*" Kuvlu warned as he stepped onto the ice. It was a thin ledge overhanging the water, where current and waves had undercut the floe's sheer edge. "Remember when Migalik jumped out onto a *kangataaq* last summer and it broke, sending him down into the water." Kuvlu laughed uncontrollably when he thought of it, and everyone joined in except Migalik. He had drenched himself from head to toe in the accident and had sat for several hours wrapped in a canvas tent while they traveled home. Since then he never failed to check overhangs by stamping one foot on them before jumping from the *umiaq.*

Sakiak stayed behind holding the boat while the others clambered up the tall hummock for a look around. Bright sunshine warmed his face, but he still shivered from the chill of traveling against the breeze in the forty-degree temperature. Like his companions, he was dressed warmly—heavy cloth parka, thick insulated pants, gloves, sealskin boots, and plenty of clothing underneath. But there was no way to keep warm in an open boat on the Arctic Ocean, even during the finest summer weather.

The old man stood quietly thinking as he watched Amiksuk's boat come nearer. How many years, he wondered, since there was a summer like this. The pack had come near land for just one week early in the season. Ever since then it had been held far offshore by wind, while the current pushed it continuously northward. Hunters from Ulurunik had taken only fifty walrus when the ice was in, scarcely a fourth of what they needed for the winter ahead. Walrus were the main source of dog food and an important addition to the people's diet. If more were not taken, many dogs would prob- ably starve before spring.

When onshore winds at last arrived, no ice appeared near Ulurunik. Old men said that the pack had already receded north of the village, but ice might still be found up near the broad headlands at Ataniq. Indeed, even before Kuvlu's crew had reached Atanik they saw the pack, lying just a few miles offshore. And this was its south margin, where walrus usually congregated in large numbers.

Sakiak felt sure they would locate a herd, and with the combined capacity of two boats they could take a fair number of animals. But many crews would have to hunt successfully to ensure a secure winter, and who could say how long the ice would remain? It was already the beginning of *Aqavirvik tat- qiq,* "the moon when birds molt," and very soon the walrus would be gone until next year.

In a moment the other boat came in toward the ice, and Sakiak caught its bow. Amiksuk called out a greeting, then laughingly berated himself for owning such a slow engine. His crew members—Talimat, Pukak, and Pamiuk—climbed out on the ice while Amiksuk recounted details of their trip north. Several miles back an *uguruk* had bobbed up near their boat and watched them pass, close enough for a sure kill. But they made no effort to chase it, and Sakiak under- stood why without asking. Today they were after more pre- cious game, and they had not come this far to load their boat down with seals.

The conversation was interrupted by an urgent call from atop the nearby hummock. "Come, look!" It was Kuvlu, pointing toward the west. Sakiak tethered the boats to an ice boulder and followed the others up the ridge.

When they reached the top, Kuvlu spoke in low, serious tones. "Look far over there." He handed the binoculars to

Talimat and indicated the direction. Everyone was silent while Talimat scanned the floes. Great fields of ice shimmered white in the sun, with dark shadows and ponds of water everywhere to confuse the hunter's eye. Then he paused for a long moment in one spot. There were two, perhaps three, small ice pans with dark mounds covering them.

"Nunavak," he muttered. "Walrus on the ice." Literally translated, the word meant "patch of earth," describing exactly what a herd of walrus looked like among the floes. Now Sakiak took the glasses, and everyone waited to hear him speak. Although he did not act as a formal leader, the old man's great wisdom and experience lent considerable power to his words.

"It is good." He spoke without taking the binoculars from his eyes. "They are in scattered floes not far from the edge of the pack, so we can reach them easily and without fear of becoming trapped by closing ice." Looking back toward shore, he continued, "The only danger is our distance from land. It will be a long, slow journey to the beach, and even longer from there back to Ulurunik. We are just south of Pingasuguruk now, and we may drift north to the Seahorse Islands by the time we finish. But the weather is good, without signs of change—I think we should go and hunt."

Without hesitating, the men climbed down and made quick preparations for departure. When they stepped into the boat, Pukak warned Pamiuk, the inland Eskimo, about his knit watch cap. *"Azaah,* look. Your hat is partly red and could mean danger for us. Some animals—like the polar bear, whale, and especially walrus—are made angry by that color. Perhaps it would be wise to take it off and hide it until the hunt is finished." Eskimos did not waste time questioning traditional wisdom of this sort, so Pamiuk removed the hat and tucked it inside his hunting bag.

Pamiuk had never hunted walrus before, and so he felt strongly apprehensive about what was ahead. The men had told him very little of hunting walrus, because old-timers warned them against discussing it. Walrus could hear people talking, they said, even from far off. And they would take vengeance if the words angered them. So Pamiuk knew only that this was a dangerous undertaking, and he sensed the powerful excitement that affected his companions. Their voices were soft and resolute, their minds were completely preoccupied, and their actions betrayed abiding fear.

For half an hour the boats made their way along wide channels of open water. They were heading straight west, and old Sakiak thought they must be getting very far from land. Finally he signaled Kavaasuk to find a hummocky floe from which they could check the walrus herds' location. Then he turned and spoke to Migalik: "When I was young we would never travel so far out to sea. We knew, long before the white men told us, that the ocean's surface was not flat. If we went out too far, the old people warned, we would go over the hump. Then we would have to work very hard, paddling uphill, to return. So, you see, the *Tanik* was not the only one to discover that the earth is round."

A few minutes later they pulled up to a small floeberg and climbed to its highest point. Kuvlu was there first, and he saw the herds even before looking through his binoculars. At the same time, faint roaring sounds drifted to them on the wind. "*Azahaa,* they are not far off," Talimat said, "and that bellowing sounds powerful, like a big bull." Looking through binoculars, he could make out individual walrus, lifting their great tusked heads above the dark aggregate surrounding them.

The hunters stood quietly for a while, watching the animals and carefully scrutinizing the entire area. The ice cover was not dense, so they would have no trouble finding paths of open water to the herds. But they would have to avoid following a channel that went upwind of the animals, because engine fumes were one of the few things that could frighten walrus away.

"We should hunt," Kavaasuk said with serious finality, turning back toward the boats. The others followed without speaking.

They traveled west along the edge of a broad floe and then angled into a lane of water that opened to the north. Kuvlu gazed ahead through his binoculars and finally turned to the others, smiling. He bobbed his head up and down, imitating a walrus, pointing straight ahead. A small dark spot was visible beyond some drifting ice cakes. Amiksuk's crew, coming right along behind, quickly saw it too.

Every man sat staring toward the herd, saying nothing, immersed in his own thoughts. The dark spot resolved itself into a wide pan of ice completely covered with inert bodies. Occasionally a head rose above the mass, then dropped from sight again. The channel widened and all three herds became visible. Finally, on Kuvlu's signal, the two boats drew up beside a small pan.

Kuvlu, Talimat, and Sakiak got out onto the ice while the others sat quietly. Binoculars passed between them. They saw one very large herd, perhaps a hundred animals, crowded onto an ice pan so small that their weight partially submerged it. The two remaining herds were much smaller, about twenty animals apiece. Sakiak pointed first toward one and then toward the other, murmuring his advice.

The large herd was out—to kill a few animals in a group that size was to risk massive retaliation from those left unharmed. One of the smaller groups was so close to the big herd that they preferred to avoid it. The other small group drifted along a hundred yards from the others. It was on a flat pan with plenty of space, so animals would not easily slide into the water after they had been shot. This was the one to hunt, Sakiak asserted, and the others agreed.

When they had finished talking, the three returned to their boats, pointing to indicate which herd they had chosen. Tension closed tightly around the men now, as they directed their thoughts entirely toward the tasks at hand. No unnecessary chances could be taken; no mistakes could be made.

The two *umiaqs* eased off and headed slowly toward the herd, engines at idling speed. In the bow of the lead boat, Kuvlu hunched over his rifle, checking to be sure it worked smoothly. Twice he sighted down the barrel, then clicked a cartridge forward. Behind him, Pukak squinted into the blinding glare of reflected sunlight and tugged nervously at loose threads on his parka sleeve.

Fifty yards from the herd they cut their engines and pulled in behind the partial concealment of a small pan. Wavelets slapped rhythmically against the ice all around them, creating a constant patter of noise. Every few moments the staccato was broken by deep, powerful roars from amid the herds.

Now, almost in the shadow of their huge prey, the hunters did their final reconnoitering. Kuvlu spoke softly, not whispering, because a hissing voice was said to make animals nervous. "The ice pan is oblong, but not so narrow that it might overturn when the unharmed ones leave it. And I see no underwater ice shelf extending from the southwest side. So it is best we approach from that direction."

To avoid unnecessarily disturbing the animals, they decided to use only one boat. Talimat and Pamiuk quietly stepped over the gunwale into Kuvlu's *umiaq,* bringing their rifles and ammunition pouches. Amiksuk and Pukak would stay at a safe distance with the other boat until the shooting was finished.

"*Angaayutaa,*" Kavaasuk muttered, looking toward Sakiak. "We will pray." Because it was fraught with danger, walrus hunting would never be undertaken without a prayer asking for protection and success. So the old man folded his wrinkled hands and began a long monotone recitation. The others sat staring downward, faces almost melancholy, listening to the prayer between lapses into their own thoughts.

Pamiuk could not help looking up at the walrus. For a

moment they all lay quiet. Then a ponderous bull lifted its head. Thick tusks flashed white against the blue sky, and it suddenly emitted a tremendous belching roar. Pamiuk was startled by its size and its arrogant flaunting of power. Never before had he seen animals like these that showed no hint of fear at the open approach of man.

"Amen," Sakiak mumbled, and the others responded chorus, "amen." Without another word they lifted paddles from the thwarts and pushed away. All security was left behind now, and nothing but open water separated the men in their frail boat from the unsuspecting prey ahead.

Pamiuk dipped his paddle noiselessly, the way he had learned for chasing whales. At forty yards he could fully comprehend the herd's enormous bulk. Nothing moved except two chocolate-brown calves that crawled around over the adults' backs. They weighed several hundred pounds apiece, but for all their size they looked tiny compared with the slumbering hillocks of flesh and bone underneath them.

As the boat drew within twenty yards, several walrus rose up to stare toward it. But they dropped back to sleep moments later. Then a gust of wind turned the boat aside briefly, so that its length could be seen, and two large females on the near edge became nervous. They raised themselves on their great foreflippers, lurching back and forth, rolling their eyes until the whites showed. Finally they settled down again, and the only signs of life were sporadic grunts and heavy breathing.

The hunters nosed their boat straight in, coasting slowly, until they were just five yards away. A massive bull suddenly jerked awake and lifted its head six feet above the ice. Its long, robust tusks looked quite different from the slender, gently curved ivory of the females. It gazed at the boat, then let out a prolonged hollow roar and tried to push itself up on another animal's back. This disturbance caused a chain reaction, and in seconds half the walrus were startled to alertness.

A spasm of loud huffs and groans passed through the herd.

Kuvlu, Talimat, and Migalik sat stiffly on the forward seats, looking up at their prey. They lifted their rifles, each aiming toward a heavily tusked animal. Pamiuk sat behind them, wide-eyed, hands perspiring, heart pounding loudly in his ears. Kuvlu looked so small, now just five feet from the long brown side of the nearest animal. Yet he sat motionless, holding fire until the last possible moment. In ten seconds he could have reached out and touched a walrus.

Suddenly the large bull threw its full weight against a smaller animal beside it, trying to open a route of escape. Ripples ran through its blubber as it pushed, and the other walrus began slipping off the ice. Kuvlu took aim at the bull, now looming above him. All fear and thought had vanished. Mechanically, he set his sight just behind one of its bulging eyes.

Crack! The bull's powerful neck collapsed and its head fell from sight. *Crack! Crack!* Almost at the same instant, Migalik and Talimat shot. The herd was plunged into pandemonium, all heads up, tusks clashing, confused animals shoving each other in vain efforts to find escape.

Along the pan's edge some walrus began diving or rolling off to safety, making great splashes and vanishing below. Rifle shots exploded again and again, as all the hunters now joined in firing. Several more heads dropped lifeless into the chaotic morass.

On the far side, half a dozen animals lunged toward the water, pushing and shoving in a frenzy of fear. A dead cow was bumped from the ice by a young bull trying to crawl over it. Pukak saw one of the calves ride off clinging to its mother's back; but another sat bawling loudly atop a lifeless carcass. He turned and shot it immediately, lest its cries incite the adults to attack. It rolled down heavily onto the ice.

The pan rocked back and forth, suddenly emptied of its burden. No one attempted to shoot the last unharmed animal as it scuttled off the edge. But at the same moment a wounded cow made its final effort to escape, squirming slowly away. It turned its head to look back at the hunters, lifting its three-foot tusks high above the ice. Talimat quickly aimed behind its eye and shot. The walrus slowly dropped its head, shaking it from side to side, and then became still.

It was over. The last shot's echo rolled away among the floes, and the air went still. What seemed to have lasted for several drawn-out minutes had taken less than thirty seconds. Five carcasses lay on the ice and one floated nearby.

But the quiet was an illusion, and no one paused to rest. "Hurry," Sakiak shouted. "Hurry!" Everyone grabbed paddles and stroked up against the ice. Looking down into the clear water, Pamiuk saw the reason for their haste. Long dark forms torpedoed across streaks of sunlight below, arcing through the silent dimensions of liquid space. Suddenly released from gravity's burden, the walrus swam gracefully beneath their pursuers, looking up toward the boat. They were full of anger and seemed to know that some of the herd were missing.

Kuvlu leaped onto the ice, followed by Talimat and Migalik. But, before the others could move, a bull walrus surfaced right beside the *umiaq*, snorting mist into the air. Suddenly it lunged upward, hooking its tusks over the gunwale, stiff whiskers bristling on its flat snout, eyes red and angry. Pamiuk instinctively moved to shoot, but Kavaasuk's frantic voice stopped him. "No! Club him, quickly!" Pamiuk obeyed without thinking. He cracked the animal's nose with the butt of his rifle, using every bit of his sinewy strength.

The walrus wheezed, and blood ran from its nostrils. Then it slowly released its hold on the boat. Sakiak would later tell Pamiuk that if he had shot the walrus its limp weight might have tipped them all into the sea.

Now everyone piled out and hauled the *umiaq* up onto the ice. Kuvlu hurried around looking at the carcasses and found one still slowly convulsing. He put the muzzle of his rifle behind its head, where a vague cross in its wrinkled skin marked the base of its skull. Then he shot. The animal gave a heavy lurch, and all its muscles stiffened. Fading heartbeats pumped thick streams of blood out over the ice as it slowly relaxed.

Meanwhile, everyone else stood on guard around the pan's edges with rifles ready. The herd was reluctant to leave, rising periodically to stare at the attackers and snort defiance. Sakiak and the others raised their arms and spoke to the walrus when they appeared. *"Tavraaqtugut,"* they implored repeatedly. "We are finished."

Several minutes passed, but the animals kept surfacing nearby, sometimes within a few yards of the ice. "Go home now. . . . that's enough," Kavaasuk said as a group came up near him. No one wanted to shoot more because they had enough for a load. The hunters knew that walrus could understand what was said, and that if treated properly they would eventually leave without further violence. It was in the order of things that humans must live by killing animals, after all, and this was something that the creatures understood.

Migalik brought two harpoons from the boat and handed one to Pamiuk. "A wounded one is still nearby," he said. "Perhaps you can harpoon it." Then Migalik walked to the pan's far side, where he plunged the other harpoon into a floating carcass. Kuvlu and Pukak helped him pull it up onto the shallow ice shelf. Then they secured it by tying the line through a loop cut in the skin of another carcass.

Pamiuk stood watching as the angry herd reappeared just ten yards from him. He saw the unharmed calf, still riding on its mother's back in the water, clinging tightly with its flippers. Then Sakiak pointed to another animal. "There! The wounded one, a cow with a broken tusk." Pamiuk saw that it swam erratically, and blood flowed into the water along its side. Two other adults were with it, trying to help it away to safety.

Without hesitating, Pamiuk aimed and pitched the harpoon. It flew in a perfect arc, straight on target. But suddenly it was caught short in midair and fell into the water. He knew his error immediately, but it was too late. The line was under his foot! Surely his *Tareogmiut* friends would tease him relentlessly for this foolish mistake.

But Sakiak turned to him wide-eyed and exclaimed with great relief, "*Azaah*, you are a lucky one, Pamiuk. That walrus is still full of strength and would surely have pulled the line away. And if you had become entangled it would have taken you along with it." The old man laughed, even though walrus hunting was a time to be serious. "We nearly lost one inlander!"

Several minutes later Sakiak killed the wounded animal with a shot in the neck, and Pamiuk then successfully harpooned it. Gradually, the remainder of the herd slowly moved off, rising occasionally to look back.

When they had pulled in the harpooned animal, Sakiak sat down on a big carcass and talked to Pamiuk. "Now you know what it is like to hunt *aiviq*, the walrus. But look at these huge animals we must cut up and haul back to Ulurunik. Walrus hunters have only a few minutes of excitement, but many hours of hard work afterward."

Pamiuk looked off toward the other herds, still crowded atop nearby ice pans, growling and roaring as if nothing had happened. Volleys of shooting and the panicked flight of another herd into the water, just a hundred yards away, seemed to have no effect on them. Strange animals, he thought.

"Perhaps now you will understand what we say about walrus," Sakiak remarked. "These animals are not afraid of people. They are like us in many ways. But they anger easily and have untold strength. When you hunt *aiviq*, you must not act like a man; instead you must humble yourself. Always respect the walrus and watch them carefully. Do these things and you can hunt without fear of their anger."

The two men stood quietly for a moment, absorbed in thought and relieved that the killing had ended without mishap. Eskimos did not share the *Tanik's* strange need to pursue the thrill of danger and to hunt for sport and trophy. Hunting, after all, was the most essential and serious activity of their lives, the focus of all their intelligence and energy. It was not idle pleasure or pastime that brought them far out among the floes to kill walrus, but the harsh, perpetual dictates of survival.

Just then they heard an outboard engine and saw the other *umiaq* coming. Amiksuk and Pukak had waited until they saw the herd leave before rejoining the others. When they pulled up, Amiksuk counted the catch and looked very pleased. "Six large ones and a calf!" he exulted. "This is very good indeed."

Everyone set to work without even pausing to talk over the hunt. The current was taking them farther north of Ulurunik every minute, and so it was essential that they butcher the catch as quickly as possible. Long knives and axes were brought from the boats. Amiksuk, who was an expert knife sharpener, ran his leathery thumb along each shining blade, testing for dull spots. When he found one he lubricated his whetstone with spit, then with a few deft strokes he honed it to a fine edge.

"Come, Pamiuk," Talimat called, "Bring an ax and I will show you how to cut up a walrus." He stood beside the largest carcass, a bull nearly ten feet long that he had shot himself. "First the *kauk,* the skin and blubber, must come off," he said, feeling the ax blade. Then he took a quick swipe, cutting deep into the animal's hide near its shoulder. To his surprise, its muscles jerked powerfully. "Danger!" he exclaimed. "Somehow this one is still alive." Pamiuk fetched a rifle, then Talimat showed him where to shoot. The great body lurched one last time.

Now Talimat cut slits across its broad, rolling belly, sinking the ax blade through four inches of hide and blubber. Pamiuk tried to cut the skin with his large knife, but the blade was useless against it. Then, after the slits were made,

Talimat began slicing beneath the fat while Pamiuk pulled it away with a meathook. Ten long strips of skin and cream-colored blubber, each weighing more than fifty pounds, were peeled from the animal's belly side. Then four men laboriously rolled the carcass over, and then more strips were taken from its back.

Sakiak came for some thin slices of *kauk* to put into a boiling pot. "You see now why the walrus is so tough?" he asked Pamiuk. "Even a polar bear is afraid of this animal. Once I saw a big bear swim up to a herd asleep on the ice, hoping to take a calf. But it was afraid to walk close, because it could do nothing against them. Finally it picked up a small boulder of ice, stood on its hind legs, and threw it into the herd. Perhaps it thought this would scare them away from the calf, or perhaps it was just angry. I only know what I saw. After this the bear gave up and started swimming away, but some members of our crew gave chase and shot it from the *umiaq*." The old man nodded his head with finality and walked away to begin cooking.

Talimat used a dull ax to sever the walrus's throat and chop through its heavy neck bones. Later he would chop the tusks free and remove the flattened teeth from the jaws. Ivory always belonged to those who owned the boats, in this case Amiksuk and Kuvlu. It was used to make carvings that would sell for good prices to the *Taniks*. Teeth were usually kept, because they could be made into little fishing lures and sinkers.

Pamiuk dragged strips of *kauk* to the boats and threw them inside, then helped Talimat cut off the foreflippers. "Ah, soon we will have rotten walrus flipper," Talimat said happily. "The smell is bad, but it runs with thick oil and tastes delicious." Pamiuk had eaten flipper only once, but he agreed that its taste was excellent.

Now they cut the thick rib bones and abdominal muscles, exposing a great cavity filled with organs. Talimat plunged his hands into a deep swill of blood, cutting between the lungs. Then he pulled out a melon-sized organ and held it up, streams of red dripping from his elbows. "The heart," he said. "Perhaps Sakiak will boil part of it if you take it to him."

When Pamiuk returned, Talimat told him to fasten a meathook into the animal's windpipe. Then he pulled hard while Talimat cut into its entrails. Two huge pink lungs came slowly out of the bloody cavity, followed by the thirty-pound liver, then finally a voluminous mass of stomach and yards of coiled intestines. Talimat leaned down and slit the stomach open, exposing a mélange of gray, black, and green matter. "Walrus food," he said. "Mostly little clams from the sea floor." Talimat picked out some large pieces and ate them, but Pamiuk did not want to try. He could eat the contents of a caribou's stomach, but this was unappetizing to him.

The two men dragged the mass of organs to the ice edge and let it slide into the sea. *"Kunnikun,"* Talimat muttered as it sank. A short while later, when they dropped some unusable pieces of backbone into the water, he said the word again. Pamiuk knew that it meant "calm water," and Talimat instructed him to say it whenever he discarded walrus parts. "These bones and innards will feed the little creatures down below," he explained, "and in return we ask them to calm the water so we can travel safely home."

An hour later Pamiuk and Talimat's walrus was reduced to a few chunks of meat and a broad red stain on the ice. The other carcasses were also nearly finished, and Sakiak was cutting the hide from the calf. He sliced in a tight spiral around the animal's body, so that its skin came off in one long, narrow strip. Later this would be dried, scraped, and cut to length for a harpoon line. Eskimos had learned through experience that no rope was as strong and durable as line made from the hide of a young walrus.

"Food is ready!" Migalik called out. "Let's eat." Everyone was hungry and tired, and the break was welcome. After Sakiak's prayer of thanks, boiled *kauk,* heart, and other tidbits of meat were pulled from the pot. Pukak, who loved to

eat, held slices of heart between his teeth and cut them off
close to his lips. Then he ate *kauk,* relishing its strong, nutlike
flavor. Grease from the rich blubber soon covered his face
and hands. When he was finished he wiped himself clean
with a piece of cloth, leaned back to rest a moment, and
contemplated his good fortune.

Sakiak brought up a broken skull and ate a few pieces of
raw brain from inside. No one showed interest in sharing his
delicacy, and it set him thinking. "The young people are
hardly Eskimos any more," he said pointedly, "because there
are many things they have never learned to eat. When I was
young, before rifles and flour and engines for boats, we let
no part of any animal go unused. That is the lesson starvation taught us."

In a short while the men finished eating and returned to
work. It took them only an hour to cut up what remained
from six of the walrus and load all but a few useless parts into
the boats. When they reached the village, equal shares would
be divided among them, except for double amounts allotted
to the boat owners.

Finally, Kuvlu looked around and spoke. "Everything
seems ready, except for the walrus that Pamiuk tried to harpoon while it was still lively. Perhaps he wanted to go down
into the sea and discover what the ice looked like from
underneath." Everyone had a good laugh, even Pamiuk, who
now realized that stories of his foolish error would `spread
throughout the village when they returned.

"We cannot haul another walrus in the boat or we will
sink," Kavaasuk laughed, "so we had better inflate it for tow-
ing." The carcass had no buoyancy, but Eskimos knew how
to solve this problem. They cut a small hole through the skin
near one foreflipper, then Kuvlu produced a hand-operated
tire pump from his boat. He pushed its hose into the opening
and began forcing air underneath the skin. Sakiak watched
the procedure with delight, recalling many times in the past
when he had inflated dead walrus the "old way," with his
lungs. Soon the chest started puffing out, and finally the

carcass floated. Then Kuvlu shoved a piece of blubber into the hole, plugging it tightly.

"Ah, the Eskimo is a smart one," Kuvlu said, smiling and pointing to his head. Ulurunik people loved to congratulate themselves this way when they had done something particularly ingenious, whether it was a standard procedure like inflating a walrus or something they had thought up on the spot. They especially enjoyed it when comparing themselves with the white man—what *Tanik,* after all, would think of inflating a walrus, much less doing it with a tire pump?

The floating carcass was lashed tightly along one side of Kuvlu's *umiaq,* where it would slip easily through the water. When this was done they climbed aboard, started the engine, and began the long journey home. It was late evening and the sun was low. Sakiak wondered if it might drop down and touch the horizon tonight, as it had not done for more than two months. He turned and watched the two remaining walrus herds become smaller in the distance, until finally he could see them no longer.

Migalik leaned against the gunwale, feeling tired but thoroughly satisfied. There was no greater pleasure in his life than to hunt far out on the Arctic sea, to eat from the fresh-killed game, and to look forward to a triumphant return home. He thought about the people who would stand atop the beach cliff many hours hence, watching their boat plow slowly along the shore. It would float low in the water, with just inches of freeboard to spare, and everyone would hope it was laden with walrus.

Then the hunters would sit straight in their seats, trying to look strong and still full of energy. They would give the yodeling shout of joy, and it would carry far over the water, sounding like a herd of walrus. The watchers, hearing them would know. . . .

Indeed, for this tiny company of men, somewhere far up along the continent's lonely edge, there would be a moment of glory. They would stand as objects of great admiration before the others; and even though the people of Ulurunik represented a mere handful in the vast spectrum of humanity, their pride would be as intense as any men's. For the Eskimo these moments would remain forever, transfixed in the gaze of time. They epitomized all that was meant by being *Inupiat,* "the Real People."

Tingiivik Tatqiq

The Moon When Birds Fly South

(SEPTEMBER)

MAIN CHARACTERS

Kiluk (*Kee*-look) *a young woman*

Masu (*Mah*-soo) *Kiluk's adoptive grandmother*

Nauruk (*Now*-rook) *Masu's adult son*

Itiruk (It-*tir*-ook) *Nauruk's wife*

Sakiak (Sah-*kee*-uk) *an old man*

Patik (*Pah*-tik) *Sakiak's grandson*

KILUK WAS WET, COLD, AND MISERABLE. Icy raindrops beat elentlessly against her cheeks and forehead. The canvas tarpaulin that covered her lap had soaked through and water saturated her legs, so she huddled against the gunwale of the *umiaq* trying to shelter them from the blowing rain. A drop of water slid down the soggy fur of her parka ruff and hung from a cluster of matted hairs. She watched it shiver a moment in the wind before it flew away. Behind her the outboard engine droned monotonously, as it had done for several hours.

There was no chance of going back now, she thought, her gloom almost as dark as the ragged scud that raced overhead. At least the water had calmed somewhat since they passed the mouth of the Ivisauraq River, so brackish spray no longer blew in over the bow. The great estuary of the Kuk River had begun to narrow, and Nauruk kept the boat near its protecting south bank. She thought of him sitting in the stern, far more exposed to the weather and unable even to turn his face from it. He would never complain, she knew. He was like all the others—tough, proud, and stoic.

She could say the same for old Masu, Nauruk's mother and her own adoptive grandmother, who sat quietly beside the opposite gunwale. Surely Masu was as wet and chilled as she,

181

but her aged face reflected no discomfort. In fact, it seemed she was either asleep or thinking placidly with her eyes closed.

And in the bow, seated so she faced them, was Nauruk's wife Itiruk. Never one to be idle, she was repairing tears in a fishnet, deftly weaving the shuttle and tying the special knots that would not slip. Kiluk watched her glistening wet hands and wondered how they could remain supple when hers were stiff and numb even inside sealskin mittens.

Both Masu and Itiruk looked quite at peace, while Kiluk suffered. She should have resisted their urgings to join them at fish camp far up the Kuk River. After all, she had refused all their other suggestions—that she learn to scrape hides, to sew boots and parkas, to prepare food in the old ways. "Come now, you try it," they always said. "You will learn to be a real Eskimo woman at last." Itiruk, who was younger and more direct, would add pointed remarks: "School taught you many things, but never how to *live*. What good is all that reading if you cannot sew and catch fish?"

The words hurt Kiluk, sometimes even angered her; but she was enough of an Eskimo to shadow her emotions behind silence and an expressionless face. What did she care for the endless labors of an Eskimo woman, working hours each day with needle and braided sinew, or bent over dried skins with a scraper . . . or shivering in the fall rain in an open boat? Eight grades in the village school had kept her away from all that; and four years at a high school for Indians and Eskimos nearly a thousand miles from Ulurunik; and even a start at college. After so much education, it was hard to be told that little you knew was of any value.

When criticism failed to change Kiluk, Masu would try other approaches. Learning the skills and ways of her people would be fun, exciting—it was a better way to live than having a job or just doing nothing. "You will see if you come with us to fish camp," she had said a few days earlier. "The river at Nunavik will be full of fish, thousands of them. We will eat fresh whitefish and grayling, and perhaps there will be caribou herds as well. When you start catching fish you will know why we love to go there."

Masu had spoken it all in her labored English, even though she knew Kiluk understood Eskimo perfectly. Kiluk had been raised with the language of her people, but after the years away at school she spoke it with a strange accent and sometimes she stumbled over the long word-phrases. People had laughed at her, so she retreated into English, which she could speak far better than they.

It was one of her few points of clear superiority. They knew little of the *Tanik's* world, and she knew it well. She had proved that by living so long away. But her heart had yearned for the familiarity of home, for people who would not insult her with foolish questions about living in igloos and rubbing noses. She had been lonely there. And now she had to admit that she was lonely here, too, that although she was no *Tanik* she was not fully Eskimo either. There were other young ones like her in Ulurunik, others who lived the same dilemma. Some stayed and some did not, but nearly all felt lost wherever they were.

Only Patik seemed to know exactly what he wanted. The years in school never took away his consuming desire to be a hunter, and to be all that went along with it. No amount of teasing by the elders for his inexperience, or jealousy from his less settled friends, could turn him from that course. Patik wanted to hunt, to drive dogs alone across the tundra, to dance in front of the drummers, to speak *Inupiat*—to be clearly and preeminently an Eskimo.

And there was something else Patik wanted. It showed in his eyes and in the way he teased her. Patik wanted Kiluk.

That thought pulled her suddenly back to the present, to the wetness that saturated her thick cloth parka and the gusts of wind that leaned intermittently against her. She looked far ahead through the haze and drizzle and saw a black speck on the river. That was Sakiak's boat, and Patik was its steersman.

The old man had requested that his grandson come with him to help out in the fish camp and to further his learning. Sakiak must have had another motive too, Kiluk thought. Somehow he knew of Patik's interest in her—nothing could be hidden from him.

Of course they were all wasting their time. Patik would need quite a different kind of woman for the life he wanted—"a real Eskimo woman." She let herself think those words, but with sarcasm and a brief flush of bitterness. A woman who had never sewn even a pair of fur socks would hardly do for Patik. And a man who wished only to go to fish camp and to hunt for caribou was not what Kiluk had in mind.

Tired of such thoughts, now colder and even less happy than before, Kiluk leaned against the heap of gear that filled the *umiaq* behind her. She pulled her hood farther up so it deflected some of the rain and stared with tear-filled eyes over the gray water. The riverbank was muddy and black in the muted light, and the tundra sloped away above it, fading into the chill mist. Before she closed her eyes, she saw a patch of willows at the water's edge, their bare, twisted branches shaking in the wind.

Kiluk ascended slowly to the edge of wakefulness. She heard a flapping noise, first softly, then growing louder as she became conscious. It was wind on loose canvas. And there was a hissing sound of windblown drizzle against the tent walls and roof. She opened her eyes and gazed into the dim light. Someone breathed heavily nearby. It was early morning, and the others were still asleep.

Cold air crept into the opening of her sleeping bag, as it had done all night. She remembered shivering for hours in the darkness, breathing inside the bag to warm it, while the others slept soundly. Finally she had drifted into a fitful sleep, awakening often and wondering if daylight would ever come. Now it had come at last, and she lifted the tent wall just enough to peek outside. A chill breeze puffed in underneath, and a few big snowflakes came with it. She could see patches of wet snow clinging to the windward sides of tussocks, but the drizzle was eating them away and they would probably vanish soon. She also saw another tent—Sakiak's—just a few yards away.

Kiluk snuggled back down into her sleeping bag, grateful for even the modest warmth it provided. She remembered last night, arriving here in the half-darkness, everyone rushing to unload the boats during a merciful break in the rain. "This is Kangich," Nauruk had shouted to her over the wind, "the old village where your grandparents lived." All her life she had been told about this place, that her ancestors had had a sod house here, that Masu and Ulimaun often camped here to fish, that its name meant "meeting-of-rivers"—the Qaolaq and Avalik, with the Qitiq just upstream. The others had seemed excited just to be here, as if Kangich was a very special place. But to Kiluk it had seemed like any other empty spot on the flat and dismal land, meaningful only because they were finally going to stop here and shelter themselves.

A short while later she heard movement beside her, then Masu's voice. She was talking softly to herself about sleeping too late, about the chill as she crawled from her sleeping bag, and then about how fine it was to be at Kangich again after a whole year's passage. This awakened Nauruk and Itiruk, who also shared the cramped little tent. "Granddaughter, are you sleeping?" the old woman asked. "We are at Kangich! And the sun is shining." She laughed at the last remark, as Eskimos often did to be sure no one ever mistook a tease for a deliberate deception.

Kiluk stretched and wearily peeked out. "Come, hurry," Nauruk admonished gruffly. "We have a long trip today while the weather is so fine." He cocked his head and looked down at her, smiling broadly. Everyone knew how wretched she had been yesterday, and now they were teasing her for it. She rolled toward the tent wall and said nothing.

"Sakiak! Patik! Wake up before the morning is gone." Masu's shrill voice filled the tent; and in a moment they heard Sakiak's reply: "I am well awake and drinking hot coffee. Only this young man sleeps, when he should be out looking for caribou. Perhaps you will come to my tent; there is plenty of coffee here."

Masu and the others had already gone by the time Kiluk got up, slipped on her parka, and ran the few yards to Sakiak's tent. She felt a rush of warmth as she stepped inside, and rich smells of fresh coffee and boiling meat mixed heavily in the air. Everyone sat around the walls, leaning against the clutter of gear, clothes, and caribou hides. Kiluk shook the water from her parka before sitting down and accepting coffee from Itiruk. The cup felt wonderfully warm between her palms, and she relished her first sips.

After several minutes of silence, Sakiak began thinking aloud: "This is poor weather for traveling farther upriver. The wind has shifted to the north and the rain is heavy. If we wait here, the water may rise and it will be easier to cross the shallows below Nunavik." Kiluk could have shouted her joy at hearing these words, but she was young and a woman, so she remained silent. It was for Masu to agree, and she did. She was anxious to see her camp, she said, but she could wait another day or two. Plenty of work could be done here, especially on the nets.

Old people were the final authorities on such matters, and so even Nauruk was quiet. He was the biggest and most powerful man in Ulurunik, one of the most successful hunters, and leader of his own whaling crew—but he always showed deference to his elders. Among Eskimos, wisdom was the most treasured virtue; and wisdom came only with age.

This was true for men and women alike, but there was also a difference. Old men eventually weakened and could not hunt or travel, so their only asset was their knowledge. But old women could still cut patterns and fit and sew, usually far better than their younger counterparts. Perhaps this was why their personalities and assertiveness often strengthened with age. None showed this better than Masu, who administered the household of Ulimaun as tightly as she stitched her seams.

Steaming caribou meat was drawn from the pot, and everyone ate enthusiastically. Even Kiluk felt almost contented afterward, and she listened closely as Sakiak recounted the history of Kangich: "When I was a boy, this was a gathering place for the *Kugmiut*—the Kuk River people— who used to make a big camp here each fall when the fish ran thick. One day they would look across the land and see people walking toward them from the south. These were the Utoqaq River people, who traveled the long overland trail so they could trade at Kangich, and dance and play games. It was especially fine for the young ones, who made new friends here, or arranged trading partnerships, or even met someone they would later marry." Kiluk was sure that she saw a mischievous twinkle in the old man's eyes when he said those last words.

Masu then interjected: "It was that way for your real grandparents, Kiluk. Atuk, your grandmother, was a *Kugmiut,* and her husband Ivrulik was from the Utoqaq. They came here with their parents, and their mothers arranged that they should marry. So when your grandfather's people left after the snows, he stayed with the *Kugmiut.* He was scarcely a man then, but already a fine hunter; and your grandmother loved to fish. Perhaps that is why they spent much of their lives here, in the country around Kangich. Both of them died long before you were born, from a sickness that came with the whaling ships. Your real mother nearly died with them, and she never was strong after that."

Masu looked to Sakiak for confirmation, then continued: "Your mother had two children already when you began growing inside her, and no one knew how she would feed you. So she and your real father, who was an unlucky hunter, asked if Ulimaun and I would raise another baby, our own children being older by that time. We agreed, and you were given to us; and although we are uncle and aunt to your parents you have always called us grandfather and grandmother."

"By your birth you are a Kangich person," Sakiak added, "because your family has always camped here. Until your mother died she came here each year, and just after your birth she brought you with her. She stayed with your father in a sod house that stood above the bank where the rivers join. It is gone now, and only a shallow pit remains. I can show it to you."

Thoughts of the cold and misery left Kiluk as she lost herself in these stories of her life and her special connection with Kangich. The bleak emptiness of the place gave way, in her mind, to something more meaningful. The land here was a part of her, and she a part of it. The earth seemed warmer in a sense, less forbidding and foreign.

Kiluk had been told the story of her adoption before, but never in such detail. She felt no antipathy toward her mother, no sense of rejection, because children were often given to others for adoption. If her mother and father were still alive, they would remain special for her and she for them. A child was given away lovingly, to a couple who could provide well but who had no children or whose children were grown up.

But sometimes, as Sakiak now pointed out, parents could not support a new child and had no one to give it to. "Long ago, in the spring of a year with little food, a woman was about to give birth. But she already had a child at her breast, and three others who were still small. Perhaps she did not ask if someone could take her new baby when it was born because it was a hard season and the burden would be too much. So when it came from her she took it outside the house, dug a hole in the snow, and left it to die quickly.

"A man and his wife were camped nearby, and the woman heard a baby crying outside. She listened for a long time, knowing what it was and thinking. She had wished for a child, but none was ever born to her. If she adopted an infant now, before summer came and the animals arrived, it would mean difficulty or even danger of starvation for her and her husband. But she kept hearing the baby and it was hard for her to wait until its crying stopped. Finally her power to resist was gone, and so she rushed out and took the infant from the snow.

"Her name was Aliksik, and she has always been very special indeed for me. You see, I was the baby and she became my mother."

There was a brief, thoughtful silence, and then Masu continued: "In the old days, before we had rifles and such things as the *Taniks* brought, there were starvation times. When food ran out in one place, people had to move, and they kept moving until they found something to eat. A woman with a baby needed more food, and she moved less easily than the others. So, although it was a terribly sad thing, she sometimes had to let her newborn infant die. She did this as soon as it was born, because if she waited she would be unable to let it go."

Infant girls were more often left this way than boys, because hunters were essential to the family's survival. But many more boys died before they became adults, because they faced the great dangers of traveling on the sea ice and hunting far over the tundra. So, although more boys were raised in an Eskimo society, more girls lived beyond adolescence; and by the time of adulthood the numbers of men and women were almost equal. Thus, as in most realms of Eskimo life, the practical dictates of survival held sway above all else. Nowadays things were less difficult, and so children never had to be left this way any longer.

Masu and Sakiak continued exchanging stories for some time, until finally the old woman said she must go to her work. "I want to be ready for fishing when we reach

Nunavik," she declared. "We will set our nets quickly so we
can eat fresh, fat fish. And in a few days the river will freeze
and we will start hooking. Then you young ones will know
what it means to fish!" Kiluk could see how real Masu's enthusiasm was, but it made little sense to her. Fishing on the
ice all day sounded cold and utterly boring.

By late afternoon she felt the same way about sitting inside
the tent with rain beating ceaselessly against it. She huddled
in a corner, half-covered by her sleeping bag, watching the
others work. Itiruk spent hours with her shuttle, gradually
closing a multitude of holes in an old gill net she had bor-
rowed from her brother's wife. In return for its use she
would give a portion of the fish she caught in it. As her
fingers darted in and out of the webbing she sang Eskimo
songs to herself.

From time to time Masu would join in, swaying with the
music and smiling in pure delight. She was sewing a pair of
waterproof sealskin boots for Nauruk, fancy ones with the
silvery fur outside and geometric designs stitched from hide
pieces around the tops. Few younger women knew how to
make such boots, and Kiluk noticed that Itiruk was watching
closely as they took shape. Masu loved to talk, and so she gave
a running account of her work as she proceeded, sometimes
complaining when she felt her stitch was uneven or too loose.

Twice she spoke softly to Kiluk without looking up from
her work: "My granddaughter, come and let Itiruk show you
how to mend the net. It will be easy to learn the knots, and
time will pass quickly if you are busy." But Kiluk made no
reply, just wrinkled her nose as children did to say no. She
was not entirely uninterested, but she would be inept at first
and the women would tease her. Masu was silent when Kiluk
refused; but she hurt inside, thinking that this girl who
meant so much to her wanted nothing of the life she loved.

That evening they all ate in Sakiak's tent, and afterward
the men began carving new sinkers for the net Itiruk had
repaired. The sinkers were made from pieces of caribou ant-

ler, cut to the length of a man's palm and drilled at each end. These were tied at intervals along the net's bottom edge; and along the top they placed floats carved from driftwood chunks. Patik watched his grandfather and Nauruk for a while, then began carving too. The older men corrected his errors, and Nauruk had a great laugh when he split a float in half just before it was finished. Patik only smiled and started over, determined to do it right the next time.

Kiluk sat beside Masu, who had insisted she help braid sinew for tomorrow's sewing. They peeled long filaments from a strip of dried caribou sinew and braided them into thick, strong thread. Twice when Kiluk glanced toward the men she saw Patik looking at her. She flushed and quickly resumed her work, feeling both perplexed and flattered by his apparent liking for her. He was very pleasant and singularly handsome, and she had to admit that she admired his willingness to become absorbed in the Eskimo ways. It was not for her, but perhaps he was fortunate because he knew who he wanted to be. She found herself looking at him again, bent to his carving, pulling the sharp blade of his knife through the weathered wood.

That night, while she lay awake listening to the wind buffet and winnow over the tundra, Kiluk thought she heard a lone wolf howling in the distance. The sound came to her briefly and faded, carried off by the swirling gusts. She wondered if perhaps it was not a wolf at all; perhaps, as Masu often said, those who lived at Kangich long ago had never left. Kiluk stared into the darkness. The storm pressed heavily around the tent, and the wind moaned and whispered and breathed, alive with something she felt but did not know. She was afraid and wished to be in the safe familiarity of the village.

The next day was much like the one before, except that the north wind strengthened and the rain turned to showers of snow. Everyone worked inside the tents, and Kiluk helped with the cooking to relieve her boredom. Confinement made her feel nervous and sullen, so near midday she went outside to look around. She walked along the steeply cut riverbank, which stood slightly higher than the surroundings. Snow had whitened the landscape, and the converging rivers stood out like streaks of black ash. Sakiak came out and showed her where her parents' house had been. The river had cut into it, and fragments of bone sled runner protruded from the mud. She wondered if they might have been from her father's sled, and she felt a growing sadness as she lingered in that silent place. Finally she returned, shivering, to the tents.

That afternoon the wind diminished, but mixed snow and rain fell heavily from a somber sky. Sakiak went to get something from his tent, and on his way back he stopped and shouted toward the sky: "Sun! Sun! Your smell is getting bad."

"*Aana* [grandmother], what does he mean?" Kiluk asked. The old woman put her sewing aside and spoke slowly: "To understand this, you must know about the beginnings of the world. A long time ago, the things we see around us were not as they are today. For example, the animals were like people and could talk. Also, the moon was a man and the sun was his wife. One day they had a terrible argument, and the moon man cut her with his knife. She ran away, up a rainbow into the sky, and there she became the sun. Her husband chased after her, and he became the moon. Today he still follows her around the sky, and sometimes he comes close enough so that we can see both of them at the same time.

"The sun is still a woman today, and she can hear us if we talk to her. When she insists on hiding behind the clouds, as she often does in the summer and fall, men sometimes insult her by saying that she will smell bad inside if she does not come out. Many times I have seen the sky clear after some-one shouted at the sun this way."

When Masu had finished, Itiruk added, "These are not just stories; they are as true as the Bible." Kiluk had heard the old people tell *ulipqaat*—ancestral stories—many times before, and she knew how strongly they held them as essential truths about the world. They had accepted the missionaries' Christian teachings, but without abandoning all their traditional beliefs. They kept their Eskimo ways to themselves, however, and let the *Taniks* believe that such things were lost long ago. Only the young people, like Kiluk, seemed to care little for the old religion. She listened respectfully to the stories but was not at all sure there was truth in them.

The day passed slowly. Evening finally came, and darkness fell early beneath the heavy curtain of clouds. Kiluk withdrew to her sleeping bag while the others played cards with a ragged old deck, drinking tea and laughing far into the night. She wondered why she did not join them, but somehow she resented their easy, simple pleasure. Alone and full of self-pity, she stared at the pattern of stains and watermarks on the tent roof, dimly lit by the gasoline lantern. One was a caribou; another was a bird flying away alone.

"Wake up in there! The wind is gone and the sky is clearing. Time to load the boats and head for Nunavik." It was Sakiak, poking his head into the tent. "Come, Nauruk. . . . You sleep too much. There is ice on the water's edge and I want to see *fish* today." Kiluk awakened slowly and saw shadows on the tent wall—the sun. She thought of yesterday's stories as she yawned and rubbed her eyes.

An hour later they slid the two *umiaqs* into the river, loaded mountains of gear inside, and pushed away from the hard-frozen bank. Cold outboards slowly came to life as the boats turned up the Avalik River. On both sides the tundra mosaic of snow white and patches of vibrant brown lifted away in protracted sweeps. High above a golden eagle circled in ascending spirals, a tiny fleck weaving its way upward in the cold blue ocean of sky.

When they had traveled only a few miles, the current increased and the river became shallow. Crystal water ran swiftly over gravel shoals, and before long the boats scraped bottom. "*Azaah,* too shallow," Sakiak complained. "We will have to drag the boats upstream until we reach deep water again. Masu and Kiluk should wade to shore and walk ahead on the bank."

The river bottom was tricky and uneven, and within a few steps Kiluk slipped and icy water soaked one of her feet. It was a bad way to start a long trek upriver. She found herself feeling miserable again, wishing this would all end quickly so she could go back home. How many miles were they going to walk? And would the others be able to pull the boats over the riffles she saw ahead? It seemed that Eskimos had to do everything the hard way, and she wished they could just live on food from grocery stores like *Taniks* in the cities.

The ground was covered with frozen tussocks that made walking very difficult indeed. But old Masu trudged along happily, sometimes singing Eskimo songs to herself and sometimes telling stories about the places they passed. She paused occasionally to look over the land for caribou and was disappointed that there were none. Near one place called Tasiq, she stopped abruptly, listened, then gazed at the sky overhead. "Do you remember," she asked, "that Sakiak told you we have nearly reached the end of *Tingiivik tatqiq,* the moon when birds fly south?" Now she pointed, and Kiluk finally saw what it was—very high above them she could make out a long skein of Canada geese, so high that they barely seemed to be moving. The old woman watched them for a time, and then mused with a soft smile. "They must be the last ones to fly away from us this year; but if I am still alive I will see them again in the spring."

When they had gone about a mile, she led Kiluk away from the bank, promising a surprise. Shortly she stopped and gestured toward the ground. "Look, *akpik!*" she exclaimed with obvious delight. Poking up through the snow was a profusion of beautiful orange cloudberries—one of the few edible plant species found on the tundra—a favorite Eskimo

treat. Both of them set to work immediately, picking berries
and putting them in the large front pouches of their cloth
parka covers. They rewarded themselves liberally as they
went along, savoring the cold, sweet, succulent berries.

Kiluk's wet foot was aching with cold by the time they
finished and walked back to the river. The boats were close
by now, but they were stuck in very shallow water and the
others had partly unloaded them. "Come, granddaughter,"
Masu urged. "We are strong enough to help." And without
hesitating she went down the bank and waded in. Kiluk followed reluctantly, wondering how she could be so unlucky,
wishing they had just stayed at Kangich.

"Ah, good, now we have plenty of power," Nauruk declared laughingly. "This young woman has been resting for
two days and must be very strong. *Ki* . . . go up near the bow,
where Patik can help you if you fall." Nauruk had gone too
far with his joking, but the others were ready, so Kiluk had to
stumble quickly alongside and start pulling.

The *umiaqs* very slowly began moving upstream, their re-
silient sealskin covers flexing as they slid over the rocks.
When they were about halfway through the riffle, Kiluk
slipped and filled her boots with numbing water again. She
could have cried, but no one stopped, and she could only
keep splashing ahead. The water became shallower, the load
heavier, and she was almost gasping for breath.

"Whoa!" Nauruk shouted as if he were driving a dog team.
"Look there, ahead of us in the river—fish!" Kiluk saw nothing for a moment, just the gentle rush of water over the
shallows. Then suddenly she realized that it was deeper
ahead, and what looked like scattered rapids were fish,
thousands and thousands of them, huge, dense schools
frothing the surface as they dashed away from the boats. The
entire river, from bank to bank, for a hundred yards upstream, swarmed with fish.

Kiluk suddenly forgot her agony, and when Nauruk gave
the word she pulled as hard as the rest. The boat moved

more easily now, and she glanced up to watch the spectacle of
the fleeing fish. For a moment the water would be calm; then
it would suddenly explode as the frenzied mass scattered first
one way, then another. She had never seen such an abundance of anything, never imagined it possible.

Finally the boats floated free, and they all went to shore.
"Now you have seen the fish!" Nauruk triumphed, looking at
both Kiluk and Patik. "And before long you will have the fun
of catching them." He punctuated that by crunching his boot
through the thin layer of ice along the shore, indicating that
the river would soon freeze. "Come, let's go for the gear. We
have an easy ride to fish camp from here."

Kiluk was thoroughly exhausted by the time they had carried all the gear to the *umiaqs*. Her back hurt, her arms were
rubbery, and every time she took a step her boots sloshed
loudly. Sakiak noticed her forlorn expression as she pulled
her boots off and poured water from them. "Ah, you work
like a young man," he congratulated, "but you don't watch
for the deep holes." Then he sat beside her, took off his own
boots, and dumped an equal amount of water from them.
"And look at that old woman . . . and my foolish grandson."
Now Kiluk saw them all begin emptying their boots and realized that everyone was suffering like her. Sakiak began
laughing; and he laughed harder and harder, until tears
began streaming down his cheeks. The others could not help
joining, and finally even Kiluk laughed.

Like a real Eskimo, she laughed with the others—at the
absurdity of their misfortune, at their icy feet and their aching backs, at the shallow water that had tricked them all into
hard work and suffering. And they laughed, too, at the pleasure of seeing the multitude of fish, which promised good
fortune and good times ahead. They laughed as those who
came before them had learned to laugh, toasting a hard life
in a hard land, that took from them payment in labor and
pain and rewarded them with the inestimable riches of freedom.

It was not long before they approached Nunavik, traveling swiftly on placid waters that mirrored the riverbanks and tundra in detailed perfection. A few upright poles marked the campsite, beside a small creek that flowed into the river. The water was very deep, Masu said, and the fish congregated here before going farther upstream to spawn. Her face glowed with excitement as they eased in to the shore, and she almost ran up the bank to look over the land. "We are here!" she sang out. "Come, old man—you, Sakiak—come and look at Nunavik again."

Everyone worked hard to set up camp quickly, but the sun touched the horizon before they finished. It was a beautiful evening, the sky aflame with orange and magenta, the air still and cold, and the indigo water dimpled with occasional swirls of fish. Patik walked far off across the tundra before darkness came, searching for signs of caribou. When he returned he found Kiluk alone by the river. He said he had seen nothing, and they sat together talking until there was no more light.

When they entered Masu's tent, where everyone had gathered to eat, they felt clumsy and embarrassed. Kiluk expected Nauruk to make a joke about them, but instead he asked Patik what he had seen and said perhaps they would walk farther to look around tomorrow. Masu added that young men were supposed to tire quickly, but somehow this one still had the energy to hunt after a long day. "*Azahaa*, you're a man," Nauruk whispered, smiling and feigning exaggerated admiration. In the end, he could not resist a tease.

After they had eaten their supper of caribou meat with seal oil, they all talked for a while and then retired to their sleeping bags. Kiluk laid awake in the stillness, thinking of the day's events and feeling almost too tired to sleep. She wondered when the first deep snow would fall so that dog teams would come from Ulurunik and she could go back to the comforts of home. But there was a vague feeling of excitement in her too; she could not deny it, thinking of all those fish. . . . When she was on the verge of sleep she thought of Patik, walking alone across the tundra in the last glow of twilight.

The sharp noise of rifle shots somewhere nearby startled Kiluk awake the next morning. She sat up and blinked at the brightness of high sun on the tent wall. *Crack!* Another shot, then silence. A few minutes later she heard Masu's voice down by the river: "Look, daughter-in-law," she called to Itiruk, "that old man can still shoot." Curious now, and knowing she had slept very late, Kiluk got up and peeked out the tent door.

Sakiak was walking along the bank, carrying two plump little animals. "*Sikrik,*" he called to her. "Ground squirrels. Fat ones ready to hibernate. They were half-asleep in the sunshine outside their burrows." Kiluk pulled on her parka and stepped outside, stiff from yesterday's hard work. Itiruk was already preparing to skin the squirrels, and Sakiak had gone down the bank to help Masu with a fishnet. "For several years I have been saving *sikrik* hides," Itiruk said as she carefully removed one of the small skins. "Someday I will use them to make a fancy parka, decorated with tails and stitched designs."

"And today we can eat fresh boiled *sikrik,* " Masu called out, "perhaps some fish too." She and Sakiak had a gill net stretched along the beach and were discussing where to set it. "Your *aana* wants it right here, but Sakiak says it should be farther upstream," Itiruk explained. "Of course she will win, because she is always the boss at Nunavik, and she perhaps knows the fish better than anyone else."

Itiruk was soon proved right. Sakiak fetched a tiny skin-covered boat that he had brought upriver from the village. Then he took one end of the net and pulled it out into the deep eddy, while Masu tended the beach end. When the net was stretched completely out, Sakiak dropped a rock anchor that would hold it in place. At the same time Masu tied the other end to a stake on the beach. A line of floats marked the top of the net, and the carved antler weights along its bottom edge made it hang vertically underwater.

Kiluk sat with Itiruk, eating a breakfast of cold meat with her coffee, watching the two elders work. They quickly prepared two more nets, then set them in the spots Masu insisted upon. When they finished, Masu puffed up the bank looking completely pleased with herself. "My *qatangan* wants to put the nets in all the wrong places," she laughed. "But then, who knows where the fish may choose to swim?"

Itiruk saw Kiluk's quizzical expression and knew immediately what to ask. "Do you know why she calls the old man *qatangan?*" Without waiting for an answer, she explained: "Your *aana* and Sakiak have always been fishing partners, but they have another special relationship as well. Long ago, before the *Taniks* changed things, men sometimes exchanged wives for a short while. Often these men were trading partners from different villages, and they might agree to the exchange without asking their wives first. After this was carried out, the children of both couples always called each other *qatangan;* and they were obligated to help each other like brothers and sisters.

"The missionaries said such things were a sin," she mused, "and because I am a woman I think it is better that husbands no longer have this right. But I have heard that *Taniks* are not free of such sins themselves, and I often wonder if their children become *qatangan* like Masu and Sakiak. I am always too shy to ask."

This started Masu on stories of her childhood, and then stories about Nunavik and the events that had taken place here. For several hours she talked, and Kiluk surprised herself by listening carefully the entire time. It was only because there was nothing else to do, she told herself. Things were especially quiet without Patik and Nauruk, who had left at dawn to search farther inland for caribou.

Late in the afternoon, Masu saw the net floats jiggling.
"Many fish have entangled themselves already," she sur-
mised. "We should check the nets—I am too anxious to wait
any longer." It took almost an hour to pull all the slippery,
wiggling fish from the meshes, and when they finished they
had almost filled a large tub with silvery whitefish and a few
grayling trout. Masu and Sakiak's enthusiasm was contagi-
ous, and when they began cleaning fish to hang on the drying
rack Kiluk let them teach her how it was done.

They were so busy that Patik and Nauruk walked into
camp unnoticed. Suddenly Nauruk's voice boomed behind
Kiluk, "*Azahaa,* look at this young woman cutting fish." His
broad hand took one of hers from the slimy fish it held, and
he scrutinized it. "Well, no fingers cut off yet. I see you are
learning how to do something important, just like this funny
little man here." He looked mockingly at Patik, who would
have blushed except that his cheeks were already red from
the cold. Nauruk's voice was hard and gruff, but in fact
teasing was his way of showing affection. No matter how
tough he sounded, there was always a gentle look in his eyes.

"Well, what did you see?" Masu interrupted. "Nothing except a few ptarmigan," he replied, "and a brown bear's tracks
near Avalitqoq Creek." He recounted the details of their day
and then announced that he and Patik had eaten nothing
except a few berries since morning. So they all filed into
Masu's tent to boil a huge pot of freshly caught fish.

In the hushed chill of evening, Kiluk walked to the riverbank. On the pretext of getting water from the river, Patik
followed shortly afterward, and they sat together as night
flooded the sky. For a while they spoke of unimportant
things, then about their lives away from Ulurunik and their
reasons for coming back. Patik was not one to speak of sadness, but his voice showed that he had struggled with the
same confusion that Kiluk knew in herself. Finally he said, "I
am an Eskimo, and I belong here. I have seen the cities,
where there is no open land to travel, no game to hunt, and
no freedom to choose your own trail in the morning. Others

may leave, but I will stay where I have all those things, and where I can laugh with people who know me well."

Stars lit the sky, and a new moon skirted the horizon. While the others played cards and drank tea in Masu's tent, Kiluk and Patik sat alone on the bank. Later, when the moon vanished, they slipped quietly into the other tent.

Hidden by the deepening darkness, an owl hovered on silent wings above the camp, then swept away in an exultant rush of flight over the undulating land.

Days seemed to pass quickly in the Nunavik camp, although the routine varied little. Fish came in greater and greater numbers, and gunnysacks beside the tents bulged with the catch. For a few days it was warm enough to allow some fermentation, which would give the fish the tangy flavor Eskimos liked. But then they began to freeze, and flurries of snow made little drifts around the gunnies.

Kiluk learned how to set and check the gill nets, and one day Masu convinced her to help with a pair of mittens she was sewing. But she still missed the comfort of the village—regular baths (even though they were in a small washtub), warm houses, well-washed clothes, and the excitement of having many people around. Sakiak said that a good snow could come any day now, and dog teams would surely follow immediately afterward to haul fish. Then, she knew, she could ride back to the village ... if she wanted to. Kiluk startled herself by thinking of it that way.

Perhaps it was Patik—she knew that something was happening to her, but she would forget about it when she left. Fish camp had become a fairly pleasant interlude, but not a life. She and Patik spent their evenings by the river, and the others let them be alone. Nauruk, of course, could not help teasing whenever he had a chance, but it was easy to see that he was pleased.

Then one dawn Sakiak woke the camp, shouting happily from outside the tents that the river had frozen. The ice was only a fragile skin of crystal, but it would thicken quickly in the growing cold. That afternoon they broke lanes with the little boat to remove their nets. Masu was almost beside herself with anticipation, and she spent the evening at work on her fishhooks and jigging lines. "Now, at last, the *fun* is here. I have a line ready for you, granddaughter, and a warm caribou skin for you to kneel on."

The next morning Kiluk awoke early, because it was very cold inside the tent. She decided to light the gasoline stove for warmth, and when she did she noticed that Masu and Itiruk were gone. Only Nauruk was there, snoring blissfully. Once the stove was lighted and coffee water was on, she poked her head out the tent flap to look for the women. A dusting of snow had fallen, and the world was a sheet of white. Footprints led toward the riverbank and onto the ice. There they were, two dark figures bent over newly chopped holes, rhythmically jigging their fishing lines.

A short while later she walked down to join them. The sun broke intermittently through running clouds, mottling the snow-covered land with patterns of bright and shadow. "At last you have come," Itiruk declared. "We checked the ice at dawn, and when we found it safe we didn't hesitate even long enough for hot coffee. Look, your grandmother has many fish already, and even I have a few." Itiruk was being overly modest, although the old woman had indeed caught considerably more.

Masu immediately called for Kiluk. "Come, granddaughter, I will show you how to fish. You can sit here and I will chop a new hole nearby." Kiluk was reluctant to try, feeling that she would be inept and the others would laugh at her. And to make things worse, Sakiak and Patik were now coming down onto the ice, the old man carrying a tangle of fishing gear. "These women must have fished all night in the darkness," he laughed. "Grandson, run quickly; get me a caribou skin to sit on, and bring one for yourself."

Kiluk escaped to the tent, with the excuse of getting her

heavy caribou parka and boots. But, instead of hiding there, she encountered a wide-awake Nauruk, who immediately asked how many fish she had caught and why she was in the tent when she should be out jigging. Reluctantly she resigned herself to the inevitable. She would try for a while, so they would have to leave her alone.

Masu taught her in typical Eskimo fashion—by handing her the jigging rod and telling her to fish. The hook looked like a small piece of ivory, slender and curved, with a sharp metal barb set out from its lower end. It was carved from a dog's tooth, Masu explained, while Kiluk lowered her line into the black water and began jigging. Much to her surprise, the old woman only laughed a little at her first clumsy attempts, and by pantomime she demonstrated how to move the line properly.

Kiluk held the jigging rod in one hand and a short stick in the other. If she caught a fish, which she thought unlikely, she was to lift the line, then loop it over the stick to pull it from the water. That way she would never have to touch the wet line. Not far away, she saw Patik making his own beginning; and when he looked at her she could not help smiling. He would surely catch many fish, she thought, and she would catch nothing. She moved her arm up and down, imitating the motion her grandmother had used. But nothing happened.

Then suddenly she felt a hard jerk on the rod, and more jerks, as the line zipped in circles around the fishing hole. She was so startled that she nearly lost the rod, but Itiruk shouted, "Pull it up..quickly!" In a moment a fat, shiny grayling flopped on the ice beside her. She shook it from the hook as she had seen Itiruk do earlier, then just sat there looking at her catch with a huge smile on her face.

"*Azahaa,*" Sakiak called from the river's far side, "a fish already. Go ahead, drop your line again." Kiluk almost quivered in her excitement, realizing she had actually caught a fish. And before she had calmed down, the line tugged again.

This time she laughed with pure delight as her fish dropped onto the ice. The next fish took longer, and she lost it by pulling it up too slowly. But she had another out of the water a short while later.

"This young woman seems to be lucky with fish," Itiruk called to Masu. "Look, Patik has yet to catch his first, and I have caught only one, while she has got three." Masu replied in a matter-of-fact voice, "Kiluk is almost certain to catch many fish. She was born just after the death of old man Kiluk, who was from the Utoqaq people and was known as a great fisherman. His name was given to her, and so we must expect that she will show something of him."

In the Eskimo world, each person's name was imbued with its own soul. When someone died, the soul wandered aimlessly, sometimes maliciously, until it was given an abode in a newborn child. Eventually the child would behave in some way like his or her namesake, when the soul manifested itself. This bequeathed a kind of immortality or promise of re-incarnation to the Eskimo people. That was why Amiksuk, who was old Kiluk's grandson, sometimes greeted Kiluk as *ataataga*, "my grandfather," even though she was young and a woman.

The fishing went on for hours and hours, with occasional breaks for hot food, tea, and the tent's welcome warmth. Everyone had caught a little pile of fish, and even Patik was quite successful. Only Masu had more fish than Kiluk, who never retreated to the tent until her hands and feet were freezing and her teeth chattered. "*Aana*," she once called to Masu, "I am having great fun, and someday perhaps I will catch as many fish as you." The old woman only laughed, but tears of happiness stood in her eyes. In all the time since Kiluk had returned, she had never before shown pleasure in learning the ways of her own people.

When dusk came, Patik and Kiluk were the last to pull out their lines and walk up the bank. Everyone else was in Masu's tent, celebrating the day with laughter and stories. The two stood for a moment listening, then went to Sakiak's tent. Eskimos had lived for many generations in small family camps, and the elders understood the need to be alone. Sakiak would not return to his tent tonight, and Nauruk would even resist teasing through the thin canvas walls . . . at least until tomorrow.

Days melted together where the calendar had little relevance. Each was a bit shorter than the one before, as they descended toward the time when no sun would appear at all. And each was a bit colder. Life at Nunavik was filled with fishing—and more fishing. Kiluk awoke with the women each morning, sometimes even before them, and fished until dusk. With Masu's help, she cut caribou leg skins for a pair of warm fishing mittens, which she would try to sew herself.

Nauruk and Patik, and sometimes Sakiak, searched far for caribou but found none. Then a blizzard came and deep snow packed hard around the tents. The next day they found caribou tracks nearby, and that night they heard the clicking of hooves almost within the camp. When they awoke the following morning caribou were everywhere, scattered herds of a few hundred each, moving northward over the tundra plain. The fall migration had reached them at last, and the men began hunting immediately. They concealed themselves below the riverbank and shot only the best animals, the fat cows and young bulls, as they walked near the tents. When they had enough they stopped shooting and everybody helped to butcher the catch. Kiluk joined in the work, though she had never touched an animal's warm insides before.

The evening of the caribou, they heard distant shots from the east, and they knew that hunters were coming. After dusk, under a high full moon that made shadows on the drifts, Patik and Kiluk saw a dog team coming slowly over the nearest rise. Two more followed, and soon they heaved into camp. It was Sakiak's oldest son Kuvlu, together with Migalik

and Talimat, who were sons of Masu. Amid the joy and excitement of greeting. Migalik's dogs pulled over to the sacks
of fish and managed to tear one open. Migalik shooed them
off and laughingly warned that they would pull the fish
home on the sled, not in their bellies.

"Tomorrow I head back to Ulurunik, younger sister," he
called to Kiluk. "Perhaps you will ride on my sled and keep
me company. Your friends have missed you in the village."
Her heart jumped, and she saw Patik turn and walk to his
tent.

Everyone stayed awake very late that night, eating fresh
meat and fish, exchanging news, and telling stories. Finally,
as the moon descended along the sky's eastern edge, they
turned off the lanterns and slept. Only Kiluk remained
awake, thinking of the weeks past and agonizing toward a
decision. She had longed for the village; she was tired of
hard work and cold; and she was almost afraid, as a matter of
principle, to stay in the camp. Deep inside, she felt she was
losing her former self—but what was that to lose, she wondered? Perhaps a storm would come and she would have
more time to think.

Dawn light smoldered dimly along the far horizon, beneath the prodigious blackness of the sky. The dense quiet
was broken by a hollow boom, as the river ice cracked in the
pinch of deepening cold. Beyond the eastern bank, a resting
caribou twitched its ears at the sound, lifted its warm muzzle
to the breeze, and stared into the chasm of darkness.

Migalik's voice abruptly ended Kiluk's sleep, which seemed
to have just begun. "Come, sister, wake up and eat. I will load
my sled soon and start for Ulurunik. The sun is bright and
there is little wind; a fine day to travel." Migalik had a curious
gleam in his smile, as if he was teasing her, or perhaps
taunting her. "Go away," she whispered hoarsely, still only
half-awake. But a few minutes later she slowly crept out of
her sleeping bag.

Kiluk dressed in her warmest clothes and walked to the riverbank, where she could look across the river and the lift of tundra beyond. She saw a small herd of caribou in the distance, and another far upriver. The snow-covered ice was dotted with fishing holes and laced with a network of footprints. Brilliant sun reflected from the white land. It was so quiet, she thought, so peaceful, here in this Eskimo place far removed from all other worlds.

She turned abruptly and hurried toward the camp, then pulled open the flap of Sakiak's tent. Patik looked up at her and their eyes met for a long moment. "Hurry," Migalik said, "Talimat is already loading the sled and I . . . "

"I will stay!" she blurted, a huge smile brightening the beauty of her face. "*Aulagnaitchunga!*" She said it again, in Eskimo. this time, because it also explained her reasons. "I will stay until I have caught enough fish to feel satisfied, and until I have finished a pair of mittens, and until everyone else is leaving."

Migalik looked down at his soup, trying to hide his satisfied grin. Patik pretended to be busy with his boot ties. And old Sakiak just looked at her with a pleased light in his eyes.

Kiluk walked slowly away from the tent. An icy breeze hushed over the drifts and stung her cheeks. She turned away for a moment, but then she faced the wind and smiled. Suddenly she thought of herself in the boat a few weeks earlier, crying tears of anger at the cold and loneliness. Now the chill felt like a friend to her, and the breeze like a reassuring hand. The land that once seemed so empty had become rich with life and meaning. She was no longer a stranger here. She was an Eskimo.

Kiluk looked over at the tents and saw a young hunter coming toward her.

Nippivik Tatqiq

Moon of the Setting Sun
(NOVEMBER)

MAIN CHARACTERS

Sakiak (Sah-*kee*-uk) *an old hunter*

Patik (*Pah*-tik) *Sakiak's grandson*

Amiksuk (*Ah*-mik-sook) *an adult hunter*

Pukak (*Poo*-kuk) *Amiksuk's formal hunting partner*

PATIK . . . PATIK! *Azaah,* you sleep like a walrus." Patik slowly opened his eyes and stared at the tent wall inches from his face. "I thought you were a man, but you're still only a small boy. Come, drink your mother's milk." Hilarious laughter followed, and Patik rolled over to face his smiling tormentors. Still half-asleep, he could make out three men sitting along the other wall of the tent, all fully dressed and holding cups of steaming coffee.

There was Amiksuk, his cousin, speaking again of laziness and of young men who caught no animals because they only knew how to sleep. He was a pleasant man, always friendly and joking, highly regarded as a hunter and respected as a leader in the settlement. His face was long and heavy-boned, with small eyes, a crooked nose that looked as if it had been broken, and smooth ocher skin that made him appear younger than his forty-odd years.

Beside Amiksuk was his hunting partner, Pukak, who looked on with a twinkle of amusement. Pukak was older than Amiksuk, ruddy in complexion, with a pug nose and broad cheekbones. He was a quiet man who listened well and smiled often; but although he worked hard he was seldom very successful in the hunt. Patik could see large scabs on Pukak's chin and nose, marking spots where he had been frostbitten while traveling in a storm several weeks before.

Finally there was old Sakiak, Patik's grandfather. He was smiling too, but the serious look in his eyes meant it was past time for a young hunter to be awakening. Sakiak was a man of great knowledge, and when there was a decision to be made people waited to hear him speak, hiding their lesser wisdom behind silence. Seventy winters had made his skin leathery and wrinkled, but his eyes were alert and his mind quick. He was also a strong man, although rather slight in build, and people said that when he was young he had been the fastest runner along the entire coast from Tikerak to Utqeavik.

The old man looked thoughtfully at his grandson. Patik was quickly learning the arts of living and would soon have skill enough to hunt without constant advice from his elders. His expression reflected vitality and confidence but also the incompleteness of youth. He had a very round face, with narrow eyes, full cheeks, and light reddish-brown skin. Already he had grown taller and heavier than Sakiak, and everyone was sure that he would someday be an excellent hunter. It was perhaps because of this expectation that people often demanded more from him than someone his age was capable of.

Patik stretched his arms from the warm confines of his sleeping bag, his mind just now pulling together to realize where he was and what he was doing. They had set out yesterday from Ulurunik, four men with two dog teams traveling north along the coast in search of caribou. But they saw nothing except a few old tracks around Nunagayak and a snowy owl flying low over the tundra near the Sinyagaurak River.

With two men on each sled, plus heavy loads of supplies, their progress had been slow—six hours on the trail before they drew in sight of the low mounds that marked the abandoned houses of Atanik. Everyone had been tired, and they had quickly staked out the dogs, unloaded their sleds, and set up camp in one of the old huts. It was not a frame dwelling like those at Ulurunik, but a small semiunderground house with a steep sod-covered roof. Because it was old and let in the wind, a tent was set up inside, and within this double shelter the men slept.

"Come, drink some coffee quickly, then load the sleds," Sakiak said in a low voice. Then it was Amiksuk's turn to laugh again. "Ah, Patik, your dogs must be getting anxious to chase caribou. Perhaps today you will fly off the sled as you did last fall when we were hunting inland at Kikiktasuguruk." Everyone shook with laughter this time, except for Patik, who smiled in embarrassment as he filled his cup. He wished that episode would be forgotten, and he knew he would never be so foolish again. Ridicule was often leveled at young men like Patik, both for the endless entertainment it provided and for the very serious purpose of teaching apprentice hunters to avoid potentially fatal mistakes. Patik had walked for two days to reach Ulurunik; and his dogs had been found a week later, far out on the tundra, two of them dead from fighting.

After a few sips of coffee, Patik slipped on his parka and ducked out through the tent door. The sod house had a long, dark hallway, so low that he bent almost double to avoid hitting his head. Outside the sky was heavy, overcast and dull. The sun would rise soon, he thought, but this would be a short day. In about two weeks it would disappear for the last time, and for seventy days they would see nothing more than twilight. He stood remembering what his grandfather had told him, that it was now *Nippivik tatqiq*, "moon of the setting sun." Then he hastily began loading the sleds—two caribou skins on each, rifles lashed on top of the skins, canvas sled bags filled with miscellaneous equipment and hung from the upstanders.

Patik has just placed the grub box on Amiksuk's sled when he heard one of the dogs whimpering in a way that indicated nervous excitement. Then he saw that it was staring out toward the snow-covered beach and the frozen sea beyond, intermittently lifting its nose trying to catch a scent. He followed the dog's line of sight but could see nothing except motionless ice and a few distant ridges. When he had finished tying down the box, the dog was still watching, as were a few others. Curious now, Patik pulled a pair of binoculars from the sled bag, then carefully scanned the area just offshore. For several minutes he saw nothing, and he was about to conclude that the dogs had heard the distant barking of a fox. Then his eye caught movement near one of the closest ridges.

Patik was young, and it was small wonder that his heart suddenly pounded very hard. The movement was a white bear, standing on its hind legs and looking straight toward shore. *"Nanuq!"* he exclaimed out loud, and at the same moment he turned and ducked quickly into the hallway.

Within a few seconds three men emerged from the house; Amiksuk and Sakiak, parka-clad, looking intently, and Patik, pointing to where the animal had been. All the dogs were looking too, and several had started barking while the men were still inside. This was an unfortunate thing, because their noise had carried out over the ice and frightened the bear. Sakiak was sure he saw it cross a ridge and lope into a narrow flat, heading seaward.

Without a word, Amiksuk ran to his sled, pulled a line of harnesses out along the snow, and began hitching his dogs. Sakiak answered Patik's questioning eyes. "Quick, fetch the rifles and ammunition while I harness the team." Pukak, who was always a bit slow, finally appeared to help his busy companions. The dogs were becoming wild with excitement, leaping and pulling at their lines trying to jerk free and pursue the bear.

In the midst of this exuberance and frantic preparation, the old hunter Sakiak had thoughts of his own. The day was good and the bear nearby indeed, but what of the signs? He had an uncertain feeling about the wind and the dangers of sea ice when the weather came from the south.

Several days before, the *ungalaq,* this south wind, had begun to blow. It brought heavy clouds and snow, the temperature went up to near zero, and the rising tide lifted anchoring ice piles so they no longer rested on the sea floor. This meant that the ice several miles out from land might no longer be grounded, and if a strong offshore gale arose it could perhaps break loose and drift seaward with the pack. Then last night, ringing in his ears, the dogs howling—these were storm signs. But he would wait and speak only if the chase took them far from the land.

In a moment two sleds rushed down across the beach and onto the sea ice. Patik stood at the back of one, clinging to the upstanders, while his grandfather rode before him on the soft skins, pointing to indicate the correct course. On the other sled, Amiksuk stood behind and Pukak sat on the stout wooden food box. For nearly half a mile both teams ran headlong, side by side, the sleds bouncing high over hard drifts. Eskimos seldom traveled anywhere without making a race of it, and Patik could not help smiling as his team drew slightly ahead.

Very shortly they approached the first ridges. Then Sakiak spotted bear tracks just as the dogs picked up a scent. "Let's go!" Patik shouted when the dogs slowed to snuffle at fresh, deep prints on the crusted snow. Taking quick advantage, Amiksuk's team sped by and galloped along the bear's trail. Now the hunters braced themselves for rougher riding as they jostled through a field of piled ice and reached the first of countless ridges they would cross that day. The tracks led northwestward, angling away from the coast rather than straight out to sea. This was a bit strange, but perhaps the bear had not been badly frightened.

For the first few miles there were scattered flat stretches, but the farther they went the less frequent these stretches became. An hour passed, but they seemed to gain nothing on the bear. As everyone knew, *nanuq* was little faster than a dog team on level ice; but among rugged hummocks and ridges no animal could catch him.

Twice they saw the bear not far ahead, standing and looking back quizzically toward its pursuers, and the sightings renewed their enthusiasm to continue the hunt. So the chase went on. Ridge after ridge passed under the sleds, until the men and dogs were exhausted and more than a little discouraged. Finally, they had gone nearly six miles, and in their private thoughts all the hunters were sure they would never catch the bear.

Amiksuk stopped his dogs near a high ridge, which he and Pukak climbed to have a look ahead. By the time Patik and Sakiak caught up they were on their way down again and Amiksuk gave their report: "It is a young male, far away from us now, heading straight to sea. Perhaps we will never catch him."

Sakiak agreed and said they had gone far enough from the land. At the same time, he looked up and pointed to the clouds. "Possibly the weather will change. The clouds are moving faster, and from the southeast instead of the south as before. Surely the tide is high, and we do not know if the ice here is fast to the land or free to move if the wind blows or heavy pack ice collides with it. If we head straight back toward land we will reach the shore at Pingasuguruk." Old men were wise, and although Sakiak spoke as if these were only possibilities, the men knew that he was giving them a strong warning.

Pukak, who was often teased because he was a hungry man, said that they had traveled hard and should perhaps eat something before leaving. Sakiak felt they should waste no time, but he said nothing. So frozen chunks of raw caribou meat and slices of fat were taken from the grub box, and Amiksuk told Patik to pour hot tea from the thermos. Apprentice hunters were expected to serve their elders, perhaps to compensate for the burden created by their frequent mistakes. Sakiak laughingly congratulated Pukak for not forgetting to fill the thermos after the bear was sighted that morning. Surely Pukak was not a man to overlook his stomach, even when a bear was nearby inspecting their camp! And Patik, how did he become so sharp-eyed that he noticed the bear? Perhaps, Amiksuk suggested, it was because he slept so much that his eyes were always well rested.

In the midst of the laughter that followed, Sakiak stood up abruptly and pointed toward the southeast. *"Azaah,* look!" he exclaimed. Everyone stared intently for a moment, then without another word they prepared for a quick departure. Stretched out along the distant horizon was a glimmering orange-red cloud, like a bright sunset; but it was near midday and the sun was still high.

The red cloud warned that a southeasterly gale was rushing down across the land. It would blow powerfully offshore, pushing against ice lifted by the tide, almost certainly opening a lead somewhere near shore. If the hunters were caught out beyond the lead they would face an ordeal of survival, and perhaps eventual death somewhere on the expanse of pack ice that covered the entire Arctic Ocean. Even Patik knew that many who drifted away never returned, so their best chance now was to make a dash for the coast.

No storm descended more quickly than the southeaster, and before a mile was behind them Sakiak felt the first gusts of wind. *"Alyakaah!"* he shouted to his frightened grandson. "This is bad!" Whips cracked at the dogs' tails, but they were already tired from the long chase. The sleds took a terrible beating as they pounded up the sides of ridges, then slid and tumbled downward again, their riders holding on mightily to keep themselves aboard. Twice Patik stumbled and fell as he guided the twisting sled, but he grabbed the upstanders and was dragged along until he could regain his footing.

Sakiak thought of the bear now, ambling seaward in its element, nose high to sniff the growing breeze. For a man there was no greater danger than being caught on the pack in a howling storm, but what did it mean for a bear? A day of sleep in the lee of a hummock, perhaps, surely nothing more.

The wind rose steadily, and by the time they were two miles offshore it was blowing with gale force. Sakiak was now certain that unless something strange happened they would not make it. Because he was a religious man, he prayed for deliverance from the ice; but perhaps the Christian God could do little to help now. In the old days the shamans had been powerful enough to change wind and current by singing songs that compelled assistance from their familiar spirits. But the last shaman had died long ago, and now people seemed to have much less control over the world.

Whirlwinds of snow blew across the ice surface, and the temperature was falling. Sakiak pulled his parka hood forward to shield his face from the biting wind. Ridge after ridge loomed out of the storm to slow them, and there was no way to find easy trails with clouds of snow obscuring visibility beyond a few yards. Finally a high ridge opened onto level ice—perhaps a broad plain that would quickly bring them nearer the land.

But it was not to be. Squinting into the haze of blown snow, Sakiak saw what he had feared so deeply. The air and sky ahead were darkening, and minutes later they had become almost black. The old man knew immediately that this was the darkness of open water, reflected by clouds and flying snow.

Patik turned the dogs aside near the water's edge and stared out over a lead filled with whitecaps and drifting pans of ice. Waves slapped noisily against the straight-sheared edge of ice, but their sound was lost in the roar and hiss of wind. They were adrift on the pack, and the lead was so wide that almost certainly there remained no points of contact with the landfast ice. Nevertheless, Pukak said that a lead was always narrowest downwind, where the latest opening occurred. Perhaps they should make a dash north along the edge and search for a bridge of ice where they might escape. Sakiak said that it was too late to hope for such a thing and that traveling near the lead edge now would be asking for trouble.

Along the windward side of a lead, growing swells and drifting floes could easily crack or disintegrate even the heaviest ice. Inexperienced men who drifted away might think it wise to stay by the lead, where they could escape quickly when the pack moved landward again. But they were likely to find themselves trapped between cracks, with ice grinding and piling all around, and they would be lucky indeed if they survived. The old man said they should quickly head out again, onto the heavy pack, where there would be safe places to camp and await the storm's end. At the same time, however, they should travel toward the south to compensate for the pack's northward drift, which would carry them farther and farther from home

It was not easy getting the dogs started again. They had been pushed hard for more than three hours through the most difficult terrain imaginable, and they clearly felt it was time for a long rest. But when the men shouted with strength in their voices, the tired animals obediently rose to their feet and shook snow from their fur. At least it was colder now, and they would suffer less from overheating. In fact, the temperature was nearly twenty below, and with a gale blowing it was very cold indeed. The men were preoccupied with other thoughts, however, as they urged the dogs to a trot and swung off toward the southwest, disappearing into a swirling void of snow.

They had not gone far at all when they were startled by a black line slicing the ice just ahead. "Open crack!" Amiksuk shouted. It was nearly six feet wide and they could see that it was growing by the minute. Sakiak pointed urgently northward along the crack, where it seemed narrower, and they whipped the dogs to a full gallop. A few minutes later they found a narrow spot, bridged by a wide pan of ice that was turning and grinding between the severed floes. Sakiak jumped off the sled and tied a long rope to the lead dog's neck; then he ran ahead onto the crushing ice cake, moving with the agility of a boy. Dogs feared nothing more than piling ice, so once across he used the rope to pull the terror-stricken animals over, Patik guidng the sled and shouting encouragement from behind.

Pukak and Amiksuk followed immediately, urging their

team ahead onto the tilting, rocking bridge of ice. Amiksuk
pushed from behind, and as he finally heaved the sled onto
solid ice deep groaning and creaking filled the air. He felt
himself being pushed upward as the ice beneath him bent,
then suddenly split. He jumped and barely managed to grab
the sled. Behind him, pieces of the broken pan drifted
slowly apart.

There was only one more crack, and it was narrow enough
to jump across. From then on the weary travelers encountered no further difficulties. When they were several miles
out from the lead they took a brief rest and discussed their
plans. Everyone was aching with exhaustion, and both
Amiksuk and Patik had painfully bruised legs from falls in
rough ice. But no word of complaint was uttered. Even
young Patik had known his share of discomfort and had
learned that an Eskimo does not bemoan such trivial matters.

They waited for Sakiak's advice. "It seems that we have
gone far enough," he spoke slowly, looking to Amiksuk for
agreement. "Now we might head more toward the south,
traveling parallel to the coast to stay as near as possible to
Atanik. We will drift north all night and will surely move a
considerable distance unless the wind or current changes."
Amiksuk nodded. "This is surely true. There is not much
time before darkness will begin, with thick clouds and blowing snow obscuring the sky. It would be good to find solid ice
very soon and set up camp."

They moved slowly southward, traveling almost into the
wind. The dogs were exhausted, and little could be gained by
pushing them now. They would be needed again, after all,
and there was nothing to feed them. So Amiksuk, who was in
the lead, stopped near the edge of a small flat to wait for the
other team. When they arrived he pointed to a hulking ridge
nearby. It was tall and broad, made up of enormous ice slabs
set at all angles, and numerous smaller hummocks surrounded it. Deep, hard drifts along its flanks and in its

chasms showed that it had formed months before. "*Eee,* it will be good," Sakiak shouted over the wind, affirming Amiksuk's choice of a place to make camp.

Many generations past, Eskimos had learned that the safest places to camp on the sea ice were the largest and heaviest ridges. Here was the thickest ice in the ocean, measuring twenty to forty feet above the surface, and extending one could only guess how deep into the water below. The geometric boulders making up ridges were frozen into a solid, unified mass. Certainly the awesome power of the drifting pack could fracture any ice, no matter how thick, but these heavy ridges were rarely broken or crushed.

Amiksuk once heard a story of two white men whose airplane had crashed far out on the sea ice. They had made their camp in the middle of a huge flat, where the smooth ice was no more than ten feet thick. During the night a crack had opened right beneath their tent and one of them had slipped to his death in the frigid water. Incidents like this certainly showed the *Taniks* to be a foolish sort and made the Eskimos wonder why these inept outsiders always considered themselves so clever.

It was only a hundred yards to the high ridge, but through very rough ice indeed, so two of the men walked ahead while the others drove the dogs along behind. At the base of the ridge, Patik and Amiksuk anchored their teams by setting the iron sled hooks into narrow cracks. The teams were put well apart from each other to prevent fighting, and the dogs were simply left in harness. Meanwhile, Sakiak and Pukak found a deep, hard drift in a swale between two peaks of the ridge, where there was ample room to build a snowhouse. In the deepening gloom of evening, their bent figures only half-visible through veils of blown snow, they set to work on a shelter.

Using large steel-bladed knives, they cut rectangles into the drift's surface and lifted out long, clean blocks of snow.

These were set on end around the hole they were taken from, making a wall several feet high surrounding a depression about six feet square. Then more snow blocks were set atop the walls and leaned sharply inward to meet in the middle, forming a gabled roof. At one end they made a snowblock hallway, also sunken into the surface, with a tiny entrance that they closed by hanging a piece of canvas over it. Loose snow was pushed into cracks and holes between the snow blocks, making a snug, windproof shelter. Ulurunik people knew from old stories that Eskimos living far to the east used dome-shaped snow houses, but their own were always built in a square or rectangular shape.

While Sakiak and Pukak finished the snowhouse, Amiksuk and Patik brought everything from the sleds. There were four caribou skins that covered nearly all of the floor, the grub box and sled bags, rifles, and a large piece of heavy canvas. They were lucky for what they had, but Pukak wished out loud that he had not forgotten the portable gasoline stove in his haste to leave that morning. And there was very little food indeed—a few chunks of caribou meat, three frozen fish, a can of rancid seal oil, a small cloth sack of biscuits, some sugar, and a box of tea.

Although these men were in a very deep trouble, adrift and lost on the Arctic pack with a terrific gale blowing, they felt strangely relaxed and secure inside their small shelter. They sat along the walls, two on each side, nearly overcome with exhaustion. Amiksuk's low voice came out of the near-complete darkness. "Let's smoke." He passed his cigarettes around and offered a light. Each man's face was illuminated in turn by the match flame, and then nothing could be seen again except little glowing embers moving about surrealistically in the blackness. They were too tired to talk, and so they listened to the muffled sounds of wind rushing through the piled ice and swirling around their shelter, each occupied with his own thoughts.

Patik finally decided to lie down, but his grandfather stopped him. "The space is small and it is best to sleep sitting as we are now. Men who lie down when they drift away bring bad luck onto themselves." So he sat up again, and before anyone else spoke he had dozed off.

Amiksuk said that no one in Ulurunik would miss them for many days, since they had expected to stay away for a week or more. Sakiak agreed but said that perhaps somebody would pass by Atanik and find that much of their gear and food was inside the sod house. Old tracks on the snow would show that they had not just left that day; and the storm, an offshore lead. . . . They would put the pieces together. It might not happen for days, perhaps weeks, but at least the people could surmise how they were lost.

Just then they felt the ice shiver beneath them, faintly at first and then growing like an earthquake, until they were shaken quite strongly. Patik jerked awake, and with fear in his voice asked what was happening. "*Ivaluktaqtoq,*" his grandfather answered calmly. "It is the ice piling." Somewhere nearby a floe was rent apart and began crushing upward into a new ridge, perhaps like the one they were on now. Sakiak could imagine huge fragments lifted in a churning mass, slabs and boulders sliding down its sides, the surface nearby buckling downward and water flowing out over it. He had seen it many times in daylight, but in the darkness it was a frightening thought. Then the quaking slowly faded.

The four men lined up along one wall and squeezed close together to share their warmth, canvas pulled over them and warm caribou skins underneath. All were dressed as in the day—caribou-skin boots with tough sealskin soles, heavy insulated cloth pants, caribou-skin parkas with cloth jackets and shirts underneath. They loosened their boot strings, pulled their arms in from their parka sleeves, and plugged the openings with their mittens. Then one by one they lapsed into fitful sleep. Sakiak was awake longest, and before he slept he silently prayed for their safety, mumbling a soft "amen" when he finished.

No one slept through the night without interruption, because the chill gradually crept into their clothing and the wind spawned dreams that made them awaken with a jerk. So it seemed a long time before the first hint of luminescence filtered in through the snow blocks. Pukak awoke thirsty, so he found a large empty can in the grub box and filled it with granular "sugar snow" dug from the lower wall of the shelter. This kind of snow, found near the bottom of drifts, contained far more water than an equal volume of powdery surface snow. He held the can inside his parka where body heat would slowly melt the snow into water. Eskimos had learned not to eat snow, because doing so would only make them thirstier. In the old days men like Pukak's grandfather would carry a small water pouch made from the skin of a seal's flipper that they filled with snow and hung underneath their parkas. After taking a drink they always stuffed a little snow inside to replace what had been used.

A short time later Sakiak awakened, drank a share of Pukak's water, then crouched out through the low hallway. Wind pushed heavily against him when he stood up outside, and his eyes watered from the brightness and cold. He saw that the sky was thinly overcast, clouds racing along from the southeast. No snow was falling, but a thick haze of swirling drift limited visibility to a few yards near the ground. The temperature had not changed. Sakiak quickly relieved himself, walked down the ridge's slope to check the dogs, then headed back to the shelter.

Inside, he shook snow from the ruff of his parka. "The wind is still powerful?" Pukak asked. "It is indeed, extremely!" the old man exclaimed. He added that unless the storm abated it would be too dangerous for travel today, because they might encounter much cracked and piling ice. But they must have drifted very far north, and if the wind continued they would have to move southward regardless of weather. Otherwise they might drift beyond the northwestern tip of the continent, which was less than a hundred miles up the coast from Atanik. If this happened they would never reach land again.

By midmorning the four men were ravenous, so they decided to eat a bit of their food. They divided the last of the caribou meat among them, dipping each piece in seal oil before eating it. The strong-smelling oil was delicious, and like any kind of fat it would generate body heat. Sakiak also thought of making a small lamp to burn seal oil in, but he remembered the old-timers' advice that oil makes more heat in a man's stomach than in a lamp. Eskimos did not like to drink seal oil, so each man ate a biscuit thoroughly soaked in it. Amiksuk said that though they had little food there were twenty dogs outside, all of them fat, and after the dogs were gone they could eat caribou skins and sealskin lines. They could get along for many days on this, and, of course, there were seals and polar bears to be hunted.

The day wore on. Several times old Sakiak broke the silence with tales about others who had drifted away on the ice, most of whom were never seen again. The monotonous periods between stories were occasionally interrupted by slight quakes running through the ice beneath them. Except for these signs of fracturing or piling ice, there was no feeling of motion whatever—nothing to keep them conscious that they were adrift on the Arctic Ocean. The great pack was so enormous, far beyond a man's comprehension, that it was difficult to imagine that any earthly force could be powerful enough to move it.

In late afternoon, just when the snowhouse was beginning to darken again, the dogs set up a chorus of howls. Sakiak listened and thought. Dogs rarely howled during a storm unless it was going to end soon. And the wind, had it not increased in the past hours as it often did before diminishing? "Perhaps I will have a look outside," he said quietly. Clouds of blowing snow obscured all but the nearest terrain as the old man emerged from the shelter. He held out the dark palm of his mitten and looked at it closely, then smiled and spoke aloud. "Ah, this is good indeed." On the mitten's surface he saw not only the grainy particles of snow that blew up from the ground but also tiny geometrical snowflakes that fell from the sky. It was snowing, a sure sign of the storm's end.

By the middle of the night the wind had dropped to half its original strength. Amiksuk and Patik went outside their shelter and looked into a clear sky. The stars, brilliant and unwavering, added to their conviction that the storm was over. A phosphorescent auroral band swung across the entire sky, from horizon to horizon, bending and swirling like a torn storm cloud. For a few moments it became five parallel curtains of luminescence, flaring bright green and silver white, with oscillating pulses of light shooting through it from one end to the other. Then it expanded, throwing off sprays of radiance that faded upward into the consuming blackness of sky.

It was difficult to believe that such wild impulses of energy were silent, yet nothing could be heard. Patik remembered how he and his playmates used to run inside the houses to hide from *kikuyat,* the aurora, when it looked as if it would descend to earth and pierce them.

Next morning the men were awake, shivering, before any hint of twilight. Amiksuk was first outside, and he reported clear, cold weather with a breeze from the northeast. One of the dogs had chewed through its line and was running loose among the others, but luckily it was a young female so there had been no fights. Sakiak said that this wind, which blew off the land, would surely prevent the lead from closing unless

there was a strong onshore current. But they were probably
drifting back southward now, which was very fortunate indeed. It would be a good day to travel toward the south and to
hunt for seals, if they could find a breathing hole or a large
open crack. Yes, they were lucky, but they must have meat
quickly for themselves and the dogs. "We can be ready to
travel at dawn," Amiksuk said, "and running with the sleds
will quickly warm us."

It was minus thirty outside, and near zero in the black
interior of the shelter. Sakiak pulled a large jar cover from
the grub box, and by matchlight he poured a thin layer of
seal oil into it. Then he tore a strip of flannel from his shirt
and laid it in the oil, one end turned up along the lip of the
cover. When it was thoroughly saturated he lighted the
cloth's exposed edge, and a very soft orange flame gradually
spread along it. The wick was only a few inches wide, so its
fire seemed insignificant measured against the dense cold
and darkness of the shelter. But for Sakiak and the others it
was a dilating heart of warmth. Patik patiently held the water
can over it, and before long they were drinking heavily sug-
ared black tea. They divided two frozen fish, and each man
ate a biscuit soaked in oil. It was very little to face a hard day
with, but they were thankful and in good spirits.

The southern horizon was pale blue with morning's first
light when the four Eskimos filed from their snowhouse.
Cold nipped hard at them for the first few minutes, but they
quickly grew accustomed to it as they straightened dog harnesses and loaded the sleds. Some of the dogs were completely covered by drifted snow, which had created little
pockets of warmth that they were reluctant to leave. They
were also hungry and stiff and lacked the excited energy of
two mornings past. But a few minutes later they were all in
harness, and when their masters shouted, *"Kya!* Let's go!
they pulled away toward the sun's point of rising.

Snow had drifted everywhere in the rough ice, smoothing
its surface and making travel easier than before. The

Eskimos let the dogs set their own pace to avoid tiring them, and by sunrise they had gone several miles from their abandoned snowhouse. It was a crystal day. A billion diamond snowflakes reflected the sun's amber; long, hard shadows stretched out in the lee of hummocks; and toward the land a cloud of black-gray fog hung over the steaming lead that imprisoned them on the ice.

They saw several breathing holes that morning, but all were covered with ice inside, showing that no seals had visited them for some time. Perhaps they were using holes beneath the piled ice or had moved to open water. There were also many fresh cracks along the way, but all were narrow and already covered with solid ice. Sakiak warned everyone to watch his step, though, because some cracks might be concealed beneath newly drifted snow that insulated them and prevented formation of safe ice. A man could easily fall through such cracks and soak himself, a very dangerous prospect in the intense cold.

About midday Amiksuk, who was traveling well ahead, saw that they were approaching a wide crack. A haze of steam rose from its surface, so he knew it was not covered with the thin black ice that looked deceptively like water from a distance. "The rifles," he said to Pukak, who was already loosening the ropes that held them.

Patik and Sakiak, coming along well behind, saw the team stop beside a thick dark line drawn across the ice. Moments later they saw the figures of their two companions move quickly from the sled and shrink to half-size against the surface, then heard three muffled thuds that set the dogs running toward what could only be the sound of gunshots.

When they came near they saw Amiksuk standing beside the crack, smiling with ostentatious pride. It was immediately clear, even before they noticed the carcass floating near the crack's far edge, that Amiksuk had killed a seal. Sakiak tailored his congratulations to the magnitude of Amiksuk's present self-esteem. In the meantime, Pukak had crossed a nar-

row spot in the crack and was waiting for the seal to drift
close enough so he could snag it with the sharp hook on one
end of his *unaaq*. "There were two," Amiksuk puffed, "but
Pukak missed the other. Too bad—it was very close."

Just then they heard Pukak moan loudly, "*Alyakaah!*"
drawing out the word for emphasis. "This is bad indeed!"
Their smiles instantly faded when they looked up, just in
time to see the carcass vanish beneath the rippling surface.
Shot seals rarely sank during midwinter, when they were
usually fat and buoyant, but now it happened right before
their eyes. Pukak lay prone on the ice, staring down into the
water, hoping it might sink only a few feet and drift under
him where he could hook it. He had seen this happen before,
but now there was nothing except the blackness of water.
Their seal was lost.

Sakiak could not help laughing a bit to think that Amiksuk
and Pukak, both grown hunters, had lost a chance for two
seals in a crack just a few yards wide. It was a joke indeed, just
when he was about to eat fresh seal fat and rich dark meat,
and now he would have to settle for a frozen biscuit instead!
"Perhaps there will be more seals in this crack," he added,
"and next time you might wait and let a nearsighted old man
shoot." They all knew that no one could shoot better than
Sakiak, even though he used an old rifle that looked worth-
less. So they stayed near the crack, hoping another seal
would appear.

But hours passed and the water was empty. A heavy mist
rose from its surface and wind ripples disappeared as the
sun fell gradually lower. Amiksuk's eyebrows, lashes, and
scraggly moustache were coated with a thick rime of frost,
and like the others he kept moving constantly to generate
warmth. He was a tall man, heavy-boned and extremely
powerful, his erect stature a visible expression of his pride
and confidence. But now he was shivering and clearly a bit
miserable, wanting desperately to see the dark shape of a seal
that would come to feed them. He warmed the stiff, numb

flesh of his cheeks with a bare hand as he walked to where
Sakiak stood.

"I thought we would shoot a seal at sunset, when they like
to come up in open water; but it is growing late. We should
find a camping spot before darkness sets in." Sakiak agreed
and pointed off toward a ridge that loomed above its surroundings. "Heavy ice is not far away. If we stay nearby we
can come to this crack again in the morning. Unless ice covers it tonight, it will be a good place to hunt at dawn." They
stayed a few minutes longer, still hoping a seal might appear,
then finally went to their sleds and hurried off to make camp.

When they were about halfway to the ridge, Sakiak abruptly
signaled Patik to stop the dogs. He jumped from the sled
and shuffled quickly to a spot some distance away, then
leaned over for several minutes peering at the surface. When
he returned he said nothing, and Patik did not bother him
with questions. Later, as they cut snow blocks for their night's
shelter, Sakiak told the others about a breathing hole he had
found, a large one probably made by an *uguruk*. There was
open water inside, showing that it was being used, and he
might walk to it before light tomorrow.

When the snowhouse was finished and the gear put inside,
the old man made a lamp again, using just enough oil to last a
short while. They divided the one remaining fish, and each
ate half a biscuit made soggy with seal oil. "Almost no food is
left, and the dogs will not pull much longer unless they have
meat," Amiksuk said. "If we have no luck tomorrow I will kill
one dog to feed the others." Sakiak knew he would have to
do the same, and he wondered which one to choose. Perhaps
the small brown male, Mamik, that always seemed to tire
before the others. He stared pensively into the lamp's yellow
light, soft shadows flickering across the deep lines of his face.

Somewhat later the old man began telling stories of the
strange animals that lived where men rarely saw them. There
was the giant shrew, called *uguruganakpak*, and the man-
eating creature of Teshekpak Lake; but perhaps the most

dangerous was *kukuiak,* the ten-legged polar bear. Sakiak leaned back against the snowhouse wall and talked softly, as if to himself: "*Kukuiak* has five pairs of legs, starting right behind its neck, and it is so huge that a man can sit cross-legged in the imprint of its foot. It lives far out on the pack, hunting seals underwater and breathing at large holes it opens through the ice. *Kukuiak's* breathing holes are easily identified because there are seal lungs floating in them. This is all that remains after it has eaten." Pukak nodded agreement, recalling the same story as he had heard it told by his father.

"One day many years ago, a man named Kusiirak was hunting on the ice south of Ulurunik, and he came upon a large open hole with lungs floating in it. He knew immediately that the ten-legged bear must be somewhere nearby, and the thought terrified him. But then he remembered his family at home, hungry for want of meat, and so he decided to wait beside the hole. Before long the animal's enormous head surfaced, and with his spear Kusiirak stabbed it in both eyes, blinding it. The enraged monster leaped out onto the ice and chased him, following his scent.

"Kusiirak remembered a strange formation he had noticed earlier—two huge slabs of ice leaning sharply together like a steep roof, with an open space underneath that was wide at one end and narrowed to a small passage at the other. He went quickly to it and ran through the space; and when the pursuing bear followed it became wedged tightly inside. Kusiirak knew that strange animals like this were practically invulnerable to man's puny weapons, because their heavy ribs overlapped to form an armor that could not be penetrated. This meant that the bear could be killed only by harpooning it in the anus, and so Kusiirak came back around and managed to spear it from behind until finally it was dead. People came from the village and hauled its meat to their homes. The animal fed them for so long that it seemed almost as if someone had killed a whale."

By the time Sakiak finished, the lamp had gone out and everyone was silent. Pukak thought of his wife, a small woman with a full, round face that nearly always wore a smile, and his four children, the eldest a young boy who was still many years from becoming a provider. Amiksuk, too, had a wife, and one could scarcely remember how many children. Small wonder that his wife was so often tired and serious, for she worked harder at home than he did at hunting, though he was one of Ulurunik's most ambitious men.

The next day was much like the one before—clear and cold, with a breeze from the northeast, a heavy fog along the eastern horizon showing that the lead was unchanged. Sakiak waited beside the *uguruk* breathing hole before the first dawn light and remained until the sun began lowering. Patik walked slowly in a great circle around him, trying to drive the seal from its other holes. But no animal appeared, and finally the old man gave up, shivering so hard he could barely speak.

Amiksuk and Pukak checked yesterday's open crack and found it covered with ice, so they traveled around the area looking for other places to hunt. They found two breathing holes, but both were frozen inside, and they saw a polar bear track that was too old to be worth following. Amiksuk had also carefully checked the lead with binoculars from atop a tall hummock. But he saw only a broad apron of young ice extending outward from its edge and a solid wall of fog rising from the water beyond.

That evening they all returned to the snowhouse. In the gloom of dusk, Pukak walked to the dogs, picked one from each team, and led them out of sight behind the ridge. Two shots rang out in quick succession, echoing in the calm of sunset.

He skinned both carcasses and saved the hides to be used for repairing worn boots or torn clothing. Nearly all of the meat went to the remaining dogs, except for two that only sniffed and nuzzled it, then refused to eat. The men, who were ravenous, boiled dog meat over the seal-oil lamp and ate it with the last two biscuits. Amiksuk and Pukak had found *piqaluyiq* ice that day, old sea ice that had lost its saltiness in the previous summer's thaw. They brought several chunks of the clear, blue-black ice to camp and melted them for drinking water and tea. After eating the men talked for a while, doused the lamp, and sat listening to the silence that surrounded them.

Patik drifted quickly to sleep but woke up a short time later and stared blindly into the dark. He could hear his grandfather's voice softly singing, a melancholy *"Ya aiya ai, Ya aiya ayanga ai...."* It was not one of the familiar songs he had often heard at village dances, and so he knew it must be a private one. Perhaps the old man had learned it from a shaman many years ago. He wondered if the song had power and if Sakiak might be trying to change the wind or current so they could return to the land. Patik closed his eyes and held his chilled arms against his belly. The singing gradually became faint and slipped into the dream side of his mind.

Everyone slept fairly well that night, perhaps because they were growing accustomed to the cramped sitting position and the constant cold. But toward morning Amiksuk awoke suddenly, feeling strange. He listened intently but heard nothing except the breathing of his companions. Perhaps, he thought, it was the motion of the pack that his body sensed but his mind could not detect.

Then he heard a dog bark, and others quickly joined in. Amiksuk knew from the sound that something must be prowling nearby—a loose dog, a fox, a bear perhaps. He shook Pukak awake, grabbed one of the rifles they kept inside the snowhouse, and ducked into the hallway. The dogs were barking wildly when he stepped outside and peered into the darkness. Finally their dim outlines became visible, all of them sitting or standing alert, looking toward the black line of fog that marked the lead. If a dog was loose he would see it scurrying near the others, but every animal was in its place. Something was out there, invisible to the human eye but obvious to the keener senses of dogs. Pukak now joined him, and the two men could only stand quietly hoping it was not a hungry bear that might charge in among the dogs or burst into their shelter. They were concerned, uncertain, even a bit afraid.

In a short while the dogs were silent again, but the men stayed there more than an hour before going back inside. Both remained awake, however, and when the first glow of dawn rose into the sky they went out to check for tracks. There, just fifty yards beyond the dogs, Pukak found the tracks of a full-grown polar bear sharply outlined on the snow. The footprints showed that it had come straight from the north and was apparently very close before even noticing the camp. It stood for a moment on its hind legs to get a better look and then ran away toward the lead, probably startled by the dogs. A bear! Pukak thought, meat and fat to last them a week plus a thick hide to sleep under. Unfortunate, indeed, that there had been no light; even a full moon would have been enough to make a kill.

As they walked back to the snowhouse, Amiksuk noticed a few high streaks of cloud toward the north, feathery wisps stretching up into the sky above. The horizon was faintly hazy too, and he wondered if the weather was changing. Those long clouds could mean a storm from the northeast, which would open a wide lead and push them far southward, or from the north, which might force the pack toward land. When he told Sakiak, the old man said they should go to the lead edge and look for seals. If a good change of wind happened to occur, they would be in the right place to make a dash for the landfast ice.

The dogs were excited when they loaded the sleds, perhaps remembering the bear and wishing to chase it. All four men checked the tracks again and discussed what they could read in them. Probably a female, Sakiak asserted, nine or ten feet long from nose to tail, judging by the size of its paws. Since it had run off toward the lead it would be just as well to follow the tracks and see where the animal went. Perhaps it slept or hunted seals somewhere ahead; if so, they might catch it.

Both teams had regained some of their strength and enthusiasm, setting off at a quick trot and sniffing at the tracks as they went. Patik watched the sun's brilliant glow spread gradually along the horizon, first a broad arch, then an oval, and finally a rounded dome. Long shadows stretched across the snow as it lifted itself above the earth's edge.

There was much rough ice to traverse, and for a while it seemed as if the fog-shrouded lead was moving away at a speed to match their own. In the midst of one particularly bad area the bear's trail cut back toward the northwest, along a line of heavy ridges. Amiksuk traced it with his binoculars but saw no sign of the animal; so the men decided there was no point in following it away from their intended line of travel.

Finally they bounced through the last rough stretch, crossed a narrow flat, and moved out onto new ice formed since the lead's opening. The young ice was perfectly smooth, creamy gray, and covered everywhere with flowery crystals of frost. A hundred yards farther out the newly formed ice became thinner and dark colored. Beyond its edge was the open water, hidden from sight in the impenetrable screen of fog. They tried to get near the water for seal hunting, but the unsafe ice kept them well back from the edge.

So they turned south, traveling on the thicker young ice, looking for a good place to hunt. They had eaten the last bits of cold dog meat that morning, and although it dulled their pangs of hunger they all felt weak and malnourished. The lead edge was remarkably straight, trending toward the southwest, and for well over an hour they faced the dazzle of the low sun. Sakiak said he feared that they would find no places where solid ice extended right to the water, and this would prevent them from hunting unless they went off looking for breathing holes.

But luck was with them. About a mile farther on the apron of young ice became very narrow and was safe clear to the water's edge. Sakiak stood looking for a moment, then commented to the others, "It has grown nearly calm, hardly a ripple on the water. And heavier clouds are moving in from the north. The weather is surely changing." Amiksuk added that it felt warmer as well, then turned and spoke to Patik. "Cousin, bring me a small piece of white sealskin from your sled bag so I can check the current."

When Patik returned they all watched as Amiksuk chewed the bit of skin and dropped it into the water. It sank vertically at first, turning yellow, then amber as the darkness surrounded it. Several feet below the surface it began drifting parallel to the lead edge and somewhat away from it, until finally it was lost from sight. Sakiak's eyes were wide with excitement. "A north current! This is very good indeed."

Comparing their direction of drift with the position of the sun, Sakiak knew that they were moving at a slight angle toward the land, mostly parallel to it but somewhat onshore. Since the ice they were on was moving in the same direction as the current, he could not estimate its speed; perhaps they were moving slowly, perhaps quite fast. There was also no way to guess how wide the lead might be—a mile, five miles, possibly just a hundred yards. Landfast ice was somewhere out beyond the fog, and that was all anyone could know.

"If we hunt here," Sakiak said, "we may catch a seal and feed ourselves. But if we go on and find a point, where the pack would touch landfast ice first, then we might find a way to make our escape. The value of a seal is quite small compared with the importance of returning to land, and with a landward current . . . I fear starvation much less than I fear remaining out here on the pack." So they went immediately to their sleds and were off again.

Not a minute afterward, perhaps attracted by the water-borne sound of runners sliding across ice, a seal broke the surface near where the men had stood. It rose chest-high in the water, curious and alert, watching the strange objects grow small in the distance. Finally it looked away, bobbed slightly as it drew breath, and slipped back into the familiar world below.

It took several hours before the men finally found what they were looking for, a long point of heavy ice thrusting far out into the lead. A slight wind had arisen from the north, and Sakiak was sure it would build to a storm by tomorrow. If they did not escape before then they would be forced out onto the pack again to wait, because a north wind did not always close the lead. They could not gamble on staying by the edge overnight to see what would happen, lest they find themselves caught in fracturing ice with no chance to reach safety. But for now they would move partway out onto the point and wait along its south side, watching and listening for signs of contact between the drifting pack and the immobile ice that gave passage to the land.

They found a good place with a narrow apron of safe young ice where they could hunt. Everyone sat quietly on the sleds, their senses carefully attuned to any sign of change. By late afternoon wind ripples chased over the water as the northerly breeze increased. They saw one seal, but it surfaced far out of range, remaining low in the water and vanishing again in a few seconds. No one shot at it, since the carcass would only drift away from them because of the current and wind.

Evening slowly drew itself across the sky, starting in the northeast and following the sun's westward descent. Very shortly they would be forced to hurry back onto the pack and await the uncertainties of tomorrow. A storm was coming, and tonight two more dogs would be killed. Everyone was quiet and troubled, thinking of the many possibilities that stood ahead. Finally Sakiak and Patik walked over to speak with the others. "It grows dark," the old man said. "We should move quickly and find a spot to camp."

Amiksuk's reply was cut short by Patik's high-pitched exclamation. "Wait! I hear something." Boys were taught never to speak without certainty to back them up, and so the others stood still, listening. A minute later they all heard it, a very faint intermittent squeaking and crumbling sound. "Young ice piling," Sakiak declared, gesturing toward the end of the point. "The pack is meeting landfast ice not far off." No one wasted time on thought or discussion, and before the dogs could stretch they were whipped to a run.

The point seemed longer than anyone had anticipated, and three times they stopped to strain into the wind, listening again for the sounds. Each time they heard nothing, and on the third stop Sakiak wondered out loud if they might have been mistaken. No, Patik was sure; so on they went.

The fourth time, they all heard it, loud and close by, hidden somewhere in the fog.

A hundred yards farther on Pukak gestured toward his right, shaking his arm up and down for emphasis. "There it is!" he shouted. "Landfast ice." Looming up in the obscuring steam and near darkness was a sheer wall of ridged ice. It was the end of a broad point that projected out into the lead, a seaward extension of the immobile ice that was anchored to the ocean floor and the land. The two points, one stationary and the other mobile, were long enough to overlap, and as the pack drifted inexorably southward they converged. The aprons of thick young ice that extended from both of them were already piling and crumbling where they met. But this was a miniscule portent of what was about to occur.

Forty yards separated the two enormous mountains of piled ice, and in a few minutes they would meet in what could only be a thundering collision. The men would have to move swiftly to cross the bridge of young ice and rush to safety before it happened. Sakiak and Pukak fastened ropes to the lead dogs' necks and pulled them ahead into the grinding morass. A low hummock halfway across was alive with motion, and both men fell repeatedly climbing it. Finally they pulled the frantic dogs over behind them.

Just thirty yards now between the two walls of ice, the one ahead standing a precipitous fifteen feet high. Pukak clambered up first, and Sakiak followed. Struggling and pulling in the darkness, they hauled the first team up the side, dogs yelping with pain as they slipped and stumbled in hidden cracks. Now Patik joined to help with the rope as they jerked Amiksuk's team bit by bit to the top, In the frenzy, one dog slipped its harness and ran off, disappearing on the pack. Finally Amiksuk scrambled up behind, with less than ten yards between the closing masses of ice.

The four men held onto the sleds with all their might as they careened down the opposite side of the ridge behind the fleeing dogs. Just seconds later they heard a low rumble behind them, then felt the ice lurch and shake. The place where they had crossed to safety was now a pulverizing mass of ice boulders, and had they arrived there a minute later they would have been forced to run for their lives in the opposite direction.

As always, a thin line was drawn between success and failure, comfort and agony, life and death.

They moved away swiftly, punishing the dogs to make them run, putting as much distance as they could between themselves and the lead. Sakiak warned that they must not stop for at least a mile, so that they could be certain the impact had not opened any new cracks between themselves and the land.

Finally he signaled, and they pulled up for a brief rest. Excited words recounted every detail of their escape, putting together the end of a story each man would tell repeatedly for the rest of his life. They laughed now at their fear, perhaps to assure themselves that the need for fear had passed.

Before the men set out again they clustered together around one of the sleds. Sakiak pulled back his parka hood and prayed fervently in monotone Eskimo, giving thanks for their safety and asking for a quick passage home. When he finished everyone repeated his "amen," and they stood quietly for a moment more.

They had nothing to eat or drink to refresh themselves, so they wasted no further time. Following the guidepoints of stars and wind-oriented snowdrifts, they set a southeastward course that could not miss the land. About two hours later, exhausted nearly to the edge of endurance, they chanced upon an insignificant streak of black etched across the snow. "It is sand," the smiling old man exulted, "and I see Nunagayak."

A new moon had risen behind them, its tilted crescent faintly illuminating the low cliff and a few ancient house mounds set at its edge. Near one of the mounds three huge whale jawbones thrust starkly upward toward the sky, their bold curves converging in an open arch. Once, in a time beyond memory, they had probably supported a burial platform; but now they served only as a lonesome landmark for hunters and travelers.

Patik watched them become small as the teams swung away southward, following the familiar coastline toward Ulurunik. Patik, who had chased a bear for the first time in his life, drifted away on the Arctic pack, endured the trial of survival without panic or complaint, and sensed the faint sound that led them all to safety. Patik, the young one, who had suddenly become a man.

Siqinrilyaq Tatqiq

The Moon with No Sun

(DECEMBER)

MAIN CHARACTER

Sakiak (Sah-*kee*-uk) *an old hunter*

D AWN LIGHT STREAKED THE SKY in shades of purple and amber. Beneath it, ice ridges stood tall and silent, their oblique faces reflecting the sky's hue. Diamond-hard cold penetrated the air. A light breeze, stirring intermittently from the west, blew glittering snowflakes over the frozen surface and around the sides of a large hummock.

Near the base of the hummock was a small hollow, protected by upturned slabs of ice. There were thousands of similar hollows in the surrounding fields of piled ice, but this one was different—it was occupied. Snowflakes blown from the hummock's crest sifted down onto a mound of thick white fur. Disturbed by the breeze, the mound shifted slightly, and a large, streamlined head lifted to peer around. It was a full-grown polar bear, a male, ten feet long from the black tip of its snout to the end of its stubby tail.

The bear yawned widely and blinked in the new light, then lifted its nose to smell the air. It had a gentle, almost doglike face, with soft brown eyes and smallish ears set far back on its head. But when it rolled on its back, stretching its legs upward, the bear revealed its tremendous predatory strength. Thick muscles rippled beneath its loose hide; each furry paw was bladed with five recurved claws; and powerful jaws opened to show long canines and shearing molars.

243

Pangs of hunger made the bear feel nervous and unsettled. Ten days had passed since it had followed a carrion scent to shore fifty miles to the south and discovered a frozen walrus carcass. After two days of laborious gnawing, it had finally had its fill of blubber, meat, and osseous hide. Then, though plenty of food remained, it had yielded to a nebulous urge to keep wandering northward.

The big polar bear raised itself slowly onto its haunches, puffing little clouds of vapor into the air. At thirty below zero, the chill caused it no discomfort but did arouse a strong desire for the warming energy of food. So it abandoned the secure hollow and scrambled down onto level ice. It headed north, shuffling along flat-footed, muscles flowing in a perfect rhythm of controlled strength. It craned its long neck from side to side, carefully surveying the nearby ice for breathing holes and testing the air for scents.

Hard snow squeaked beneath the half-ton bear as it walked. Half a mile from the hummock it stopped for a moment, teetered back, and stood on its hind legs to stare off toward the distant land. It balanced there briefly, huge and magnificent, overseeing its frigid domain. From afar it might have been mistaken for an upthrown fragment of ice, except that its fur looked yellowish against the more perfect white of the snow-covered floes.

If its vision had been keener, the bear might have seen a row of tiny dark spots along the beach cliff far to the northeast; or if the wind had been right it would surely have detected the strange smells of human habitation. But instead it dropped to all fours and continued on its way, totally unaware that danger waited ahead along its intended path.

A few sprays of thin, wispy cloud glowed brilliant orange, high above the horizon. The invisible sun crept slowly upward beneath the earth's rim but was foreordained not to appear. This was one of the shortest days of the year, in the midst of the sun's two-and-a-half month absence. Still, four hours of twilight each day, and periods of midwinter moon-light, staved off the specter of total darkness.

An angular ridge of ice stood in stark silhouette against the sun's corona, and halfway up its side was the motionless figure of a man. He brushed glittering crystals of frost from his parka ruff, then sat quietly on a slab of ice, looking over the deserted pack. His eyes were alert, narrow and mon-goloid, with sharp crow's-feet at the corners. Frost covered his long moustache and clung to the scraggly hairs on his chin. When he smiled, talking to himself, there were spaces where he had lost some of his flat-worn teeth. Clearly he was old, but just as clearly he was full of the vitality normally reserved for youth.

The Eskimo pulled one hand from the warmth of his caribou-fur mitten and held it first against his nose, then against his cheekbones. The air was very cold on bare flesh, but he was dressed well. His wolverine-fur ruff helped keep the wind off his face; and his parka, made from heavy, winter-killed caribou hide, held a layer of warm air around him. Caribou-skin pants and boots did the same for his lower body. Over his parka he wore a white cloth tunic that matched him to his surroundings. And on the ice beside him were his sealskin hunting bag, long-shafted *unaaq,* and rifle, the tools that marked him as a predator.

Indeed, there were few predators as cunning and deadly as this man, who was at once also gentle and full of laughter. This was Sakiak, the greatest living hunter of Ulurunik, who had killed more animals in his lifetime than any two or three other men combined. And if Sakiak was known as a hunter, he was most famous as a hunter of bears.

Once, many years ago, Sakiak had been traveling with his dog team south of the great point at Qayaqsirvik. He had left his dogs behind and walked over the ice to Solovik Island, thinking he might spot a polar bear. As he approached the

low-lying island he looked through his telescope and saw
three bears. Then, coming closer, he was shocked to see that
there were many more bears, fifteen in all.

Some men would have unashamedly turned away and left
the gathering completely alone, but not Sakiak. He had
stalked methodically, carefully, so none of the animals would
see him and alert the others. Then, after he had crept within
easy range, he began shooting. Each shot was aimed precisely, without thought for the one preceding or the one to
follow. After every shot, a bear had fallen. Sakiak fired eight
times in all, and when he stopped nine animals lay dead. Two
were cubs—he had shot them when they were lined up so
that one bullet had killed them both. The remaining six bears
he had left alone because they ran onto thin sea ice where he
could not have retrieved them.

This had been Sakiak's greatest feat as a hunter, but what
mattered most were his less spectacular day-to-day successes.
When the other men brought in game, Sakiak brought more;
and when they brought nothing, Sakiak usually had some
small kill to offer. Now, in his old age, he not only continued
to hunt but also devoted part of each day to passing his
wisdom on to others.

The old man finished scanning the pack from horizon to
horizon, and then turned and climbed down to the flat ice
below. He was out just beyond the edge of the landfast ice,
and had decided to continue westward, heading out to sea.
An onshore wind would hold the pack tightly against the
coast today, so there was no danger of drifting off on a severed floe.

Sakiak followed a trail through the rough ice, where several hunters had driven their dog teams on previous days.
There was a scarlet streak on the snow, indicating that someone had pulled a seal home behind his sled rather than
loading it aboard. This was sometimes done when bears were
known to be around, in the hope that one would follow the

enticing track toward the village, where it might be shot. Because he was on this baited trail, Sakiak kept a watchful eye around him at all times.

He had been especially careful two hours earlier, when he left Ulurunik with only dim moonglow to light the way. The moon was nearing its last quarter and no longer traced a high circle around the sky. "It is getting lazy now," the people said, knowing it would soon disappear for two weeks before showing its face again. Eskimos were likely to become nervous and edgy during these dark times, when they were trapped inside their houses for the better part of each day.

But Sakiak knew that, although it was *Siqinrilyaq tatqiq*, "the moon with no sun," this was still one of the best seasons for hunting polar bears. "Go and hunt now," he told the younger men, "because *nanuq* is migrating north, traveling out there not far from the edge of landfast ice." In fact, several bear trails had been seen out on the pack, but the only successful hunter had made his kill without traveling anywhere.

Three nights ago it had happened. Kakivik had been asleep in his house when he was awakened by a great commotion among his dogs. He could tell by their noise that they were not simply fighting or barking at a loose dog, so he had picked up his rifle and gone to have a look. There, not twenty feet from the door, was a polar bear pilfering seal meat from his cache. Luckily there had been moonlight and he could see well enough to aim. He fired twice. The animal had run a few steps toward the ocean and then fallen dead. So Kakivik had taken the only bear this winter, and he had done it without even pulling on his boots!

Sakiak smiled as he recalled Kakivik's excited accounts of the experience. Of course this was not the first time bears had visited Ulurunik—they did so nearly every winter, when protracted winds closed the leads, making it difficult for them to catch seals. In the old days, when Sakiak was growing up in the village at Qayaqsirvik, it had been common for

bears to wander in among the sod houses. There were no
bright lights to scare them away, and bears were more abundant before the *Taniks* came in airplanes to shoot them.

When he had gone nearly a mile the old man spotted a
high ice pile that he could climb to look over some flat areas
nearby. He left the trail and made his way toward it, watching closely as he went but still absorbed with thoughts of the
past. So many remarkable things had happened at Qayaqsirvik. He remembered the time his old uncle Ipuun had killed
two polar bears with a shotgun.

Ipuun had been driving his team toward Aqoliaqatat Inlet
on a day in early spring, planning to hunt ducks. Just beyond
a place called Nipailuktak, he had spotted a she-bear with a
yearling cub; but he had only his shotgun with him. There
was no time to return to the village for a rifle, so he looked
for a round stone to use for a slug in one of his shotgun
shells. Finding none small enough, he had made an un-
successful attempt to shove his ivory pipestem down the gun
barrel for a projectile. Finally he had decided to make some
extra-powerful shells by taking the cases apart and packing
double loads of gunpowder and shot in each one.

When this was done he set off in pursuit of the bears,
which had gone far out onto the sea ice. But he could not
gain on them, so he had released two specially trained dogs
from his team. They had sprinted after the bears, quickly
overtaken them, and started biting at their flanks, darting
away when the big animals swatted at them or attacked. Finally the bears had been forced to stop, and Sakiak's uncle
was able to catch up. He first went to the female, shot it at
close range, and ran off to a safe distance. It was badly
wounded, so he had let it weaken before coming in to kill it
with a single shot in the chest. The cub would not run from
its mother, and he easily killed it with a blast at close range.

Sakiak thought fondly of his old uncle as he made his way
through some rough ice. Before long he reached the high ice
pile and began to scale it. Large boulders of ice protruded

from its sides, making the climb difficult, and he was very warm by the time he stood on top. But the west wind would cool him soon enough as he meticulously glassed the miles of ice set out before him.

The old man stood quietly, minute after minute, tireless arms holding binoculars to his eyes. He turned gradually, tracing the horizon's arc from the south, around by west, and up to the north . . . then back again, pausing at each irregularity in the labyrinth of floes. But he saw no movement, no indication of life, only a steaming pond of open water in the far distance to break the white monotony.

Sakiak might have paused there, when he saw the water, to check more carefully. But he did not, and his eye passed over a creamy yellowish speck, motionless beside the dark pond. Instead he turned away, then came down off the hummock and continued west into the trackless ice. He was quite unaware that each step narrowed the distance between himself and his intended prey, steadily increasing the probability of their encounter. Whether by design or by chance, the two creatures were drawn slowly within destiny's narrowing circle.

A wide apron of gray young ice encircled the pond. Little rosettes of frost crystals, scattered everywhere on the ice, quivered in the breeze. Ripples chased over the water's surface, beneath rising streamers of fog. In the darkness of early morning a seal had risen to breathe near the middle of the pond, but it had remained empty ever since.

The polar bear had found the pond an hour ago, attracted by the cloud of vapor that always hung above open water during cold weather. It walked to the downwind side and began scratching a large hole through two-foot-thick ice well back from the water's edge. When this was done the bear lay down facing the pond, with its chest and forelegs over the hole to conceal it from below. Then it waited.

Bears always tried to avoid lying down on young salt ice,

because it was wet and cold. But there was no choice, unless the animal went off to hunt at breathing holes instead. Chances of making a kill were much greater at open places, however, and so the big male waited patiently, ignoring the damp chill under its belly and legs. It rested its head on its paws, conscious of sights and feelings, but not of time.

Then, after a long while, the rippled surface was suddenly broken. A small black head popped up—a seal, half-hidden in veils of fog. It glanced this way and that but saw only vague outlines of piled ice through the haze.

The bear moved its eyes but did not lift its head. Then it hunched slowly back and slipped down through the hole, careful to make no sound. It swam powerfully toward the unsuspecting seal, enveloped in silence, peering ahead into the gray gloom.

The seal rested placidly for a moment, until cold air began stinging its nose. Then, at the very instant it ducked under-water, the bear's enormous weight slammed into its side. Crushing teeth fractured the seal's ribs and shoulder bones as it struggled wildly to escape. The two forms turned and twisted, slowly becoming obscured in a cloud of blood. Above, the surface was whipped to a froth. In a few minutes it went still.

The bear surged abruptly from beneath the water, snort-ing puffs of spray from its nostrils, limp seal held firmly in its jaws. Then it swam toward the pond's nearest edge, broke a path through the apron of young ice, and lunged effortlessly onto the surface, still carrying its bulky prey. Moving quickly, before the water in its fur could freeze, it dropped the seal, shook itself violently, then found a bank of snow to roll in. When this was finished, almost all the excess moisture had been blotted from its fur.

Now the bear returned to its catch. It nuzzled the carcass hungrily, then held it with a massive paw and began tearing at the hide. Blubber and skin peeled easily from the seal's body, coming away in a single piece like a sock turned inside out. Chewing the thick hide, shredding hot red meat, and crushing bones, the great predator hurriedly devoured all but a few scraps of tasteless viscera. The accumulated energy and anger of hunting waned and was consummated as the animal fed.

When it had finished, the bear rested nearby, licking its jowls and moaning contentedly. A little white fox that had trailed it for weeks sneaked cautiously in to clean up what remained of the seal. A short while later the bear lifted itself slowly to its feet and ambled away toward the northeast. Satiated now, it gave no further thought to hunting. But it felt somehow restless.

For years the bear had wandered and hunted over the pack, traversing the wide frozen expanses freely, without ever knowing fear. Never before had it approached an inhabited coast, so it understood nothing of man. But now the course it followed took it across time and space toward an unlikely meeting on the lonely world of ice. Perhaps soon it would know the one Arctic predator more deadly and masterful than itself.

After leaving the large hummock where he had stopped to scan the ice, Sakiak made his way to a nearby flat. It was easy walking here but this was *sikuliaq,* unpiled ice formed during the previous few weeks. Because it was only four or five feet thick, this ice was susceptible to rafting and piling under the pressure of wind or current. So the old hunter walked carefully, especially when he began encountering fresh cracks.

The first few cracks were sealed over with gray, day-old ice, thick enough to walk safely across. They were "dead," indicating that no further pressure was being exerted on them. But then he came upon a narrow crack with no ice covering it, obviously formed within the past hour or two. He bent over, watching it closely for several minutes, and he saw that it jiggled very slightly. This was not a good sign. The ice was piling somewhere not far away, transmitting vibrations along the frozen surface.

Sakiak chewed a bit of sealskin thong and let it sink down through the crack. It was swept off toward the east, landward, indicating that the pack was being pushed strongly against the coast. There was no chance of drifting away; but it would be wise to stay on heavier floes. Sakiak knew that sea ice was moody and could change without warning. Cracks could shut so fast that water spurted high into the air. Flat ice could suddenly buckle downward, salt water rushing out over the surface. Or, most dangerous of all, it could begin piling tumultuously underfoot.

He remembered a time in his youth when he had foolishly crossed a fresh crack that ran parallel to the coast, breaking the bond between landfast ice and the pack beyond. He had gone many miles out, looking for bears. Then the west wind suddenly died. Without even stopping to check the current, he immediately began running shoreward. But when he reached the crack, his worst fears were realized. It had opened and was already too wide for him to jump across.

He had looked around very quickly and had seen a floating chunk of ice an arm's length wide. Using his *unaaq,* he had pushed it to the middle of the crack, then thrown his rifle and hunting bag to the far side. Fear and determination had charged his body with extraordinary strength as he went back from the edge, turned, and sprinted straight toward it. He had leaped far out over the water, landing on the stepping-stone of ice with one foot and instantly pushing off. The chunk had been so thin that it broke in half under his weight, but he still had managed to reach the far side.

That small piece of ice had saved the young hunter's life, because the lead continued to open and did not close for weeks. Since then he had warned others, "Never cross a fresh crack that parallels the coast unless you know the weather and current to perfection. If you do so, you are throwing your life away."

Sakiak now angled toward safer ice, but he soon encountered a wide crack that was thinly frozen over. It ran for miles at a right angle to the coast and had many fresh breathing holes in it. "Ah," he thought aloud, "here is a fine place for *nanuq* to hunt seals." He followed the crack seaward, looking for bear tracks, but there were none. The wise old Eskimo was not discouraged, however. Cracks and young ice would attract bears—if not today, then tomorrow. This was the right area, and one had only to find the right moment to be here.

It would be good to scan the floes from a high place and see if anything might be nearby. Sakiak squinted toward the bright southern sky, looking for an ice ridge, and subconsciously recognized by the invisible sun's position that it was almost midday. Toward the southwest he saw what he wanted.

Shortly he walked over strange topography, a floe covered with low rolling hillocks, quite unlike the jumbled, angular ice that surrounded it. Eskimos called this *piqaluyiq*, meaning old ice that had survived the weathering of one or more summers. Its ridges had been eroded into soft knolls, and its salt had disappeared in the thaw. *Piqaluyiq* was often massively thick, but lack of salt made it so brittle that heavy pressure from surrounding ice could easily fracture it.

Straight ahead, Sakiak saw a place where this had happened. The floe's entire west side was rent apart, with colossal jagged fragments tilted on end and yawning fissures running between them. Where the ice had split, its face was a deep, lucid blue, unlike the milky gray of broken salt ice.

Piqaluyiq was just one of many different kinds of ice that Eskimos recognized and dealt with in special ways. In fact, elders like Sakiak used well over a hundred specific terms for sea ice, according to its age, thickness, topography, and other features. "There is so much to learn about the ice," he often joked, "that by the time we understand it we are too old to hunt."

Sakiak jumped a narrow crevasse and made his way to a mountainous chunk of *piqaluyiq* that had been pitched upward and frozen into place. It stood fifty feet above the nearby ice, surrounded by smaller fragments the size of houses. One face was a steep, smooth escarpment, covered with snowdrifts formed when it had rested horizontally. Sakiak tracked up it toward the peak, carrying his hunting bag and rifle. Once there, he would scan for a while and perhaps snack on the frozen fish and biscuits he had brought along for refreshment.

The polar bear lowered its head to snuffle at faint tracks in the snow. Little scent remained in them, but it recognized the smell of its own kind—a female and its two large cubs had passed this way earlier. Bears often preferred walking on a beaten path, and so the animal changed its course slightly to follow the prints. They led onto a broad flat area that stretched north for half a mile.

It had not walked far when the trail abruptly ended. The ice had split apart, opening a crack fifty yards wide, which was now covered with dark, thin ice. The bear stood on its hind legs to stare across, shuffled back and forth reluctantly at the edge, then stepped onto the fragile surface. When the ice bent and flooded beneath it, the animal kept on, spreading all four legs wide to distribute its weight over a larger area. It moved steadily forward, without stopping, until it reached thick ice on the far side. A motionless weight of several hundred pounds would have sunk through this ice. But the bear, weighing nearly a thousand pounds, was able to cross without mishap.

Years before, at a place not far from Ulurunik, a female polar bear had been pursued by a low-flying airplane. Inside it were two white hunters who had temporarily mastered the sky but knew nothing of the ice below. Circling repeatedly and roaring just over the bear's head, they had driven it toward a flat where they could taxi in and shoot it. It had finally reached a wide expanse of dark ice, which it began crossing in spread-legged fashion.

Sensing their moment, the hunters had landed for what looked like a sure kill. Ice that could support a full-grown polar bear, they thought, was clearly strong enough for a light airplane. But as the plane coasted to a stop it had jarred suddenly and plunged through the ice. The female never returned to that spot; but another bear passed by a week later and discovered a man's body, frozen into the ice. Foxes had gnawed part of it away, but the bear only sniffed it and walked on.

After crossing the frozen crack, the big male continued northward. Before long it came onto the old tracks again, and so it followed them at a leisurely pace. Although the day was now full, darkness hung along the northern horizon and the air remained as frigid as in the night. From time to time the animal paused to lift its nose and test the breeze, but there was nothing to smell except snow and salt ice.

Another hunter was not far off now, below the wind and hidden from the bear's sight. Despite the acuteness of their senses, neither of the predators knew of the other's presence. But the circle surrounding them continued to narrow.

Sakiak saw no bears from atop the mountainous *piqaluyiq,* but he did spot something that excited him—tracks, wandering along very near his scanning place. So without pausing to eat he climbed down from the ice, and within a few minutes he stood over the footprints. "A big female," he whispered, "with two fat cubs." From the size and depth of the prints, Sakiak knew that the she-bear was about eight feet long and in excellent condition.

He quickly pulled off a mitten to feel the tracks, pressing his finger into the little ridge of snow between the foot and toe prints. It was frozen and crusty, hard enough to indicate at least twenty-four hours since the tracks were made. And there were feathers of frost in the claw marks, which again indicated a full day's passage. He looked off along the trail, thinking. It wandered toward the north, perhaps into a large flat that he had noticed while scanning. It might be worthwhile to follow and see if the animals had hunted there.

Several hundred yards along the track he found a pile of excrement. It was light-colored and felt rock hard, showing that enough time had passed for it to freeze solid. Nearby, he saw that one of the cubs had licked snow to quench its thirst. Then, somewhat farther on, the female had suddenly turned to look toward the land. Afterward, all three bears had broken into a run, making long drag marks with their heels. When they finally resumed walking, the female had stood on its hind legs staring landward again.

Sakiak studied each detail of the tracks, and like a master detective he analyzed their meaning. The bears had been startled by a noise, perhaps dogs howling miles away in the village, perhaps a seal hunter shooting out on the ice. They were not badly frightened, but long strides indicated a fast pace even after they stopped running. Healthy animals like these could travel many, many miles in a day's time, especially if they sensed danger. And now the track angled westward, heading out to sea.

"It's no use," Sakiak mumbled to himself. Following these bears was probably futile and might lead him dangerously far out onto the pack. The short day was passing quickly, so he made an immediate decision to abandon the tracks and continue looking for fresher signs.

He turned south, went through a field of low ridges and ice piles, then walked along the edge of a flat. The tracks had encouraged the thought that perhaps other bears would move through this area. So he walked slowly, keeping a watchful eye all around, staying near rough ice so he could hide quickly if he saw something.

There was no way for him to know that the big male bear

had been following the same trail he was on, or that it had abandoned the trail almost when he did. And he had no idea that the bear was not far away at this moment, walking almost straight toward him. It was still an open question whether the two would meet, and, if so, who would play the role of predator and who would be the prey.

Indeed, polar bears were among the few animals on earth that would stalk a man. Sakiak himself had seen it happen, only a few years before. He had been standing beside a narrow lead watching for seals when a bear spotted his dark figure from the other side. It had walked down the lead and swum across where he could not see it, then carefully stalked him on the flat young ice bordering the water's edge. Sakiak had felt a little uneasy, and so he looked around to see what was wrong. There, fifty yards away, was the bear, crawling toward him on its belly.

The wise old Eskimo had remained completely calm. He lifted his rifle slowly, aimed for the animal's shoulder, and shot. But he had been thoroughly startled when it leaped up and charged. Again he shot, but the bear kept on as if nothing had happened. Now Sakiak realized that it must have come out of the water and stalked him without rolling in the snow to dry itself. He knew that bullets often could not penetrate a wet bear's hide, and now there was no time for another shot in any case.

When the animal was nearly upon him, he had jumped away to its right. The furious bear took a wild swipe with its paw as it ran by, missing him by inches. Then, before it could turn to come at him again, Sakiak had unfalteringly shot it through one ear. The animal had collapsed in a lifeless heap, its skull shattered. And the man it had undertaken to hunt watched, unharmed, as it fell.

The outcome might have been reversed, however, had he not followed two traditional edicts. First, bears are left-handed, so an attack is best avoided by dashing off to the animal's right. And, second, a wet bear must be shot where there is little or no fur to impede the bullet, preferably in the ear or the anus.

Sakiak thought about the incident as he approached hummocky ice along the flat's south end. He could see it all vividly even today, the bear stalking, charging, then suddenly still and lifeless before him. In characteristic Eskimo fashion, he explained the event unphilosophically. The bear was in poor condition, so skinny that he did not even use its meat for dog food. Its hide was poor as well, though a trader in Utqeavik gave him four hundred dollars for it. Hungry bears behaved in strange ways, coming into villages, following dog teams, or stalking men out on the ice. That was their nature, and one could say nothing more about it.

The day was passing, and Sakiak felt hurried as he climbed a low ice pile for a look around. In another hour he would be forced to head back toward the land. His cheeks and nose stung in the cold west wind as he stood watching. The sky was a deepening red orange, a great frigid dome sucking the last bits of warmth from the earth's surface. Beneath it he saw the ice, immense and silent, a frozen landscape adrift on an unseen ocean.

He saw a long ridge, a flat, a tumbled ice field, another flat, another ridge . . . passing through the binoculars in slow, monotonous repetition. Then he stopped moving, except for his lips, forming words but making no sound. Straight south, at the edge of a narrow flat, nearly hidden in the dull orange of reflected light, something small and rounded was set apart from its geometrical surroundings.

Minutes passed. The glass fogged and he took the binoculars from his eyes, at the same time holding a warm hand on his numb face. Looking again, he saw it . . . move. "*Nanuq!*" he whispered. "*Nanuq!*" Watching its direction of travel, he projected his mind into the bear's, to predict where it would move and how quickly, glancing over the floes between to set his own pathway and find a place to wait. "*Nanuq!*" he whispered once more as he turned and hurried down from the hummock, charged with excitement.

The old man had lived his entire life for these moments. The thrill never diminished. The times between were taken up only with waiting and with recollection of the times before.

The bear ambled lazily across a small flat, then entered a broad isthmus of piled ice. Hummocks and ridges interlaced before it, with steep rifts between. It was as if the horizontal dimension no longer existed. Few men would have tried to walk through it, but the polar bear was perfectly at home. It climbed effortlessly over thirty-foot hummocks, leaping cat-like between tilted slabs of ice, flowing over the morass as quickly as it might cross an equal distance on the level.

From atop one ridge it picked up a strange scent. Standing balanced on a small ice boulder, the big carnivore snaked its head back and forth, nose held high. Then it came rambling down into the valley between two ridges, following the smell. Suddenly the snow before it exploded upward, scattering fragments into the sky. The bear was so startled that it turned in a quick circle and then sat on its haunches, looking upward.

The fragments disappeared, flying off toward land, making raspy noises as they went. Six ptarmigan in white winter plumage had been rudely frightened from their protected roost in the rough ice. Perhaps henceforth they would stay on the tundra, where there were only foxes to disturb them.

Moments later, after nuzzling the drift where the ptarmigan had been, the bear resumed its trek. Finally it reached another flat, a very large one indeed, and stood peering northward. It was somewhat myopic, or it might have noticed a slender figure atop a ridge in the near distance. Perhaps it did see the figure but mistook it for a pinnacle of ice. Then, after the big bear started north along the flat's edge, the

figure descended and disappeared. Now the improbable
meeting had become almost inevitable.

Sakiak knew he would have to move quickly. The bear was
not far away and would soon pass by to westward. His heart
began pounding as he made his way through a stretch of
hummocky ice. Several times he stumbled in the rough terrain, his awkward human gait showing little of the bear's
graceful power. Yet this man, who might appear weak and
inept, pursued the mightiest of Arctic predators without
hesitation or fear.

Finally he clambered up a low ridge that flanked a narrow
stretch of young ice. He stopped just below its crest, where he
could look without silhouetting himself conspicuously
against the sky. Nothing appeared to move nearby, and after
catching his breath he took out his binoculars. Again, nothing, so he moved atop the ridge for a better view. From there
he looked across the narrow flat and the encircling rough ice
to a glimmering plain of level ice beyond.

The bear must be on that big flat, he thought, and so he
watched carefully. Near its southernmost end he caught
glimpses of motion, something appearing briefly in the
spaces between ice piles. *"Kiviakatitaktok,"* he muttered. The
word meant "it alternately appears and vanishes," and it was
one of many Eskimo terms for concepts not expressed in other
languages. The bear was still moving northward, right along
the flat's near edge. Sakiak wished he could see it better, to
assess its size and learn how often it stopped to look around.
Each bear had its own pattern; some were cautious and some
were not. A wise hunter determined these idiosyncrasies and
planned his stalk accordingly.

But this time Sakiak could not wait for a clear view. He
rushed down onto level ice and angled toward the northwest,
hoping to reach a place of concealment well ahead of the
animal. Before he got far, however, he came onto a wide

crack covered with dark ice. He jabbed his *unaaq* to test its thickness, and the sharp iron tip went clear through. *"Azaah, very thin,"* he remarked softly. Nevertheless, he would have to cross or accept a long delay trying to find a way around the crack.

The old man spread his legs wide, just as a bear would do. Then he stepped onto the dark, moist surface and began sliding his feet along, quickly, evenly, maintaining a fluid, rhythmic motion. He could feel the ice bend under each foot, but he moved steadily so that it only flexed without breaking. If he fell through, death from the frigid black water or the subzero air was almost certain. But he moved flawlessly, never looking down lest he panic and lose his momentum.

In less than a minute he was safely across. Glancing back, he saw his tracks, still depressed and filling with water. When he was younger and more supple, Sakiak could walk on much thinner ice, even crawling spread-eagled on all fours if necessary. But now he was more careful, and a few agile young hunters could walk where he dared not follow.

Sakiak entered rough ice again. This time he was lucky, because the hummocks were scattered and he walked between them with little climbing. There was no time to waste, so he moved fast even though his legs were tiring. Perspiration soaked his inner clothing. His breathing was heavy. Still, the old man gave no thought to such trivial concerns. All that mattered was the bear, now walking toward him unseen in the flat just ahead. He could feel it drawing nearer, sense its presence, see in his mind the great animal he would confront at any moment.

When he came near the flat he turned north and paralleled its edge, holding to the concealment of ridges and ice piles. Not far ahead he saw where the flat narrowed, then ended against a wall of hummocks. If he could get there and wait, the bear would walk right to him. Surely it would stay on level ice, and as the corridor narrowed it could hardly pass by out of range. An impetuous young hunter might have gone straight toward the bear, to confront it aggressively on the open field of ice. But not the clever old man. He would pick his place and his moment and let the animal walk to him where the balance weighed heavily in his favor.

Now he drew even with the flat's north end. He turned and moved toward it, threading his way among the silent surrounding ridges. He crouched low, stepped quietly, looked around and behind to be sure he was not seen. It was as if he were the hunted one, creeping away to hide in a safe crevice. Finally he reached an open place, a valley between hummocks, where he could peer out along the entire extent of the flat.

There it was . . . clearly visible to his naked eye, striking and alone amid the snow-covered waste. The bear was still several hundred yards away, moving unhurriedly toward him, straying occasionally to one side or another. Its broad, flat feet shuffled over the drifts. Facing straight on, it appeared massive and wide, shoulder muscles rippling beneath its loose hide with each step. When its head drooped low, Sakiak saw the globed skull, the dark eyes set well apart, the overgrown dog snout.

The bear stopped for a moment, turning this way and that, lifting its nose to the fading west wind. Deep amber filled the sky behind, tinging its furry outline with luminescent gold.

Sakiak pulled slowly back to hide himself but still peeked over the shoulder of ice. A powerful surge of energy pulsed through him. Tingling sensations ran to his extremities. He was afraid, excited, resolute, nearly devoid of conscious thought. He was a predatory animal, fixed on the edge of attack, quiet rage burning at the core of his heart.

The bear sensed nothing unusual. Snow squeaked softly under its thick paws. Darkness crept up the sky and shadows hung deep among piles of ice. Then it encountered a faint ribbon of scent drifting on the breeze. Its muzzle searched to find the smell again, then caught and savored it. The acid odor of a male seal—its breathing hole must be nearby. Uninterested, the animal swayed heavily on its feet and gazed ahead.

Hummocks loomed before it, with steep gaps between. It walked slowly toward them, looking closely, choosing a path to exit from the flat. Then something dark and small caught its eye, moving abruptly out of sight behind a corner of ice. Something moving in the empty quiet, where an instant before the great bear had felt alone and secure. Cocking its head, unafraid but hesitant, the animal looked where the dark thing had been and where now there was nothing. Another bear perhaps, as it dimly recollected the tracks it had followed earlier.

It stood up on its hind legs, ten feet above the surface, forepaws extended for balance, straining to see. Then it pitched downward again and stepped slowly ahead, paused, stepped . . . paused.

Sakiak cringed back; pulling his rifle before him. Without making a sound, he slipped a cartridge into place and closed the breech. His hands were steady. His heart raced but did not pound to distraction. He had learned to contain the storm that anxious anticipation could create in a hunter's mind.

Now he crouched down and crawled to a new vantage, low on the hummock's opposite side, where the animal might not see him again. Somehow it had noticed before; he knew this. Evening light favored the bear's eyes. He should have hidden to the side. But the animal was not frightened, only unsure, inquisitive. The old man knew he must stay concealed, let the thought of another presence dissolve. "Come, *nanuq*. It is nothing," he thought, slowly rising to peer through a narrow cleft.

The bear was just seventy yards away, still meandering toward him. It appeared very large now, swinging its head continuously, sometimes craning back over its shoulder as if to consider a route of escape. Then it stretched forward, reaching out for a scent. But the west breeze held and it found nothing.

Sakiak carefully moved his rifle up and held it ready to shoot. Watching intently, he saw more than the flowing movement of the animal before him. During his lifetime he had cut under the hides of many bears, and each time he had studied the structure of their bodies. So as he looked now at the living animal, his mind saw beneath its surface. He saw bone fixed to bone, muscles flexing and relaxing, vital organs caged within heavy ribs that could deflect a bullet. He saw vertebrae running through the neck's thick flesh, joining to the skull. Pierce the spine, he thought, and the living machinery stopped instantly; miss it and the entire mass would come charging in a frenzy of anger.

The bear was too far away for a neck shot, which was deadliest but most difficult. So he would aim for the shoulder, if the animal would turn and present its side. A bullet there would shatter its upper leg, tear through ribs into the lungs, perhaps sever arteries, and break more bones on the other side. The bear would be slammed sideways and down. It would be alive, enraged, scrambling to rise and attack. But splintered bones and quickly waning strength would deprive it of movement. It would die shortly, or he would end the waiting.

Nothing moved in the ice ahead. The bear stopped to listen, but there was no sound. Finally the whole perception began to fade and it ambled forward. It came ten yards nearer, twenty yards . . . then abruptly stopped and raised its nose. A pungent odor wafted shoulder-high on an eddy of wind, curling and spinning like smoke in a gentle draft. The bear found it, lost it, then found it again. It was a heavy scent, not animal, a mixture of blood and breath and strange body smells. A twinge of apprehension ran through the bear, coming not of foreknowledge, not of experience, but of instinct, a deep-seated memory spun by inheritance into the nerves of its brain.

The bear moaned softly, peering from side to side, trying to find the smell's nebulous origin. When the wind eddy vanished the odor was gone with it, leaving no clear signal to follow. The animal wavered between arrogant approach and flight, then stepped haltingly ahead, deepening the certainty of its error. Inch by inch, moment by moment, the two creatures drew in upon each other, merging their destinies within the tightening circle.

Suddenly, as if recognizing what it should have known long before, the bear wheeled on its hind legs and ran. But it seemed momentarily confused, first angling straight seaward, then turning south down the long flat. Its gait was only half-speed, a bouncing trot that looked almost playful. Perhaps it was still caught between conflicting emotions of fear, curiosity, disdain, and the anger that lurked eternally at the root of its predatory mind.

The hunter had watched silently, unmoving, as his prey took its last questioning steps toward him. He felt strong, certain. The tiny bead of his sight rested beneath the animal's humped shoulder and moved to follow each step. His finger was hard and cold on the trigger. In a moment he would cough to make the bear stop, giving him an instant to aim exactly where the foreleg and shoulder blade articulated.

Then he was taken completely by surprise when the bear abruptly turned. Wide-eyed, he watched for a split second as it flexed its powerful legs and bounded away. Springing like a wolf from ambush, he leaped over the barricade of ice and ran toward his fleeing prey. But, for the hunter's ten steps, the bear took twenty.

Then a flash of recognition entered Sakiak's mind; it had

happened before. There was a quick and easy resolution. He
dropped to one knee. Rifle up. Breath held. Sight on
haunch. *Crack!*

The bear's patterned gallop was suddenly disarranged as it
scrambled to a halt amid clouds of snow. Sharp pain cut deep
into the large muscle of its hind leg. Rage and bewilderment
blurred its mind as it spun around and bit the wound, sinking
long canines into already-bleeding flesh. It let out a tremu-
lous roar, then turned, charging over the flat. A little figure
was there, just ahead. Claws would cut it to bloody shreds
and scatter them over the ice.

The hunter's calculating mind anticipated what would happen next. He watched the disheveled lump of muscle and
hide draw itself together, swinging around to charge. He
waited as it began its furious rush. Then he stood, rifle
cocked and ready, hands now warm and strong, acting without thought or hint of fear. And he began walking straight
toward the oncoming animal.

The intensity of the bear's fury suddenly waned. The little
figure had risen and answered its charge. Instinctive patterns
were snarled in the bear's mind, and the cascading momentum of its attack was lost. It faltered and slowed, nearly tearing at itself in an agony of uncontained frustration.

The hunter knelt and aimed again. The bear faced head-on.
Its vital parts were nearly invulnerable. Only the skull was
exposed; but it was small and continually moving, and even a
good shot might glance off its thick bones. Sakiak expected
all this and knew how to react. He could see the bear's hind
leg muscles bulging beyond its flank. It was a precise shot,
and now the animal seemed to become narrow. He dropped
his aim momentarily, knowing it would make his target

widen. Tradition was right. At twenty yards the muscle stood out clearly. He squeezed the trigger.

Crack! The bullet crashed and flattened deep within hot, moving flesh. Sakiak reloaded and aimed, knowing what would happen next. The bear was powerless to vary from the dictates of its animal mind. Turning on its heels, it bit the wound, exposing at close range a full view of its neck. *Crack!* The rifle kicked hard, and he shoved in another cartridge without dropping it from his shoulder.

Hide was pierced, and meat, and thick bones split, and shattering fragments bit deep within the flesh. The thick cord of nerves was torn and rent apart. Muscles collapsed. Mind clouded. Light faded. Numb body toppled limp. Heart pulsed, pulsed . . . pulsed . . . stopped.

The circle burned hard and fused.

Sakiak slowly rose to his feet, heart now pounding in his temples. Carefully, without haste, he walked to the motionless heap of fur. Blood stained its flank and neck. He reached out and touched the bear's open eye with the tip of his rifle barrel. The clear cornea felt soft. There was no twitch or blink.

"*Tavra,* " he muttered. "It is finished." And he prayed for a moment to express his thanks. His hands were shaking a little now, as restrained emotion flooded into his consciousness. He breathed heavily and his body felt weak. Every predator, including the human carnivore, mixed a part of its soul with the blood of its prey.

There was no time to waste. Deep scarlet flamed along the southwestern sky, fading to silver and gray above. The moon's crescent was already visible among stars in the east. And Sakiak was miles from the land. He guessed it was three

o'clock in the afternoon, and winter's early night was sweeping down in a hush of cold.

He poked the huge carcass once more to be sure, then
went to fetch his hunting bag and *unaaq*. When he returned,
he lifted one foreleg and managed to roll the limp bear onto
its back. "*Azahaa*," he whispered, "this one has a fine skin and
plenty of fat."

The knife flashed in his deft hands, splitting the hide inside the legs, down the belly, up the chest and neck to the
chin. Flesh steamed as the hide peeled away, exposing the
hot carcass to hard-cold air. He rolled it over now and sliced
along the back, until finally the great luxuriant pelt lay separate from the animal that had worn it. Then he folded it into
an elongated square, propping the nose end upward so it
would pull over the ice like a flat sled. Minutes later it was
solidly frozen into this shape.

Working bare-handed, Sakiak now sliced the shining muscles of the animal's belly and severed ribs from sternum.
Then he pulled the mass of organs from inside. Curious to
know what it had last eaten, he cut the stomach open. Soft
pieces of fresh meat and sealskin were inside, and he knew it
had made a kill that day.

Finally he dismembered it, skillfully severing joint from
joint. Legs, shoulder blades, ribs, pelvis, sections of backbone—all were placed separately on the ice to freeze. Although it was nearly dark, he took a few moments to see
where the bullets had gone and what damage they had
caused. Both shots in the bear's hindquarter had created
massive hemorrhaging wounds, and he marveled that it
charged him with such strength after it was hit the first time.
By looking to see the results of his shooting, Sakiak added to
his knowledge of how best to kill or immobilize game.

Now he cut a few large chunks of meat from one of the
bear's legs and placed them on the hide to pull home with
him. Tonight his daughter-in-law would boil them so everyone could enjoy some reward for his success. Thinking of

food, he remembered that he had eaten nothing since before dawn. This made him feel hungry, but now it was too late for a break. If his kill had been caribou he could have enjoyed warm raw meat. But bear was never eaten uncooked.

Somehow, many generations in the past, ancestral Eskimos had learned that humans should never eat raw bear's flesh. People who did were later stricken by a painful illness. Eskimos knew nothing of the parasite that caused it, which the white man called *Trichinella*. But they were somehow able to correlate the onset of sickness with the raw bear meat they had eaten long before. And they had also discovered that cooking would prevent it.

The dangers of bear liver, which contained a poisonous excess of vitamin A, were less subtle, as Sakiak knew from experience. He was told from boyhood that *nanuq's* liver could kill a man, or at least make his hair fall out and possibly blind him. Starving Eskimos who violated this prohibition always found that it was true. And a younger Sakiak, who fed it to his dogs, learned that they were also affected. From a team of seven, three died and the rest lost much of their fur.

When he finished cutting up the bear, Sakiak looked all around to memorize the patterns of terrain surrounding this place. He would pull only the hide to Ulurunik tonight— saturated with moisture and fat, it weighed just under a hundred pounds. Then tomorrow, if the weather held, he would send his son with a dog team to pick up the meat.

The old man bent over and attached the line on his seal-pulling harness to the hide's nose end. Without pausing to look back, he slipped the harness over his shoulders and trudged off landward. Overhead, a dim glow of aurora hung in the darkening sky.

Full blackness of night came. Stars traced glittering arcs above the earth's turning surface. The moon rose to its zenith and began to lower. The wind shifted and blew from land to sea, whispering among the houses of Ulurunik.

Near the village's east end, where the land rose toward a
gentle knoll covered with silent gravestones, throbbing drum
sounds came through muffling walls. Inside a crowd of
people dressed in bright cloth parkas celebrated the coming
of midwinter.

"*Ak-sainga, singak-sainga, soak-sainga, ay. . . .*" Six old men
sat near one wall, legs outstretched, wide-hooped drums held
before them. Their low chanting mingled with the shrill
voices of three elderly women seated behind. "*Ak-say-ak-
sainga. . . .*" Slender withes beat in unison on the drums, their
heads of tight-stretched membrane from the liver of whales
vibrating in deep-toned staccato.

In front of the singers, surrounded by a ring of delighted
onlookers, one man danced alone. It was Sakiak, who had
killed a bear on the ice the same day. Sakiak, who knew the
words and meanings and intricate dance steps for hundreds
of ancient songs. Sakiak, the Eskimo, quintessence of the
hunter in a society of hunters.

His body bent sharply forward, feet pounding rhythms,
arms stretched up before him, gloves held tightly in bare
hands. He gazed up and away, beyond the confining room,
eyes glistening, lips expressing serene confidence. He gave
the yodeling shout, the walrus cry, that meant "Come!
Dance!" But no man or woman was proud enough to join, so
they only watched, transfixed in the spell of his motion.

This was the dance of a man, his clenched hands and
strong body throwing images of the hunt into the pounding
of drums. This was the song of heavy voices that flowed with
the motion and sound. This was the expression of all that was
Eskimo, in a land where none other could live.

And as the old man danced to the pounding ebb and flow of
drums, to the merging flow of music, outside in the winds
snow was flowing and sifting across the tundra. It spun and
wove in the darkness, down the sloping drifts of the bank,
out over the frozen sea. And here snow merged with ice,

each flowing into the other, and ice flowing into the water below.

And beneath the ice were the seals, flowing with the currents of water. Here the two worlds, the silent sea and the quick of life, the twin streams, flowed together. Fish and drifting plankton became the blood of seals, and the blood of seals became the blood of bears and of men. One into the other, the flow continued.

Each living thing flowed from life to death, but the flow of Life Itself was from life to life, as a torch in ancient times was passed from hand to hand. Thus was the perpetual transmutation of Life, from one form to another.

The dance, the music, the pulsing thoughts and lives of men—all were born of the same fountain. A man would live in the flow of that stream, in the endless drift of sun and earth, of stars and moon, of ice and sea . . . and of the blood of Life that flowed from darkness, into light, and into darkness again.

The Setting

The North Slope of Alaska, the setting for this book, falls somewhere between the extremes of environment in which Eskimo people live. It is sometimes bitterly cold, but there are colder places; it is sometimes poor in game, but there are other places much poorer. In any case, the *Inupiat* do not judge the land around them as good or bad, hostile or friendly, rich or poor. It is the Land, and it is theirs . . . and that is all.

If anything dominates the Eskimos' environment it is the weather, and if any season dominates the weather it is surely winter. Temperatures in midwinter average close to minus twenty and sink to minus forty or fifty with chilling regularity. During the coldest months it is rare indeed for the temperature to climb above zero. But even this would seem comparatively mild were it not for the winds. Pounding gales rake the tundra and the coast throughout the winter, as storms pass over in monotonous succession. These high winds greatly intensify the bitter cold, blind travelers in clouds of blown snow, move and crush the pack ice, and imprison hunters in their dwellings. For seventy days the sun remains below the horizon, though twilight always appears for several hours around noon.

The Arctic summer provides a brief period of respite and

revitalization. Along the coast, midsummer temperatures average in the low forties, and in rare heat waves they reach the sixties or seventies. Constant cloudiness and sea winds add to the coolness of summer, but still it is warm enough so that the snow disappears for several months. Compensating for winter's darkness, there is perpetual sunlight and twilight from May to August; and for seventy days the sun never sets.

Anyone who has seen the North Slope understands why it is a place of winds. Over most of its length and breadth, an area of some seventy thousand square miles, the tundra prairie is nearly flat. There is nothing higher than a rounded knoll or deeper than a shallow ravine. Sometimes the plain is so level that even an upturned rock stands out as a dominant feature on the landscape.

No trees grow this far north. The nearest stunted spruces are found across the distant mountains. On the North Slope there are only willow bushes, tall as a man's head near the mountains but barely ankle-high along the coast. And beneath the willows is the tundra, a potpourri of grasses, mosses, and tiny flowering plants that burst with color during their moment of summer.

The mat of tundra vegetation provides a livelihood for a variety of small animals and a single large one—the caribou. This graceful member of the deer family wanders in great herds over the North Slope and is food for wolves, grizzly bears, wolverines, and the predatory Eskimo. Recently, the large and ungainly moose has spread northward onto the Slope, adding an entirely new animal to the fauna. In addition to these creatures, there are abundant waterfowl in summer, nesting on thousands of lakes and ponds. And, in the rivers, great runs of fish swim each year to spawning places at the headwaters.

Far out across the Slope, away from the flanking wall of mountains, the thin veneer of land finally ends against the Arctic Ocean. To the north it is called the Beaufort Sea and to the west, the Chukchi Sea. The demarcation between these bodies of water means little to the Inupiat, however, who refer to it all as *Tareoq*.

In winter the sea is hidden beneath a limitless expanse of ice, a continent unto itself, a forbidding moonscape of upthrown ridges, frozen plains, and open cracks that steam in the cold. This is the Arctic pack, ice continuously in motion at the will of wind and current. Only along its edges, where it becomes grounded in the shallows near land, is it immobile. This shelf of quiet ice, only a few miles wide, is the margin of safety that Eskimos depend on when they hurry out to hunt at the pack's fringe.

During the cold months, only seals and polar bears live on or beneath the ice. But in summer the pack thaws and loosens, finally becoming a mass of fragmented floes adrift on the frigid sea. With the turn of seasons, animals arrive in profusion—migrating whales, abundant waterfowl, increasing numbers of seals, and great herds of walrus. Using skin-covered boats, the Eskimos hunt ceaselessly until the pack drifts away to the north. After this the open water is empty of game, and so they await the return of winter before venturing onto the sea again.

This, briefly described, is the environment in which the *Inupiat* and their ancestors have lived for thousands of years. Over the long passage of time, they have gradually perfected an adaptation to the extraordinarily difficult conditions surrounding them. Many facets of this adaptation are widely known, so captivating have they been to the outsider's imagination.

Before they saw white men, the Eskimos had developed a technology so masterly that it would bewilder an engineer. They paddled far out to sea in kayaks, nautical perfection to the last miniscule detail, designed for maximum speed with minimum effort, able to be capsized and righted again without peril or discomfort to the paddler. They glided swiftly over the snow on sleds pulled by harnessed dogs. They built snug houses with blocks of snow carved from the drifts underfoot. They hunted the mightiest of polar animals, whales and walrus, with harpoons almost as complex and deadly as the rifles that replaced them. And they met the inhabited world's most extreme temperatures with animal-hide clothing so efficient that Western man has never produced its equal.

But there is far more to the Eskimos' ingenious response to the challenge of their environment. Implements, after all, are only the tangible results of human thought. The most powerful tool used by the *Inupiat* was, and still is, knowledge. Throughout the long succession of generations, they have sought to increase their understanding of the world around them and to devise new methods for dealing with it. As a result, the Eskimos have a great body of traditional knowledge surrounding every significant plant, every animal, and every feature of landscape, of the sea, of the atmosphere, and even of the heavenly bodies.

All this existed before the white man came, and the *Inupiat* spread and prospered. The inland people lived in tiny camps strewn widely across the tundra, following caribou on their nomadic wanderings, trading hides for seal oil with their coastal neighbors. The coast people built larger villages, a few families in each, at the best places for hunting seal or whale or walrus, according to the season. When scarcity arose in one place, the people moved. Such were the freedoms and the demands of life.

Then a sail appeared on the horizon, and a floating village of strange white men hove to off the shore. Soon more of them followed, chasing bowhead whales along the coast, trading for furs, bargaining for women, leaving behind sacks of flour, bottles of whiskey, rifles, and bits of cloth. Later there were still more; the white men came to live, and they were named *Taniks* by the Eskimos. They brought stores to be filled with goods, schools to be filled with children, churches to be filled with salvation. The missionary-teachers imposed new taboos no *Inupiat* had ever dreamed of, even a day of the week when one could not hunt because the Lord required that one rest instead.

Today there are frame houses, cloth shirts, eyeglasses, blue jeans, radios, strawberry soda pop, outboard engines, iron stoves, comic books... and whatever else can be loaded aboard the annual supply ship or the weekly airplane. The *Inupiat* have left their nomadic camps and crowded together in a few villages, places with names in English and in Eskimo, places where the two worlds intermingle to produce a new culture that is neither fully one nor fully the other.

Yet the people still hunt and fish and travel across land and sea. They still share that enormous body of knowledge that is essential to their traditional livelihood. The knowledge is passed on in the same Eskimo language that was used by forgotten ancestors. Personality, world view, social interaction, instruction, and authority—much of it remains as before. The trappings are changed, but underneath it all the people who have not forsaken their villages remain *Inupiat*.

This modern society of Eskimo hunters is the one I entered in 1964, fresh from a beginning semester of graduate school, ready to spend my first year away from home. I had been in Alaska before, working two summers as an assistant for zoological and archaeological researchers. These experiences, combined with a great deal of reading and much stimulation from teachers, led to my deep fascination with Eskimos. Above all, I was impressed by their ability to understand their environment and make a living from it.

I had chosen to become a cultural anthropologist, to study the ways of living people outside the sphere of Western culture. And I planned to focus on human ecology, the relationships between people and their environments. I suppose it was inevitable that I would eventually go to study Eskimos, but when the chance came I was reluctant and afraid rather than excited. I was twenty-two years old, and the thought of spending a year alone with strange people in that hard land was in some ways unattractive. But I had always believed in the value of new experiences, and so the decision came almost automatically.

The study would focus on Eskimo methods of hunting, traveling, and surviving on the sea ice. It was funded by the Air Force, with the practical aim of gathering information for survival manuals. My personal goal was to observe these activities, then write ethnographic accounts of them. Perhaps these would later become my thesis—I scarcely let the thought of a book enter my mind, though I had often dreamed of writing one.

After many months of preparation, I was finally ready to head north. It was muggy August weather when I left Madison, Wisconsin; when my plane landed at Barrow, Alaska, it was dark, windy, and snowing. The prospect of the year ahead suddenly appeared dismal, and homesickness swept over me. But it was replaced by excitement a few days later as I flew down the coast in a light plane piled high with my gear.

An hour after we left Barrow a little group of houses appeared along the sea cliff ahead. We circled once, then made a bumpy landing on the soft sand of the beach. My heart was pounding, but the crowd of friendly children that surrounded the plane made me feel somewhat at ease. Older people, perhaps fifty of them, stood along the top of the cliff and watched quietly. Minutes later my gear was on the beach and the plane flew off, leaving me behind in a cloud of sand.

It did not take me long to settle into the small house that had been prearranged for me and to begin meeting the people. They were kind and friendly, though reserved and uncertain of my reason for being there. Nearly everyone spoke English, so I could explain my interests and ask that I be allowed to live among them as a hunter. With a great deal of help from the people, and from two schoolteachers who had spent several years in the village, I soon had my own dog team and was participating in the daily activities of village life.

In the months that followed I devoted myself to becoming

an apprentice hunter. My goal was to write accurate descriptions of methods for subsisting on the sea ice, and so it seemd essential that I learn them myself. The common anthropological method of gathering information through interviews and conversations simply would not be adequate for this undertaking. And of course it was infinitely more exciting to hitch up my dog team, head out onto the sea ice, and spend the day hunting with the other men.

My routine in the village centered on daily hunting activities. In the course of a year I participated in hundreds of hunts and shared experiences so profound that I cannot begin to measure the changes they wrought in me. But I was too busy to philosophize at the time. I was almost continuously exhausted from the long days of hunting, from cooking meals and maintaining my house, from endless rounds of visiting, and from late nights spent writing down what I had learned.

There were times when I could scarcely contain my enthusiasm for what I was doing; but there were also times when I felt the opposite. The Eskimos correct foolish errors by teasing, and I made many errors. On occasion I grew impatient with this and became sullen. Or I felt lonely and homesick and retreated from their kindness.

But as time passed I began to see that my Eskimo companions were giving me the most important lessons of my life. I developed tremendous respect and admiration for them, feelings I still hold strongly. They taught me to become self-sufficient, to live off the land and sea, to think practically, to respect the wisdom of the old, to appreciate the knowledge of other people, to persevere in all endeavors, to laugh when things go wrong, and to find deep pleasure in sharing.

The year I spent with Eskimos changed the course of my life and made me a very different person. I can only hope that what I have written of them shows that I watched carefully and learned well.

Glossary

Allu (*A*-loo): A small hole through solid ice, made by a seal to permit breathing.

Alyahaah (Ahl-yuh-*kah*): "Too bad!" An expression of displeasure or dissatisfaction.

Arigaah (Ar-ee-*gah*): "Good!" An expression of satisfaction or pleasure.

Azaah (A-*zah*): An expression of surprise or amazement, usually (but not always) related to something negative.

Azahaa (A-za-*hah*): An expression of surprise, pleasure, and admiration.

Eee: Yes.

Floe: An expanse of sea ice, varying in size from an acre to many square miles.

Floeberg: A large fragment of piled sea ice, floating free in the water, usually seen in summer.

Grub box: A wooden box used to carry food and cooking utensils.

Hummock: A ridge or pile of crushed sea ice.

Kauk (Kawk): Walrus hide and blubber that has been cut into strips.

Kï (Kee): "Go ahead."

Landfast ice: An expanse of ice extending outward for one-

281

half mile to many miles from the coast, anchored in place by large grounded ice piles.

Lead: A crack in the sea ice, from a few yards to many miles wide. Usually separates landfast ice from pack ice.

Maktak (*Muk*-tuk): Whale skin and blubber, a prized food.

Nanuq (*Na*-nooq): Polar bear.

Natchiq (Na-*chiq*): Ringed seal, a small seal weighing 50 to 150 pounds.

Pack: The expanse of sea ice that covers northern oceans for most of the year; ice not anchored to the coast.

Piqaluyiq (*Piq*-al-oo-*yiq*): Sea ice more than one year old that has become fresh owing to summer thawing.

Pan: A small fragment of floating sea ice, usually large enough to support a man.

Tanik (*Ton*-eek): White man.

Tareogmiut (*Tar*-ee-ohg-*mee*-ute): "People of the Sea"; coastal Eskimos.

Tundra: A treeless Arctic plain.

Tuvaq (*Too*-wuq): Landfast ice (see definition above).

Uguruk (*Oog*-oor-ook): Bearded seal, a large seal weighing several hundred pounds or more.

Umealik (Oo-*may*-lik): A skin boat owner and whaling crew leader.

Umiaq (*Oo*-mee-ak): A large open skin boat used for sea hunting.

Unaaq (Oo-*noq*): A long wooden shaft with an iron point on one end and a sharp hook on the other, used during sea ice hunting.